Framing the Bride

Framing the Bride

*Globalizing Beauty and Romance
in Taiwan's Bridal Industry*

Bonnie Adrian

UNIVERSITY OF CALIFORNIA PRESS
Berkeley · Los Angeles · London

University of California Press
Berkeley and Los Angeles, California

University of California Press, Ltd.
London, England

Library of Congress Cataloging-in-Publication Data
Adrian, Bonnie, 1970–
    Framing the bride : globalizing beauty and romance
in Taiwan's bridal industry / Bonnie Adrian.
        p.   cm.
    Includes bibliographical references and index.
    ISBN 0-520-23833-8 (alk. paper). —
ISBN 0-520-23834-6 (pbk. : alk. paper)
    1. Wedding supplies and services industry—Taiwan.
    2. Weddings—Taiwan—Equipment and supplies.
3. Bridal shops—Taiwan.   4. Wedding photography—
Taiwan.   I. Title.
HD9999.W373 T283   2003
338.4'73925'0951249—dc21   2002153270

Manufactured in the United States of America
12   11   10   09   08   07   06   05   04   03
10   9   8   7   6   5   4   3   2   1

For Michael, Nathaniel, and Maya

Contents

Illustrations

Acknowledgments

Though this work's shortcomings are mine alone, its accomplishments came to be only because I have been the recipient of tremendous generosity.

Various stages of this project were funded by the J. William Fulbright Foreign Scholarship Board and the American Council of Learned Societies/Chiang Ching-kuo Foundation Fellowship Selection Committee, with funds provided by the Chiang Ching-kuo Foundation, a National Science Foundation Graduate Fellowship, the Council on East Asian Studies of Yale University, the Williams Fund and the Mellon Fund of Yale University's Department of Anthropology, and the Rosenberry Fund of the University of Denver.

Numerous businesses and organizations in Taiwan facilitated my research: A Romantic Life Bridal Photography, Beauty and Joy Beauty School, Becoming Bride and Groom Bridal Photography, Charlie's Bridal Photography, Chuech Color Photography, Cinderella Bridal Photography, CKF Fashion Design Workshop, Dream Workshop Beauty School, Forum Bridal Photography, France Bridal Photography ("French Classics"), French Superstar Bridal Photography, G. P. Wedding Shop and Photo Studio, Gill and Simon Body Art Photo Studio, H. K. Broadway Photo and Bridal Center, H. P. Photography, Imminse Photo Studio, I-Piin Photography, Jealoucy Photo Studio, Josephine Bridals, Joyce Bridal Photography, Love in Venice Bridal Photography, Mantor Wedding World, Mr. Ms. Wedding, Old Mai Photography, Photographic Association of Taipei, Queen's Closet Bridal Photography, Romance Bridal

Photography, Sesame Bridal Photography, Sophia Wedding Studio, Spring Bridal Photography Limited, Suzuka Style and Design, Treasure Our True Love Bridal Photography, Truelove Cherish Wedding Photo, Vogue Lady's Club, Wang Sir Next Generation Photography Independent Photo Studio, Warm Life Women's Association, Weiwei Bridal Photography, Women's Romantic Feelings ("France"), Very Man-Woman Wedding Plaza, Young Life Styling Consulting Co., Zhongshi New Bridal World, and others not named here.

Many teachers have worked with me on this project, foremost among whom are the women and men in Taiwan who took the time to chat with me, granted me interviews, shared their photographs with me, allowed me to watch them at work and play, and made my fieldwork not only a successful research experience but also a meaningful personal experience. Looking back upon this project, I marvel at the generosity of time and friendship new acquaintances in Taiwan showed toward me. I cannot thank these individuals by name for reasons of confidentiality but am most grateful for their support.

Hal Scheffler's unwavering support and enthusiasm sustained me through many crucial moments. My work has benefited much from the clarity of his thinking and the kindness of his mentorship. Susan Brownell and Linda-Anne Rebhun offered thorough criticism and important insights. Lisa Rofel and Laurel Kendall provided critical assessments that considerably sharpened and improved the manuscript. I thank them for their careful work with the manuscript and for their warm encouragement. I wish also to thank teachers Helen Siu, Deborah Davis, Josh Gamson, Bill Kelly, and Hu Tai-li.

For their support and assistance in Taiwan, I thank the staff of the Foundation for Scholarly Exchange, Academia Sinica's Institute of Ethnology, the Center for Chinese Studies of the National Central Library, the Fototek School of Photography, the Council on Cultural Affairs, Emily Chen, Gao Mei-yan, Guo Hui-ying, Alice Huang, Huang Yu-zhen, Lydia Jian, Li Bi-hua, Ma Hen-ting, Anne Ragoschke, Roberta Rosenberg, Tao Yi-feng, Constance Woods, and Zhang Yuan-ling. For support and guidance during write-up, I am grateful to Lydia Breckon, Chen Ming-chi, Ian Condry, Susan Cook, Karen Horwitz, Sherry Koch, Li Jin-mei, Lin Hsuan-hsiang, Joseph Lipton, Celia Lowe, Shanti Parikh, Alberta Scasino, Susan Sterett, Sun Qixiang, Hsiu Ju Tsao, Augustana Early Learning Center, the Children's Cooperative Daycare, Morningstar Preschool, and members of the Yale University anthropology dissertation writing group. Thank you to the University of California Press, especially

Sheila Levine, Reed Malcolm, Laura Harger, Carolyn Bond, Sarah Skaggs, and Vicki Kuskowski. I owe special thanks to my *xuejie* Perri Strawn, whose wise counsel and critical feedback were indispensable.

Emily Chen inspired my curiosity about romance and changing familial relations in Taiwan when I met her in 1992, and she has helped me countless times on this project ever since. Our *yuanfen* keeps drawing me back to Taiwan for more.

Family creates the foundation that makes this kind of work possible. I am grateful to Karen and Jeffrey Horwitz and Paul and Minnette Graver. Family also creates the obstacles that make completing one's work all the more challenging. Thank you to Michael, Nathaniel, and Maya Koch, to whom I dedicate this book.

Framings

Taiwanese bridal photography captured my curiosity on the first glance. I was Hui-zhu's English tutor, visiting her at home weekly to help her practice English conversation skills. This was in 1993, when I lived in Taipei for a year, studying Mandarin Chinese at a local university and supporting myself by teaching English. After several weeks of lengthy conversations on a variety of subjects, Hui-zhu and I were becoming well acquainted. One day, I passed by her bedroom and looked inside. Centered directly above her full-size bed hung an enormous portrait of a bride in a white gown and a groom in a tuxedo, framed in ornately carved, gold-painted wood. I paused. The bride, I thought, looked nothing like Hui-zhu. Who could she be? The three-foot-tall portrait was a familiar enough object, but its placement here in Taipei, hanging above a young couple's bed, was disorienting. It looked, to me, like something that belonged in a museum or a castle, not in a modern Taipei flat.

I went back to the den to ask Hui-zhu about this wall hanging. Who is that in the picture? Is it a painting or a photograph? She took me back to her bedroom and explained it was her "wedding photo." I could not believe my eyes. Hui-zhu had been married less than a year before. How could she possibly have looked like that? Why, I wondered, would she want this photograph that looked nothing like her, that made her look like a generic Beautiful Bride—soft and sweet, so different from her everyday tough appearance and attitude? Recently married myself, I knew that if I had ordered a photograph of that size from my wedding photographer, it would have cost over a thousand dollars. Why would Hui-zhu and her husband want a larger-than-life photograph of themselves framed in ornately carved, gold-painted wood? And why would they hang it over their bed, of all places?

Back in the den, Hui-zhu took out an enormous and extremely heavy album of bridal photographs. With each turn of a page, I was more baffled. Each page featured a fifteen-inch-high photograph, large enough (by my standards) to be a framed wall hanging itself. The photographs showed the bride and groom dressed in numerous costumes. She appeared in white, pink, yellow, blue, and red formal evening gowns with fitted bodices and puffy skirting. He wore a Western business suit, a black tuxedo with tails, a white tuxedo with blue cummerbund to match the bride's blue dress. Some photographs were decorated with graphic designs along the edges and featured English text, some of it nonsensical and misspelled. Overlaid on one romantic photograph was a poem about a forlorn lover whose beloved had left him. After flipping through the album's forty or so portraits, I wondered about photos of the bride and groom's families. Page after page featured pictures of the couple or of the bride alone—close-ups, full-body shots, photos taken against a studio backdrop, photos taken in a flower garden—but their families were nowhere to be seen. I had so many questions running through my mind that I could not ask them all. When did you cut off your long hair? Did the photographer retouch the photographs to remove the mole from your cheek? Retouching, the cash register in my mind took note, adds exponentially to the expense of wedding photographs in the United States.

Hui-zhu became *my* teacher that day, which turned out to be the start of my multiyear engagement with bridal photography. She told me that the photographs had cost a total of about $2,000 U.S., that they were indeed retouched, and that she had worn a wig. In response to my queries about family members' photos, Hui-zhu took out several small books of four-by-six-inch snapshots stored in plastic sleeves. She showed me pictures of her parents and siblings, and her husband's parents and siblings, in addition to grandparents and various aunts and uncles at her wedding ceremonies and banquet. They were absent from the larger, more formal photo album but were by no means absent from her life. In fact, the wedding photos[1] and my questions prompted Hui-zhu to tell me about problems with her in-laws.

Hui-zhu had met her husband, Zhi-xiu, at work. He is a middle manager and she is an executive secretary for a successful, medium-sized local company. Both are college-educated. Hui-zhu's father is a successful

lawyer, her mother a homemaker and instructor of Japanese-style flower-
arranging arts. Zhi-xiu's father is a wealthy entrepreneur, his mother a
lay devotee of Buddhism who spends much of her time organizing phil-
anthropic projects with other women from her temple. Zhi-xiu is their
eldest son. Before the wedding, Zhi-xiu's parents purchased a spacious
three-bedroom, two-bath apartment and renovated it for the couple.
Hui-zhu and Zhi-xiu were to pay monthly rent to his parents, which
would cover the monthly mortgage payments. The couple was allowed
to select paint colors, bathroom tiles, plumbing and light fixtures, and
household appliances, including a costly Japanese air conditioning system to tame Taipei's fiercely hot and humid climate. An allowance from
Hui-zhu's parents permitted the couple to appoint their home with stylish furniture, area rugs, electronic equipment, and other furnishings. Zhi-
xiu's parents, who had put down deposit money on the flat, retained
ownership of the property.

Hui-zhu had recently stopped using birth control in response to pressure from her husband's mother and grandmother, which began shortly
after the wedding, to get pregnant. She told me that she was reluctant to
become a mother for fear of losing her job, where she worked long hours
and held much responsibility, but she could no longer endure the pressure from her in-laws. She was extremely frustrated by this and many
other demands that Zhi-xiu's family made upon her. The Tomb Sweeping
holiday- -a time for tending family gravesites and making offerings of
food and paper money to the dead—had recently passed. Hui-zhu complained that her mother-in-law had assigned her the task of preparing
numerous dishes to offer to Zhi-xiu's ancestors. Hui-zhu spent an entire
day cooking under the watchful, domineering command of her husband's
grandmother while her mother-in-law worked on a project for her temple. The grandmother was too frail to do the cooking herself but sharp-
minded enough to exact control over Hui-zhu's every move in the
kitchen.

Hui-zhu's complaints did not stop there, however. Shortly after she
and her husband had moved into their beautiful modern apartment, her
in-laws had announced that when Zhi-xiu's younger brother married, he
and his future wife would live in the apartment too.[2] They had let Hui-
zhu and Zhi-xiu believe they would live independently as a modern,
nuclear family *(xiaojiating)*, and their choices when arranging the apartment had reflected that assumption. They occupied the master bedroom.
The other bedrooms served as a home office and a television-equipped
den. All of their furnishings were modern-style and light-colored (in con-

trast to the dark colors and dim, fluorescent lighting of most older Taiwanese homes). Their kitchen was twice the size of most old-style kitchens and—rare even in Taipei—featured a General Electric dishwasher and a Maytag clothes washer and dryer. Hui-zhu's in-laws had laid out a lot of money for the apartment, so Zhi-xiu felt he could not protest. Besides, he was the first-born son, and filiality had been ingrained in him since early childhood. Hui-zhu believed their only hope for keeping the apartment as their own was if her brother-in-law refused the arrangement when the time came for him to marry.

The enormous portrait hanging over the bed and the bridal album kept in the den clearly represented Hui-zhu and Zhi-xiu's marriage in individualistic, romantic terms. In the photos conjugality took precedence over extended family in the same way generic bridal beauty took precedence over Hui-zhu's real-life looks. The circumstances of their married life, however, suggest that they were far less independent of family than Hui-zhu had hoped. The fantasy world depicted in their photographs was fractured before Hui-zhu and Zhi-xiu reached their first anniversary.

METHODS AND SUBJECTS

I first saw Hui-zhu's wedding photographs during my year's study in Taiwan in 1993. On subsequent summer language-study trips I encountered such photographs again. At my first Taiwanese wedding banquet *(xiyan)* the next year I learned that bridal portraits are taken in advance of weddings and displayed at wedding banquets. The following year I attended my first countryside wedding banquet, held under a tent across the way from the groom's family home, and found the rural couple's bridal photographs even larger and more elaborate than those I had seen in Taipei. In fact, bridal albums and wall hangings similar to Hui-zhu's have adorned the entryway to nearly every wedding banquet in Taiwan since the early 1990s. Now the framed portraits hang above these couples' beds and the hefty albums are tucked away for their future children and grandchildren to admire. Intrigued, in 1996–1997, I conducted anthropological field research in and around Taipei's bridal industry to discover why this new cultural practice is so popular and what it reveals about marriage and families.

The best place to study Taiwanese bridal photographs, I reasoned, was in the bridal salons *(hunsha sheying gongsi)* that produce them. My first forays into these salons were unsuccessful; curt saleswomen brushed me off and refused to put me in contact with salon owners. The process of working my way in, though frustrating, turned out to be revealing. I called many old friends, teachers, and acquaintances from previous stays in Taipei and asked for help in locating contacts in the bridal industry.[3] I also introduced myself to neighbors I met in the supermarket, on the street, at the morning fresh foods market, and in playgrounds. New and old acquaintances of every sort introduced me to soon-to-be-photographed and newly married couples who talked to me about their photographs and bridal salon experiences. Various friends and acquaintances took me along as their guest to wedding banquets, where the products of the bridal industry—costly gowns and photographs—were inevitably displayed. I attended consumer bridal fairs, introducing myself to salon managers and photographers. I was granted some salon tours and even some interviews, but still, bridal salon staff kept me at a distance.

I persisted, and one day I got lucky. I had called the office of a local bridal magazine, asking to interview magazine staff about the bridal photography industry. When the editor, Qiu Li-ru, took my call, I explained that I was an American doctoral candidate from Yale University studying modern weddings and that I would like to interview her. She refused to grant me an interview but complained that she was badly in need of an English teacher. She explained that the magazines she was editing (a fashion magazine, a celebrity gossip magazine, and the bridal magazine) must have English headlines in them and that these often contained errors.[4] Her boss had admonished her to improve her English. I met her for lunch the next day and refused to accept money for the English lessons. As payment, I told her, I wanted help making contacts inside the bridal industry. Li-ru turned out to be too preoccupied to commit to regular English lessons after several weeks, but one of her underlings, Xiao-lan, took her place as my student. We met once a week for English conversation and American coffee. Xiao-lan's already excellent English skills permitted basic conversations, and our "lessons" often revolved around my research interests, as these were her business interests as well. Xiao-lan forged many initial research connections for me. She called bridal salon owners, dress designers, photographers, and stylists with whom she had recently worked on magazine layouts, arranging interviews for me. She also took me along with her on magazine shoots (many took place at bridal salons, with bridal stylists and photographers working on professional models paid for by the magazine). During these shoots, Xiao-lan often sat down with me and a bridal salon owner or employee and helped me conduct interviews. Suddenly, through her sponsorship, the guarded doors of Taipei's bridal salons flew open for me. Saleswomen, stylists, photographers, and owners cheerfully welcomed me, introduced me around in their circles, and forged more and more contacts for me. Xiao-lan and I met at least once a week for most of the year, even after my research schedule filled up and overflowed with all of the interview and observation opportunities she helped me make.

I wondered, though, why it had been so difficult for me to get an "in" without Xiao-lan. As an American with blue eyes, fair skin, and curly, reddish-brown hair, I was used to enjoying a special status in Taipei. Strangers were curious about me. People often struck up conversations with me on the street, in buses, in shops. During my first year in Taiwan, I found the attention exhausting and missed the quiet anonymity that crowded public spaces afford at home. Very often, once locals heard me speak Chinese, I became an object of intense, curious scrutiny and received invitations, aid, and small gifts of many sorts. Although every Taipei resident has seen Euro-Americans not only on television but around and about the city, many had never before met one who could really speak Chinese (and therefore answer their litany of questions about the United States and adjustment to life in Taiwan). I studied standard Mandarin in college and at three different language programs in Taipei, where all of my teachers taught a Beijing accent and its "standard" grammar—even those teachers who had never set foot in Beijing. The Beijing accent sounds foreign to most Taiwanese.[5] Once I began preparing for field research, I worked at cultivating a Taiwanese accent and using the "incorrect" grammatical forms and pronunciations spoken by people in Taiwan—much to my teachers' dismay. I studied Taiwanese briefly, such that I understood bits of Taiwanese conversations and spoke enough that I could flourish a few phrases when I wanted to demonstrate my commitment to Taiwan as unique place distinct from China.[6] (Readers unfamiliar with the history of Taiwan and its differences from and with China will benefit from careful attention to the primer on Taiwan's history given in chapter 1.) My Taiwanese-ified Mandarin was a huge hit with people in Taiwan, and I was accustomed to charming my way through all kinds of social interactions and cultural faux pas. Why had my experience with bridal salon saleswomen been so different?

Xiao-lan explained that due to intense competition in the bridal industry, saleswomen were instructed to protect their salons from intruders. Ten years previously, bridal salon owners had been extremely successful. There were fewer salons then, and as the use of bridal salon services became nearly universal among the to-be-married, business had been phenomenal. Salon owners—many of them photographers who had received only a vocational high school education—became fabulously wealthy overnight. News of their successes caught on, and more entrepreneurs opened salons of their own. In fact, bridal salons had proliferated too quickly; now competition was intense. Salons competed not only over ways to draw in new customers, but also over experienced bridal salon employees.

The competition, moreover, has an international scope. Taiwan-style bridal salons were being opened throughout the region, especially in the People's Republic of China, but also in Korea, Japan, and in Chinese communities in Southeast Asia. Bridal salons with close Taiwan connections also exist in New York (Flushing), San Francisco, Los Angeles, Vancouver, and other North American cities. Chinese, Korean, and Japanese entrepreneurs eager to repeat the successes of the Taiwanese bridal industry avidly consume books, courses, and supplies (photo album covers, studio backdrops) from Taiwan. Many owners of salons in Taiwan have opened bridal salons in the People's Republic of China and today have their hopes for great fortunes pinned to those investments rather than to their local salons.

Xiao-lan surmised that I had been treated with high suspicion because owners instruct sales staff to keep out all noncustomers for fear that they are industry spies. Even with Xiao-lan to introduce me as an anthropologist, salon owners and photographers continued to assume that I intended to open a bridal salon of my own once I finished my doctoral degree. Many anthropologists have been suspected of being CIA agents, development workers, or missionaries in disguise. That the bridal salon owner's worst fear is industrial espionage by an American posing as an anthropologist is telling. It speaks to the self-confidence that some people in Taiwan can enjoy in globalizing processes, including the one that this book presents. Once it was established that, indeed, I was just an anthropologist in pursuit of a doctoral degree, people in Taipei accorded me the same treatment that local students receive: pity and respect. Students are respected because their work is honored, but pitied because their long work hours and meager budgets are looked upon as "bitter." Whereas many North American anthropologists working in poor countries tell of the pressures locals place upon them to offer gifts beyond what their research budgets allow, my experience was just the opposite: I had to fight to pay for meals, even when I had invited another for a lunchtime interview. "You're a student," interviewees would argue, "you don't have any money!" Educational degrees are a major marker of status in

Taiwan. Some of the people I interviewed outside the bridal industry seemed to be willing to aid me in my research efforts not so much because they took interest in my project but because they wanted to assist a student in the pursuit of a degree.

I conducted interview and observation research in about three dozen Taipei salons, plus some in Taoyuan city, Taichung city and county, and the city of Tainan. My salon-based research consisted of informal interviewing, formal interviews, and participant observation research in the various salon departments (sales, gowns, makeovers, photo sessions, and retouching/graphics work). When I could do so without intruding upon the smooth functioning of business, I also casually interviewed couples as they moved through the bridal photography production process. One very generous salon owner, Manager Huang, offered to make me a bridal album to commemorate my fieldwork and, hence, provided me with the experience of direct participation in being made over and photographed. In exchange, she asked if I would mind if a copy of the album were used as one of the salon's dozens of sample albums on display for customers.

I engaged in numerous research activities related to the production of bridal photographs and their social contexts outside bridal salons, too. I interviewed photographers, stylists, and owners of glamour photography (yishuzhao) studios that produce glamour photographs for unmarried young women and girls similar to those shot in bridal salons. I also tracked down a photographer whose small studio specialized in glamorizing portraits of young men and gay or lesbian couples.[7] I took beauty school classes and interviewed beauty teachers to learn more about makeovers. I interviewed photography teachers to learn more about photography. I visited dress factories and interviewed bridal gown designers to learn more about that end of the bridal industry and its early roots in producing wedding gowns for export to the United States. I observed professional modeling shoots to compare them to bridal shoots and interviewed several models and a modeling business owner to learn more about the broader beauty scene and its emphasis on Caucasian models. I interviewed local employees of a multinational fashion magazine headquartered in Paris. I talked to a marketing survey research firm manager and was treated to lunch by an expatriate executive for a multinational cosmetic company, who talked about the Taiwan market for beauty products and how it has changed over time. Finally, I conducted archival research on weddings and photography at a variety of research and archive collections.[8]

In addition to these site-specific research activities, I used a snowball sampling technique to gain interviews with recently married couples and to learn about the consumption of bridal photography. Whenever I met someone who was recently or soon to be married, or close to someone in that category, I not only asked questions but asked to be introduced to others. I sought out couples willing to bring me along on their photo shoots to gain participant observation experiences in a variety of bridal salons. I attended many wedding banquets. I relied on previous contacts and neighbors to help me arrange many of these, but I also generated many new contacts through bridal salon employees and women I met in beauty school classes, in department stores, and at markets. To hear numerous and varied opinions on general matters regarding bridal photography, marriage, and family, I chatted up strangers and acquaintances nearly everywhere I went. Accustomed to being approached by curious strangers at bus stops, in stores, and at restaurants who wanted to learn more about me as a foreigner, I began to turn these brief interactions into research opportunities. I learned to quickly explain my purpose for being in Taiwan and to ask questions such as "Did you have bridal photographs taken when you got married? Why?" or "I hear the divorce rate in Taiwan is getting higher; why do you think that is?" I changed my standard questions for these on-the-spot interviews from week to week, covering questions that emerged from my research. I sought out the perspectives of old people (the parents and grandparents of newlyweds when possible, but also other old people who lived in my neighborhood and had married children whom I had not met). I also made special efforts to track down women and men who had *not* had bridal photographs taken at the time of their marriage. These are the experiences from which this book grew.

Ethnographic research requires the researcher to develop deep familiarity with research subjects, to participate directly in their everyday lives. I relied on certain key "informants," many of whom grew to be much more than research subjects to me. These include two stylists, two dress designers, several saleswomen and sales managers, six photographers, three salon owners, two bridal magazine editors, several mothers of married children, and perhaps a dozen young women who were single or recently married. These women and men provided me with detailed and vivid accounts of the bridal business and of marriage and, whenever possible, allowed me to shadow them at work and invited me to spend time with their friends and family. I cross-checked what I learned from these folks in interviews with others and confirmed (or contradicted) much of what they said with participant observation data. In this book, I use pseudonyms when discussing all of the men and women I worked with, and I alter aspects of their stories to disguise their identities. Some, especially photographers, talked to me, in part, out of their interests in publicity. I use their real names selectively, only where acknowledging an individual's art or achievement is appropriate.

GLOBALIZATION AND THE BRIDAL PHOTOGRAPH

Observers might look upon Taiwanese bridal photographs, with their Victorian-inspired wedding gowns, tuxedoes, and mass-media-inspired poses, as evidence of Taiwan's Westernization. The move toward the individualistic pursuit of romantic pleasures in marriage and the de-emphasis on extended kin ties, too, looks like Westernization. Taipei residents themselves, even, talk about bridal photography in this fashion. There are too many problems with this analysis, however. "Westernization" does not accurately capture the complexities of Taiwanese bridal photography, and besides, the very concept of Westernization does not stand up to rigorous analysis. Hui-zhu's experience of marriage was Westernized more on the surface than in substance.

Photographs often lie, and not just in Taiwan. Family photography in Europe and North America grew in popularity in lockstep with the demise of the interdependence of extended family members. Photography became a "rite of family life" and photographs became tokens of family unity because real-life experiences of extended family unity were increasingly rare (Sontag 1977: 8–9; see also Bourdieu 1990). Photography is prized not for its ability to capture lived experience but for its capacity to create "memories" markedly different from the goings-on of everyday life. The photographs on display on my mantel are certainly not typical of my life. They do not picture me at activities such as eating, working, and sleeping. Instead, they picture rare moments, such as vacations, weddings, and gatherings of extended kin. If an anthropologist from Taiwan came to my house and took the photographs as representative of my life, she would be mistaken.

Given the propensity for photography to focus on that which is uncommon, perhaps Taiwanese bridal photography's focus on individualistic pursuits of beauty and romance bodes well for the state of the extended family there. If extended kin are absent from their photographs, it stands to reason that they may be very much present in young couples' lives. Similarly, the photographic focus on the bride seems to suggest, on the surface, that women predominate in marriage. The elevation of the bride—not only above the groom but also to the heights of celebrity status—contrasts with the widespread cultural belief in Taiwan that marriage constitutes a downward movement in status for women. Many view the photographs as the bride's "last time" to enjoy high status as a young, attractive, independent woman before she becomes burdened by household work and familial demands. The substance belies the surface in Taiwanese bridal photography. Much more is going on *around* the photographs than *in* them, as the ethnography that follows reveals.

As an explanatory framework, "Westernization" is not able to handle the ethnographic facts of Taiwanese bridal photography. One of the problems with the term is that it skirts the heart of the issue: the globalizing reaches of capitalism, a set of processes dominated (though never entirely controlled) by multinational corporations, many of which are based in the United States. Upon closer inspection, the problem is not merely cultural, as Westernization suggests, but political and economic. Many go so far as to speak of "cultural imperialism." The idea of cultural imperialism is that U.S. domination of globalizing processes leads native peoples to abandon their traditional cultural practices to consume Hollywood movies and McDonald's fries.[9] In this understanding, globalization engulfs the local. It is important, however, to remember that globalization does not only happen *to* people; it happens *by* people. Global capital requires national governments to pave its way—through state repression of labor organizing activities, for example, as was the case in Taiwan. Taiwan's export-substitution strategy of economic national development made the "Made in Taiwan" label ubiquitous in North America. Global capitalism did not simply arrive on Taiwan's shores and engulf the island; Taiwan actively courted and absorbed global capitalism into its fold (see Yang 2000). Its clamoring for admission to the World Trade Organization is a case in point. Nor did multinational capitalists simply swallow Taiwan once on shore. Corporations were forced to localize their practices in order to wrest labor away from Taiwanese family farms and enterprises (Kung 1983; Ong 1987 describes a similar case for Malaysia). Taiwan having transformed itself from a poor agrarian country to a wealthy industrialized one, the next wave of multinational corporations sought the island out not for its labor but for its consumers. Corporations like McDonald's and Coca-Cola had to localize, tailoring their business practices, goods, services, and marketing strategies for the Taiwan market (see Watson 1997: 10–14; Wilson and Dissanayake 1996: 4).

On the surface, photographs like Hui-zhu's depict a Taiwan that has lost its uniqueness, gone Western. The ways in which the photos are Western, however, are complex and full of Taiwanese agency. Taiwan's bridal industry and its consumers appropriate key symbols of the West from transnationally circulating mass media and put them to their own uses. In so doing, young women and men in Taiwan domesticate the West and localize the global, as do people, young and old, all over the world (e.g., see Tobin 1992; Tomlinson 1991). Taiwanese bridal photography is an important case study in globalization because it reveals not only how people receive and decode mass media images that traverse the globe but also how young people in Taiwan talk back to global capitalism and bring it into *their* world. Bridal industry producers and consumers are neither resisting global capitalism nor being victimized by it. They *are* it; they are globalizing Taiwan in their very actions.

It is more accurate, then, to understand Taiwan as consuming global capitalism than as consumed by it. Globalization is a set of processes, human processes—constantly being made, unmade, and remade by human actors. By describing globalization as a machine that is somehow larger than life—beyond the control of human hands and human intelligence and all encompassing—we unwittingly contribute to the political/economic strength of the multinational corporations whose interests dominate key globalizing processes (Gibson-Graham 1996). Multinational cosmetics companies—take Revlon, for example—engage in globalization when they deploy visual images created in New York advertising firms to bolster demand for cosmetic products in Taiwan. Women like Hui-zhu, however, also engage in globalization when they deploy cosmetics in bridal portraits that emulate the poses and backgrounds featured in transnational Revlon advertisements. Clearly, Hui-zhu and Revlon are not equal players in the processes of globalization. Yet to dismiss the globalizing activities of Taiwan's bridal photography industry and its consumers is to dismiss too much. Multinational cosmetics companies "encode" their advertising messages for a desired response but ultimately have little control over how people interpret their messages, let alone over how they respond in action (see Hall 1980). It turns out that women like Hui-zhu, upon viewing a Revlon billboard, are much more likely to buy a bridal photograph composed of the same pose, background, and quality of focus than they are to purchase the latest shade of green eye shadow. Hui-zhu globalizes even as she is globalized.

Discussion of Westernization and cultural imperialism is often born of fears of a homogenous global village to come, where people the world over work in the same companies, live in the same nuclear family households, wear the same clothes, rely on the same Internet sites, and eat the same foods. These fears—which critic John Tomlinson argues are primarily European and North American worries about maintaining a rich array of "ethnic" consumer goods for decoration purposes—are misinformed. People the world over are domesticating the American television shows, movies, and restaurants that show up in their neighborhoods. They arrive at radically different understandings of *Dallas* episodes, and they turn McDonald's into youth activity centers where customers linger for hours over fries, taking the "fast" out of fast food (Liebes and Katz 1990; Watson 1997). Globalization brings about new modes of diversification because the peoples of Tokyo, Cairo, and Mexico City engage in globalization in myriad ways that produce hybridized modernities (Canclini 1995), not one big McWorld.[10]

Westernization is more than fear of a future devoid of beautiful ethnic crafts and clothing to decorate the homes and bodies of the world's wealthy; Westernization is also a long-standing fantasy about the place of the West in human history. Observing the breathtaking diversity of human beliefs and practices found worldwide, powerful Europeans came to make sense of what was spatial diversity through temporal stories (see Errington 1998; Fabian 1983). Cultural differences, though coexisting, were placed on hierarchical scales that labeled some peoples backward, stuck in the past, primitive, and barbaric while assuming the European storytellers to be the apex of human development. Europeans (and others) fantasized that they knew the future of all the backward peoples of the world: They were going to repeat European history and end up more or less just like modern Europeans and North Americans. Modernization theory imagined non-Western peoples catching up with Europe by replicating its historical trajectory and called this process "development" (see Escobar 1995).

Many of the victims of such thinking probably saw through its illogic and arrogance long ago, but it took intellectuals with Western educational training to articulate and deliver the lesson now known as postcolonial theory: Europe and its progeny outside Europe are not the center and apex of humanity by natural right but by political/economic might (see Chakrabarty 2000). European historical experience is not universal; it is every bit as particularistic or "provincial" as every other people's history. By the time this message sank in among intellectuals, however, the fantasy of modernization was no longer mere fantasy. Explicit national policy in post–World War II Taiwan aimed to develop the country according to modernization theory's blueprint of industrialized capitalistic production and its assumed accoutrements like love marriages and nuclear families. Given first European and now U.S. domination in globalization, no nation can industrialize, modernize, globalize without reference to Eurocentric visions of what counts as modernity. The fantasy of a modernized world that is, at core, accessible to multinational capital—the ability to sell everyone a Coke—today is not just fantasy; it is a political and economic project well underway. Globalization is not new; it began at least four hundred years ago (Wolf 1982). Most agree, however, that its rapid pace and its domination by comparatively few global powers in the past fifty years are historically unique and uniquely disconcerting. Under these conditions, worries about cultural imperialism are what Renato Rosaldo (1989) calls "imperialist nostalgia"—nostalgia for that which one has just destroyed.

Worries about Westernization, then, are misplaced though well-founded. Clearly Taiwanese bridal photographs have something to do with the West. How else can one account for the Victorian-inspired white gowns and veils? My point is that "Westernization" is an imprecise concept, based on false premises and arrogant views of those outside the West. To the extent that Taiwan can be said to be engaged in a process of Westernization, this is not inevitable, not predictable, and not as complete or totalizing as the notion of Westernization suggests.

What, or where, *is* the West, anyway? The "uniqueness of the West" is a cultural construct that overlooks similarities in societies found across continents and greatly exaggerates the pervasiveness of individualism and capitalism in Western Europe, while underestimating the significance of individualism and capitalism in Asian history (Goody 1996; see also Frank 1998). "The West" also assumes there is a discrete, stable, unified entity—the West—while in practice this is not so. The vast network of transnational flows of goods, people, and ideas facilitated by modern air travel and electronic media renders the notion of a distinct, discrete West absurd. Transnational flows circulate in every direction (Appadurai 1991). People regularly eat Chinese food in Rome and wear Italian shoes in Taipei. Just as ideologies of romance and standards of beauty developed in New York advertising firms and Hollywood production studios have taken on lives of their own in Taiwan, Chinese cultural practices like Feng-shui and acupuncture have taken on lives of their own in New York and Los Angeles (not to mention Toronto and St. Louis). Victorian-inspired bridal wear in Taiwan and the Chinese medicine college in Santa Fe are both simultaneously Western and Chinese, casting doubt on the usefulness of these categories.

Yet it is difficult to let go of these conceptualizations. In writing this book, I often struggled to find a more precise, more accurate term than "Western." I tried writing "Western European and North American" only to realize that this phrasing left out Australia and New Zealand, which in Taiwan are important Western places. Johannesburg, too, has been an important player in Taiwan and is regarded there as very much Western. I tried "Western Europe and its former colonies." This phrase seems much too heavy a substitute for "Western" in the phrase "Western-style bridal gown," however. Besides, my maternal grandparents emigrated to the United States from Eastern Europe nearly a century ago. Am I, like millions of other American, British, and French citizens, not Western? The more one inquires into "the West," the more clearly one sees that it is a problematic label, though a powerful one. Though inadequate, it is indispensable.[11]

"The West" is a powerful label precisely because the transnational flows of goods, people, and ideas that we call globalization are not conducted in a balanced or egalitarian fashion. Multinational corporations headquartered in North America, Western Europe, and Japan orchestrate much of that capital and dominate many conduits for the traffic of globalization. Hollywood film production companies rely on the sheer weight of their enormous capital investments to marginalize the significance of competitors. Few Chinese or Taiwanese films can meet the high production standards and spectacular visual effects that cosmopolitan viewers in Taipei have been conditioned to expect when they go to the movies. American advertising firms set the bar for ad photography in Taipei and other "global cities," including those in Western Europe (Sassen 1991). Already Western, the French need not worry about Westernization, though *American*-ization is of great concern.

The power imbalances that drive globalization are precisely what makes "Westernization" a seemingly useful analytic tool. When Da-song, a Taiwanese bridal photographer, studies visual images created in New York to guide and inspire his work, something like Westernization is happening. Yet to stop at this label is to miss what is going on. The images he studies are not merely Western; they have been produced by individuals with particular training and particular life experiences who create their images in particular business and cultural contexts. Class, gender, race, and ethnicity greatly influence which photographers' images get published in the major fashion magazines that traverse the earth and end up in the hands of Da-song. The magazines he studies certainly do not represent *my* worldview and aesthetic tastes. Nor are they all published in the United States; a few are from Western European publishers.[12] The bulk of the photographs contained in them are advertisements for several dozen multinational cosmetic and fashion corporations. Da-song's search for ideas is not limited to international fashion magazines. He takes ideas for abstract backgrounds from music videos, finds inspiration for trendy color combinations on billboards, and borrows poses from movie posters. Da-song looks at these images through eyes produced in a Taiwanese cultural context and structured by his own life experiences. What he, and hundreds of Taipei bridal photographers like him, take away from glossy international fashion magazines is something we may call "the West" but in fact is far more particular and complex than this conceptualization allows. The West as embodied in the creative work of Da-song is the product of particular powerful business leaders and the photographers they commission to promote their names and sell their wares. Most importantly, the West here is also a product of the imagination—of many individual imaginations in concert constructing a transnational community that exists nowhere but is known virtually everywhere.[13] In his work, then, Da-song acts neither "as a freewheeling agent, authoring worlds from creative springs within" (Holland et al. 1998: 170), nor as a passive conduit for the dissemination of worlds authored by others in the West. In Mikhail Bakhtin's (1981) words, the process is "dialogic." Photographers, drawing from all of the various "languages" or worlds they have encountered, assemble or "orchestrate" a set of ideas about how modern Taiwanese couples ought to look.

Of course, not all of the various visual languages known to bridal photographers carry equal weight. In the art of competitive consumption, consumers emulate their perceived superiors in the effort to climb status hierarchies. Transnational media flows alter consumers' reference groups such that we—whether in Denver or Taipei—compare ourselves and our acquisitions to far-flung people, many of whom are fictional characters whose lives we watch unfold on television (see Scor 1998). Keeping up with the Joneses, or in Taiwan's case, keeping up with the Wangs, takes on global dimensions. In the globalizing community that is thus imagined, the emulation of "superiors" crosses nations, leaps continents. While Taipei bridal photographers like Da-song look to the United States and Western Europe for fashion trends, bridal photographers in the People's Republic of China look to Taiwan for images to emulate (cf. Yang 1997).

Da-song and his fellow bridal photographers are not the only ones looking at global mass media images, of course. Hui-zhu and many other women in Taipei flip through the pages of magazines produced by transnational publishers, such as *Vogue, Bazaar, Elle,* and *Non-no* (Japan). Though these magazines are often published in Taiwan, the bulk of their pages, too, are filled with images promoting multinational fashion and cosmetic companies like Dolce and Gabbana and DKNY, Christian Dior and Clinique. Many women never look at more than the cover of fashion magazines, but they, too, see the images. Television commercials rely upon female faces and figures to promote everything from beer to automobiles. Advertising images saturate the urban landscape of Taipei— images of female bodies decorate billboards, bus placards, calendars, and cigarette lighters.

One cannot navigate Taipei's streets without absorbing dozens of images of Woman each day. I capitalize the word "Woman" because cosmetics and fashion industry images (not to mention the kinds of erotic photographs popular on calendars and cigarette lighters) tend to picture women not as real individuals in possession of subjectivities but as abstract, essential Woman (Goffman 1979). With sadly few exceptions, the images partake of visual codes and conventions popularized by multinational corporations and their advertising directors (though with much deeper historical roots in European painting), regardless of where they are produced. John Berger's (1972) famous observation that "men act, women appear" is borne out every day in the constructed images of advertisers. Scholars of consumer cultures in the United States and Great Britain have extensively documented the peculiar gendering of consumption wherein Woman is constructed as an object of consumption, a site for the work of commodities (namely beauty products), and the consumer-agent (Lury 1996).[14] Many who believe that mass media images of Woman have harmful, even fatal, influence on actual women who struggle (and usually fail) to measure up to media norms cite eating disorders and the demand for cosmetic surgery as products of Woman in the media. Will globalization amount to the transnational promulgation of particular practices in U.S. beauty culture that feminist scholars and activists identify as dangerous? If women the world over take up wearing high-heeled shoes, we can expect women the world over to experience the foot, knee, and hip problems that often require surgical repair later in American women's lives. The globalization of beauty is an important concern that merits empirical study. Just because images of skinny, high-heel-clad, makeup-doused women now enjoy transnational circulation does not mean that people everywhere will respond to these images in similar ways. Do women in Taipei find transnational mass media images of Woman foreign, irrelevant to everyday modes of femininity because the Woman in transnational advertising usually has facial features, body shapes, and hair unlike those of any woman they know personally? Or do they, too, try to achieve mass media standards of beauty, even where mass media images frequently picture Woman as white?

If Argentineans, Indonesians, and Pakistanis attribute different meanings than Americans might to the plot lines of *Bay Watch* and *Lethal Weapon,* what of the visual codes of these and other transnationally circulating visual texts in which women are pictured as visual spectacles— conveying "to-be-looked-at-ness" (Mulvey 1989)—rather than as agentive subjects? Previous work by anthropologists and cultural studies scholars indicates that it is a safe bet that people around the world will come to very different readings of any one episode of *Bay Watch.* But the reception of its underlying visual codes, shared with so many other media images of Woman, is more difficult to study. If one takes seriously Stuart Ewen's (1988) claim that visual texts have overtaken written ones as the most important form of education about the world, the question of what happens when visual images travel is of critical and pressing importance (see also Lutz and Collins 1993; Schein 1994).

Taiwanese bridal photographs are homegrown responses to life in the media-inundated environment where transnationally circulated images of Woman prevail. This ethnography studies how women in one global city, Taipei, engage globalization by transforming themselves into Woman and deploying the resulting images. Taiwanese bridal photography replicates objectifying, mass media constructions of femininity in its beauty practices and visual codes but then puts its simulations of Western Woman (herself always already a simulation) to new uses. By making the visual imagery itself into a consumer good necessary to a proper wedding, the bridal industry provides recently married women—who, in de Lauretis's (1984) terms, know themselves to be historical subjects with their own desires and sources of agency—with their very own representations of themselves as mass-mediated, objectified Woman.

AUTHENTICITY AND CONSUMERISM

Though I have long been convinced of the importance of Taiwanese bridal photography as a case study in gender and globalization, people I met in Taipei often told me I was studying the wrong thing. "Study 'traditional' weddings," they told me. "Go to the countryside." But rural couples, too, wear Western styles, so one informant suggested that I go to the television film studios to see a *real* traditional wedding being filmed for a soap opera. Some had a hard time understanding why I would study this topic because they perceived their photographs to be exactly like those kept in American homes. Making lavish bridal photographs and displaying them are understood as acts that unify members of a global, cosmopolitan culture. One informant's husband even questioned whether Yale University would confer a degree on a student whose thesis concerned such a trivial topic. Though these reactions may sound discouraging, I found them greatly encouraging. I hope that this book will help readers, in the United States, Taiwan, and elsewhere, to denaturalize and question cultural beliefs and practices about gender and beauty that, too often, go unexamined.[15]

Many readers might, at first, agree with the people in Taipei who said that an anthropologist ought to go to the countryside to seek out the most traditional wedding practices, not set up her study in the heart of a global city and focus on the production and consumption of a consumer product. They assume that consumer commodities and consumer society are dull and devoid of meaning, that consumption individualizes and atomizes people, that consumption destroys culture (see Jameson 2000: 57). In short, the anthropologist should seek out that which is old because modern consumption—even and especially conspicuous consumption (Veblen 1925)—is vapid. A parallel assumption is that cultural practices outside consumer society, such as traditional wedding ceremonies, contain cultural meaning and social value beyond mere status competition. Daniel Miller (1995b) argues that this very logic stunted the development of the anthropology of material culture, which tended to avoid the study of consumption. The discipline, he argues, became mired in moralizing distinctions between gifts and commodities that took the commodity form as inauthentic (empty of meaning, devoid of social value) and the gift form as authentic (loaded with meaning, full of social value). A central tenet of the present study is that bridal photographs in Taiwan defy the commodity/gift binary. They are very much "beyond commerce" (Douglas and Isherwood 1979)—they are rich with cultural meanings and textured by social relationships even as they are bought and sold on the consumer marketplace.

Taiwanese bridal photographs are unique in the world of commodities in that consumers directly participate in their production. The bridal photography production process of dress selection, makeovers, and

photo sessions has become a consumable in and of itself. The process is
today as much a part of wedding rituals as are customary family wedding
rites. As such, they are gender rituals and rites of passage as central to
modern life in Taiwan as are the temple and ancestral rites more conventional to its anthropological literature. Though these rites are performed
in the service of commodity production, they do not lack meaning.

Despite their willful excesses and joyful artifice in representation,
Taiwanese bridal portraits possess a kind of authenticity and originality
that the mass-media visual forms they emulate lack. Walter Benjamin
(1985) argues that, in mechanical reproduction, art is simultaneously
democratized by widespread dissemination of artwork and desacralized
by the ripping of the art object from its social context. Benjamin contends that, prior to mechanical reproduction, art objects often have "cult
value" and, due to their deep embeddedness in particular social contexts, possess an "aura" that is lost when they are mechanically reproduced and thereby decontextualized from their social setting. The
decontextualization of the person by the mechanical/chemical processes
of photographic portraiture produces objects similarly lacking in aura
and authenticity. This is certainly the case in, for example, advertising
photography. In Taipei's bridal salons, bridal images constructed by the
photographer in the studio have little relationship to real-life experiences. In this regard, Taiwanese bridal photographs suffer a profound
lack of authenticity. Benjamin would add that the nature of photography
is to refuse the very notion of authentic artworks. Photographic negatives
give us the possibility of creating countless prints, none more original or
authentic than any other. By destabilizing the relationship between
authenticity and art, photography seizes art from elite hands, delivering
it to the masses and creating space for critical consciousness.

Of consumerist society, David Harvey argues that "the greater the
ephemerality, the more pressing the need to discover or manufacture
some kind of eternal truth that might lie therein." Looking for authenticity, people turn to photographs and other items tied to memories to
generate "a sense of self that lies outside the sensory overloading of consumerist culture and fashion . . . [and] the ravages of time-space compression" (1989: 292). Brides anticipate that in time all will forget that
she never looked as beautiful as her bridal photographs render her, never
had real-life claims to the opulent riches implied in the portraits. The
photos' lack of authenticity is not a problem; in fact, that is their very
appeal. Moreover, bridal salons sell not only the photographs but also
the "once in a lifetime" experience of making them, where brides are

treated as celebrities, the princesses of late capitalism. Though lacking in authenticity, the photos are full of authentic social value and meaning.

The social value invested in bridal portraits is made clear by their treatment relative to other commodities. Martyn Lee (1993) notes the turn away from consumer durables toward disposables (short-term or holiday-use goods) and the miniaturization of many commodities in order to make room for more goods in living spaces overcrowded with stuff. The willingness of people in Taiwan to accommodate the enormous size and weight of bridal albums in the face of the miniaturization of other possessions is striking. So, too, is their willingness to leave the bridal portrait hanging above their beds for many years, even as they grow tired of other home furnishings and replace them with new colors, updated styles.[16]

Though the bridal photography production process involves many elements of mass production, bridal portraits are nevertheless considered singular and original commodities. The framed wall hanging and the bridal album are rare, one-of-a-kind objects for the women and men they picture, even though a quick glance at the photos of a dozen couples reveals how formulaic they are. In important ways, bridal photographs differ from the vast majority of consumer objects in that they are not, in Karl Marx's language, alienated goods. The labor of photographers, assistants, and stylists in the production of bridal images is, of course, alienated, in that they produce the objects for "exchange value" and their labor generates profit for the salon owner. But brides and grooms, too, take part in the production of their photographs, and their labor is not alienated because they produce the photographs for their own use.

Because the photographs are made in advance of weddings so that they can be displayed publicly at wedding banquets, putting down a deposit on a bridal package is often a couple's first public act declaring their intentions to marry in the near future. Bridal salons sometimes dramatize this point; at bridal fairs, staff may applaud and launch fire-crackers, shouting out congratulations to the couple who has made a purchase—just as future wedding banquet guests will applaud, launch firecrackers, and shout out congratulations when the newly married couple enters the banquet. In her makeover, the bride undergoes a ritual of transformation that separates her from her former status as a single young woman and changes her into a disguised and immobilized bride for her rite of passage into wifedom. In the photo shoot, the groom performs a ritual of romance where he makes a to-be-publicized expression of adoration for his bride. The photographs picture only the highly constructed, commodified marriage rites of the bridal salon that are far removed from the lived social realities of familial obligations and family ritual. Nonetheless, they serve to memorialize those modern, consumerist-oriented rites of passage, which may often be more meaningful and exciting for young people than are their family wedding ceremonies. Wedding ceremonies are planned and orchestrated by the older generations, reflecting the old view of marriage as the exchange of the bride between two families. Young people prefer the way the bridal industry sees their relationships, in individualistic, romantic terms rather than as part of the familial obligation to reproduce. Bridal salons are often the only place where the view on marriage that young people prefer is enacted. Though the images delight in artifice and eschew the very notion of authentic representation of experience, they are authentically meaningful anyway because producing them is, itself, a lived experience that is often fraught with meaning for the bride.

Taiwanese bridal photography is contradiction-bound. Photographs that mimic aura-less, rootless transnational mass media images and homogenize individual, unique women into the generic Beautiful Bride are nonetheless original, one-of-a-kind cult objects that exude a sacred aura. The photographs stand as rare examples of the products of unalienated labor even as they simulate the visual codes of transnationally circulating mass media forms that conflate Woman with Commodity and, many believe, alienate real women from their real bodies in the United States today, where self-starvation and cosmetic surgery are lauded practices in some social groups. The enormous photographs at first look like testaments to individuality but, as this ethnography demonstrates, what makes a bridal album successful is the photographer's ability to portray the bride in multiple, constructed personae, as different from one another as possible.

Taiwanese bridal photographs are at once profoundly full of and devoid of meaning. They are full of meaning because they ritualize the transformation of women and men into wives and husbands. They are full of meaning in that people in Taipei today deploy them as status markers and because they mark changing gender relations and changing definitions and evaluations of femininity in intergenerational family conflicts. They are devoid of meaning in that people viewing them take for granted that the images are *not* representations of lived social realities. Like advertising and other mass media images, they carry no promise of substance. They are surfaces only, utterly detached from substance, moral character, and material social relations. In their miming of the

West, the bridal photographs reflect the profound emptiness that I think people in Taiwan often see in the transnational imagery that is, quite often, all that they know about the people of that imagined place. The bridal photographs are superficial, then, precisely because the West that they imitate is superficial, too.

CHAPTER I

How Can This Be?

Ethnographic Contexts and History

In Taiwan today, a proper wedding is not complete without the services of a bridal salon, which provides rental gowns, studio portraits, a bouquet of flowers, car decorations, and other goods, including a book for recording gifts and stretches of pink satin for banquet guests to sign. Bridal salons offering these products and services can be found throughout the island—in big cities and remote townships alike. The use and display of bridal salon products and services cut across class, ethnic, regional, and city/country social divides. I found it difficult, in fact, to locate a couple married in the preceding seven years who had *not* engaged bridal salon services. After asking almost everyone I met during a period of several months whether they knew of anyone who had not displayed professional bridal portraits at their wedding banquets, I found only two such couples. Both described to me the embarrassment their families loudly suffered over the couples' refusal of the bridal photography custom. To my surprise, instead, I found couples who had skipped the customary wedding rites and banquet but commissioned bridal portraits anyway.

This chapter begins with the story of one of my early encounters with Taiwanese bridal photography, over cappuccinos in a fashionable Italian coffee house tucked away from the roar of traffic in the back alleys of Dinghao, an exclusive shopping district in central Taipei. Thereafter I describe the general ethnographic and historical context for this study, focusing on the development of the modern bridal industry.

AN ALBUM ON VIEW

Cultural anthropologists often find that the finest moments in ethnographic research happen by mistake. The most illustrative moments in fieldwork often occur without (or, perhaps, in spite of) the anthropologist's plans for meddling in human affairs. Participant observation research—hanging out alongside the "natives" while they carry on with their lives—is similar to eavesdropping: One waits around until something interesting spontaneously occurs. Anthropologist Sally Falk Moore (1994) describes such moments as "diagnostic events," which lay bare social processes and cultural assumptions so taken for granted or naturalized that they are difficult, if not impossible, for most people to articulate in interviews.

The evening I spent in a high-class Dinghao coffee house came about, for me, by accident. It was 1996—very early in my fieldwork, when my primary research strategy was to talk to anyone and everyone in hope that someone with connections would befriend me and facilitate my entry into the bridal industry. Curt saleswomen had just turned me away from several bridal salons, and I was beginning to feel desperate. A close friend, Mei-hua, belonged to a small college alumni club. Back in 1993, while some of the younger members were still in college, I had joined them for dinner at a far less fashionable student-budget eatery. Later, Mei-hua had invited me to join about thirty club members on a chartered bus to the countryside outside Tainan to attend the open-air wedding banquet of two alumni group members, Xin-de and Yu-ling. Now, in 1996, I looked forward to chatting again with Xin-de and Yu-ling, whose rowdy wedding banquet had initiated me into the world of rural weddings.

At the coffee house, which was appointed with murals depicting sites in Italy, the group pushed several small tables together to form one long table to seat the dozen or so friends in attendance that night. There were two young, married couples and one couple that was soon to be married. Others were young, single men and women. After answering numerous questions about myself, especially about how I had come to speak Chinese, I attempted to engage the attention of Yu-ling. But I was interrupted by something even more interesting.

The wedding of one of the married couples had been held just a few weeks before; they had their huge and heavy bridal album in tow, with plans to show it off. The groom, Ben-ming, had grown up in a rural county in northern Taiwan, attended college in Taipei, and gone to law school in Beijing, where he met his wife, Jing, who had grown up in Beijing. At present, they were staying with his parents in Taiwan but were soon to move back to Beijing. Their wedding had been held at Ben-ming's family home, and they had rented gowns and posed for photographs at a bridal salon in a small town nearby. Only a few of Ben-ming's friends had attended his wedding banquet, as it had been held at an inconvenient time on a weekday, following a fortune-teller's suggestion for the luckiest date for the wedding. When Ben-ming pulled out the enormous photo album of about sixty prints, each twenty inches high, many in the group gasped in joyful surprise at the chance to view the photographs (and perhaps at the size of the album, too). Yu-ling, seated at the center of the long table, laid the photo album down in front of her where all could see the photographs. While many in the group discussed the photographs, several people at my end of the table continued their conversations and paid attention to the photographs only intermittently, when laughter broke out.

Initially, the conversation concerning the photos centered on the locations of the nonstudio shots. Ben-ming explained where they had been taken—some against stretches of bright-green rice paddies, others along the seaside, still others outside an old brick factory. Turning pages, the group paid little attention to the many studio portraits interspersed among the fewer outdoor shots. They then came upon a set of photographs in which the bride and groom were dressed in casual attire—T-shirts and jeans—and were shown hitting each other with huge inflatable baseball bats. The group laughed at these, particularly at one where the groom posed on hands and knees while the bride sat on his back. Ben-ming told us proudly that his grandmother had scolded them for this photo. My puzzlement must have shown, because he looked at me and explained that it is supposed to be the other way around: the woman should serve the man.

Some of the photographs had English phrases on or around them. One, for example, said "Betty Blue." Perhaps because of my presence, a few at the table read these words aloud. I asked what "Betty Blue" means. Two women seated near me said, "It doesn't mean anything." Then someone else teasingly commented, "It *really* must not mean anything if even the foreigner doesn't know what it means!" I blushed, embarrassed to have called attention to what, in my mind, was the fact that these newlyweds had spent a fortune on bridal photographs decorated with nonsensical and often misspelled English words and phrases.

Figure 1. Bridal salons decorate many photos with graphic art and English, Chinese, or Japanese text to make the bride appear as if she is a model in a magazine. (Image courtesy of Luomen Bridal Photography Co., 1997.)

Ben-ming, however, did not seem embarrassed. Nevertheless, I did not mention the English text around the photos again.

Some photographs elicited teasing comments about the groom. In one photograph Ben-ming's face looked fat, remarked one friend. In another, someone said, his facial expression was too serious. As they talked, those seated closest to the album touched the photographs, pointing to an odd profile shot of the groom or feeling the surface of a photograph taken on green pastures. I noted that my own cultural training had taught me to avoid touching anything but the perimeters of photos, especially, I thought, with such an obviously costly photo album!

No one teased about photographs of the bride, but neither did I hear viewers praise the bride's beauty, which I had often heard when women discussed their friends' photographs. Jing looked on in silence, smiling occasionally. I found myself looking down at the photographs, up at Jing, and back down to the photographs in amazement. In the photos she was stunningly beautiful. She looked just like a fashion model. In the close-ups, her eyes appeared an unusual light-brown color. Sitting before me, however, was a rather plain-looking woman with very ordinary eyes. As I pondered the improbability of the light-brown eye color in the close-ups, Yu-ling turned the page to a photo in which Jing's eyes were emerald green to match the emerald-green ribbon trim on her white gown. Clearly, her eyes had been overpainted to match. No one discussed the lack of resemblance between Jing and her image that night. (The subject came up, however, the following evening at my house, when I invited two of these friends over for dinner so that I could grill them about the photographs and parts of the conversation that I had missed or misunderstood. I return to this post-event interview later.)

Next, the group came upon a set of photographs showing the couple from mid-abdomen up in a standing, embracing position. The bride wore a satin spaghetti-strap nightgown. Unlike most of the other shots, in which the bride's hair was done up in cascades of sculpted curls piled atop her head, in these her hair hung down in loose curls. The groom wore no shirt and had removed the eyeglasses he wore in all of the other shots. When the group saw these photos, many began talking at once. I heard one person say that the groom looked fat. Xin-de said, several times, *zeme keneng? zeme keneng?* ("How can this be?"). At the time I interpreted him as saying, "How could you do this?" because *I* found the partial nudity and sexy overtones shocking. Later, Mei-hua explained to me that the comment *zeme keneng?* in fact referred to the appearance of the groom's skin in the photograph. The groom's old friend was teasing him by suggesting that his skin was not really so perfect. The surprise at the sexual content of the photograph was mine alone. For the other viewers, the seminude photo was not unusual or out of place. What was strange, rather, was that the photographer had improved upon the quality of the groom's skin when usually touchups are reserved only for brides.

Later, when Yu-ling lifted the album to hand it back, Ben-ming commented on how heavy it was. Yu-ling agreed and said he and Jing had the most photographs of all the couples in the club. Someone else asked how much Ben-ming had paid for the photographs. (I missed the answer, as did those seated near me at the far end of the table.)

Curious about what else I had missed, I invited Mei-hua and Fang, her friend from college, to my apartment for dinner the next night. I asked them to clarify parts of the conversation I had not fully understood. One joke they recounted for me regarded a double exposure print of the groom. Someone had quipped that one image was his actual self and the other was his spirit self. The wisecrack referred to a recent scam in which worshippers were tricked into giving money to a temple leader who proclaimed to have two such selves. The point of the photograph, however, was probably to create the appearance of the bride being doubly courted by her suitor. While such photos are not found in every bridal album, I later saw similar ones on display at bridal salons. Once, a woman viewing a similar double exposure shot in a salon's display album at first glance assumed that two different men had posed for the shot, as if vying for the woman. I pointed out to her that in fact only one groom had knelt before the bride in the photo studio but the photographer had doubled the effect. These double-groom photographs, like many more ordinary ones, dramatize the groom's subservient position to the bride as he courts her for her beauty.

In the relative privacy of dinner with Mei-hua and Fang, I inquired about the shockingly perfect beauty of the bride in the photos in contrast to her actual plain looks. Fang explained that her beauty was due to makeup and photographic manipulations. He opined that these tricks are why young women love these types of photographs so much. I argued, in good feminist form, that grooms and their parents seem to be equally invested in Taiwan's bridal photography craze. Fang dismissed my point, insisting that women's love for beautiful pictures of themselves alone drives the bridal industry.

Although Fang and Mei-hua agreed with me that the bride, Jing, did not look like herself, they found her transformation totally unremarkable because it is a standard feature of bridal portraits. More remarkable, they thought, was that Ben-ming looked fatter in the photographs. Also unremarkable to them were the provocative photographs I had found so striking. I imagined that the groom's grandmother, who had scolded him about the photo of the bride sitting on his back, would have complained. Probably not, thought my friends. Ben-ming had mentioned trouble only over that one photograph. Later in my research, I learned that provoking the disapproval of parents and grandparents is a common feature of Taiwanese bridal photography. Had his grandmother complained about the intimate pose, surely Ben-ming would have bragged about this point, too.

Bored with my questions, Mei-hua and Fang went on to chat about the newlyweds. Jing's parents, it turns out, are high school teachers loyal to the Chinese Communist Party. They had named both of their daughters for Communist causes, one having to do with struggle against class privilege and the other to do with factory workers. The whole family, Ben-ming had complained to Mei-hua, is very quiet. Every night after dinner each goes off alone to read. Sometimes the house is silent for as long as three hours, even when everyone is home. In Ben-ming's family everyone eats together, watches television together, even goes shopping together. Hearing this, I tried to return to my argument with Fang, who had maintained that women were the sole driving force behind Taiwanese bridal photography. To me, it seemed unlikely that this woman named after the struggle against class privilege, who likes to spend her free time reading in silence, was the one who wanted such glamorous, expensive photographs. Admittedly, the former state policy of repressing consumerist fantasies of feminized beauty in the People's Republic of China seemed to have backfired when, in the 1980s, the state began its retreat from this area of ideological rule (Honig and Hershatter 1988). However, a young Beijing woman of the late 1990s, who remained as subdued and studious as her consumption-oriented husband described her, struck me as an unlikely candidate to demand the largest, most elaborate photo album yet to emerge among Ben-ming's alumni club friends. I argued that it was the groom who had wanted the photos. At least in this instance, *he* was clearly the one who had wanted to show off the album to his friends. My friends disagreed. They imagined that Jing, who had remained silent that evening among new acquaintances, was just as excited to take the photos back to China to show her friends. In Taiwan, women always bring their albums to work to show off, they argued. Only much later in my field research, through more "diagnostic events" and overheard statements, did I come to realize that men who express excitement over their photo albums risk being seen, by standards of masculine behavior, as overly enamored with their wives and too interested in this feminine pursuit. For Fang and Mei-hua to have agreed with me would have been to insult a dear friend of Mei-hua's.

ETHNOGRAPHIC CONTEXTS

Ethnographic and historical contextualization can further illuminate the discussions provoked by Ben-ming and Jing's bridal album. To make sense of the coffee house album-viewing event—and of Taiwanese bridal photography as a cultural practice more generally—it is necessary to locate it in historical time and cultural space.

Taiwan is an island, in area slightly smaller than the Netherlands, about eighty miles off the southeast coast of China. The first European records of Taiwan date from the late sixteenth century, when Portuguese, Dutch, and Spanish traders took interest in the island and called it Ilha Formosa, meaning "beautiful island." Austronesian-speaking peoples lived there, and the Dutch colonized a small area and established a trading port in the south. Deerskins and camphor were among Taiwan's desirable exports. In 1662, a Chinese pirate and Ming dynasty loyalist known as Koxinga (Cheng Cheng-kung) ousted the Dutch as the Manchus established the Qing dynasty in China. Taiwan served as a Ming enclave under Koxinga until 1683, when Qing forces overthrew him. Chinese settlers from southeastern China also began arriving in Taiwan in the seventeenth century, their numbers increasing rapidly at the end of that century. Most of the island's indigenous peoples were eventually assimilated into communities settled by speakers of two southeastern Chinese dialects, Minnanyu (now known as Taiwanese) and Hakka. Aboriginals who lived in Taiwan's mountain areas did not assimilate as readily and even today retain distinct ethnic identities (see Shepherd 1993).

In 1895, China's Qing dynasty ceded Taiwan to Japan as a war reparation, and Japan made the island into a sugar-, rice-, and tea-producing colony (see Ching 2001). In 1945, Japan retroceded Taiwan to the Allies. Revolutionaries had overthrown the Qing dynasty in 1911, so at the time of Taiwan's retrocession, China's government was the Republic of China, controlled by the Nationalist Party, also known as the KMT. In 1949, the Chinese Communist Party defeated the Nationalists and established the People's Republic of China. The Nationalists fled to Taiwan, establishing Taipei as the new capital of the Republic of China—now commonly called Taiwan. They brought with them approximately one million refugees from China, many of them soldiers. Chiang Kai-shek ruled by martial law in Taiwan, claiming sovereignty over all of China and planning to take back the motherland. Chiang's key ally, the United States, provided economic and military patronage until 1971, when the United States shifted diplomatic ties to the People's Republic of China and forced the Republic of China out of its United Nations Security Council seat. Taiwan renounced claims to the mainland and ended martial law in the late 1980s. Full democratic reform was completed in 1996 with the first multiparty presidential election.

The conflict across the Taiwan Straits between Taiwan and China (the People's Republic) persists. China still regards Taiwan as a renegade Chinese province and periodically reminds the world of its intention to bring the island under its governance. Before the realization of Taiwan's democratic reforms, the conflict had reached a comfortable point of stasis. Taiwan's political leadership was dominated by the KMT, which agrees with the People's Republic in its goal of reunification. The KMT strictly opposes the notion of an independent Taiwan, arguing that Taiwan is and must always remain a part of China. The KMT position is that reunification must wait until the Chinese Communist Party falls, while the Communists' position is that reunification should bring Taiwan under its authority as soon as possible. The sale of U.S. arms to Taiwan, then, is a bane to China. During the 1990s, the quiet stalemate between Taiwan and China led to the development of extensive unofficial economic linkages, particularly in the form of Taiwanese business investments in China. Taiwan's democratic election process troubles China's political leaders because it fears the Taiwanese people will demand the declaration of an independent country called Taiwan. China maintains that if Taiwan attempts to declare independence, it will wage war on the island. As a reminder, China conducted threatening military exercises in the Taiwan Straits just prior to the 2000 presidential elections. Nevertheless, the people of Taiwan elected Chen Shui-bian, a member of Taiwan's pro-independence Democratic Progressive Party. The United States is implicated in the conflict between Taiwan and China; many American political leaders maintain that the U.S. military must defend Taiwan if China acts upon its threats. There are very few nations that lack official diplomatic ties with the United States. Among them are Iraq, Libya, North Korea, and, oddly, Taiwan.

Taiwan's twenty-first-century claims to fame are its unique political situation and its remarkably successful economic development that started in the early 1960s. Its economic growth—remarkable for its fast pace and equity—have made it a model for Third World nations. Taiwan became a household name in the United States for its export of cheap commodities such as T-shirts and Christmas tree lights. Today, Taiwan is better known for manufacturing computer hardware. It is also an important market for American and European retail goods and services, including everything from Starbuck's coffee to Rolex watches. Nearly 70 percent of the population now lives in urban areas, and the population of 22 million is highly educated, with an illiteracy rate of only 6 percent in 1999. Taiwan is among the world's thirty richest nations by GNP per capita (just over $13,000 U.S. in 1999) and has one of the largest foreign exchange reserves at over $100 billion U.S. (Government Information Office 2002). Its wealth, however, is very recent, and most middle-aged and older residents remember times of poverty.

My field research was centered in the national capital, Taipei, which is also the island's economic and cultural center. Taipei has one of the highest population densities in the world ("Taiwan, Facts and Figures" 1999). Over 40 percent of the island's urban residents live in the Taipei metropolitan area (Government Information Office 2002). Taipei is what sociologist Saskia Sassen (1991) calls a global city—markedly different from most of the island. Many multinational corporations have offices in Taipei, and its shopping districts are crammed with cosmopolitan consumer places such as the Virgin Records Megastore, Watson's drugstores (of Hong Kong), Sogo department stores (of Japan), and, of course, a Hard Rock Café. Bridal photography salons like those I describe in chapter 2 are not exclusive to Taipei; they can be found even in rural townships. But Taipei is Taiwan's bridal industry capital.

As Taipei-centered research, this ethnography is located in Taiwan in specific ways. When young people migrate in search of career opportunities, they are likely to migrate to Taipei, not away from it. When trends in international youth popular culture take hold in Taiwan, they most likely start in Taipei, where connections to Singapore, Tokyo, New York, and London are strongest. When news organizations report on developments in the bridal industry, or when television serial dramas include a scene in a bridal salon, the bridal salons in the spotlight are overwhelmingly those of Taipei. Similarly, when bridal photographers and entrepreneurs scout out new ideas, their notions of prestige prescribe the routes they follow: Bridal photographers and entrepreneurs in Taiwan's smaller cities look to fashion developments in larger cities to inspire their new offerings each season. Taipei photographers, meanwhile, look abroad for inspiration.

Taipei is a nexus of mobility. There I interviewed young women and men with family roots in many rural areas of Taiwan, both north and south. Approximately 40 percent of Taipei residents are recent migrants from elsewhere in Taiwan (Speare, Lin, and Tsay 1988: 63). For example, the friends gathered at the Italian coffee house that night in 1996 were alumni of a Taipei-area university, though most had roots elsewhere and had taken up residence in the Taipei metropolitan area upon graduation. Yu-ling and Xin-de lived in the south and had driven up to Taipei just for the gathering. Ben-ming had spent most of the preceding several years in Beijing and was soon to return there. My location in Taipei brought me in touch with residents of many Taiwan counties and with nationals of at least a dozen countries who, in one way or another, were involved with Taipei and bridal photography.

Taipei is a rich city. The bridal salons I came to know most intimately were centrally located and therefore among the island's most expensive. Most (but not all) of the bridal consumers I met had purchased their bridal photography packages in Taipei, where even the least expensive salons charge higher rates than those outside the city. Young women and men raised in smaller cities or in the countryside often move to the Taipei metropolitan area for schooling or work opportunities, meet their future spouse in Taipei, purchase central-Taipei bridal services, and get married at the groom's countryside family home. Such couples choose Taipei's bridal salons for their higher prestige and trendsetting styles. Other couples with non-Taipei roots prefer to save money by using the bridal services of salons in smaller towns. Or, like Ben-ming and Jing, they spend as much money in a smaller town as many couples might spend in the city, but their money buys more photos, bigger photos, more styles, and more settings. Some Taipei residents choose suburban Taipei salons for convenience or lower cost, or both. My research methods afforded me opportunities to talk to women and men who fall into all of these categories and to visit rural and small-town bridal salons on several occasions, but my observations stem primarily from my experiences in central Taipei salons.

Locating this ethnography in a particular class context is complex. In the recent past, class mobility in Taiwan was extremely high, such that the class system was considered "open."[1] The real miracle of Taiwan's economic development is that industrialization occurred rapidly *and* distributed economic prosperity relatively equally. The Republic of China's inheritance of the Japanese-designed infrastructure for colonial extraction, together with its policies of land reform, export-oriented industrialization, and universal education, helped foster this process. Research indicates that the movement of farmers into industry produced much of Taiwan's initial economic mobility and that inequality is now on the rise (Tsay 1993). Nonetheless, it is not uncommon to meet women and men attending Taiwan's most prestigious universities whose fathers are manual laborers and mothers are roadside betel nut stand operators, educated only through middle school. Though many bridal photographers were educated only through high school, they earn salaries higher than college professors. Manager Li, owner of French Riviera Bridal Photography, is the daughter of pig farmers. Her mother, who had cash reserves from land sales, gave her seed money to start the business. Today, Manager Li is a wealthy woman who travels abroad (often with her aging, country-dwelling parents as her guests) four times a year, lives in a ritzy Taipei neighborhood, collects precious gemstones, indulges in luxury beauty treatments and designer fashions of every sort, and has investments in the growing bridal photography industry in China. She lacks the prestige or "cultural capital" of a professional with a graduate degree, but she rivals them in economic clout (see Bourdieu 1984). Stories like hers are common. The pace of upward mobility, especially in the service sector of the 1990s, was dizzyingly rapid (Sheu 1993).[2]

The status marker people in Taipei refer to most frequently is education. Those with university degrees are said to enjoy a higher status and be more refined than those lacking in education. Many of my informants who were not bridal industry employees held college degrees. A brief look at the four women who most influenced me is telling. Mei-hua is the daughter of a successful businessman and has a college degree. Jin-yi is the daughter of a farmer and has a vocational high school degree. Florence is the daughter of a wealthy Taipei family and has not only a prestigious university degree but also a master's degree in business from an American university. Yu-ling is the daughter of a rural banker and graduated from the same university as Mei-hua. Most of my bridal industry informants held only vocational high school degrees; few had university degrees and most came from humble origins. However, three former bridal photographers, who were teaching photography and practicing commercial photography at the time I interviewed them, had university degrees. Xiao-lan, the bridal magazine editor who helped me to make contacts, has a university degree, too.

Ethnicity remains a salient issue in contemporary Taiwan but is not particularly important in the realm of bridal photography. Some background is in order here. Approximately 84 percent of Taiwan's population consists of native Taiwanese (speakers of Minnan or Hakka

dialects)—descendants of immigrants from southeast China who settled
in Taiwan roughly three hundred years ago. Two percent of the population consists of Austronesian-language-speaking aborigines. The remaining 14 percent consists of Mainlanders (and their descendants) who
moved to Taiwan with the KMT between 1945 and 1950 ("Taiwan,
Facts and Figures" 1999). The ethnic divide between the Mainlanders
and Taiwan natives is at times sharp—particularly in the political arena,
as Mainlanders tend to support reunification with China. For many
years, Mainlanders kept Taiwanese out of high-powered positions in the
state sector, which included the postal service, telephone service, television networks, and news organizations. In response to state domination
by Mainlanders, Taiwanese managed to develop powerful business networks and excluded Mainlanders from them. In the 1980s and 1990s,
Taiwanese converted their economic capital into political power, culmi-
nating in the presidency of Lee Teng-hui, a Taiwanese man who rose
through the ranks of the KMT and served as president from 1988 to
2000. In Taiwan's first multiparty presidential election in 2000, Chen
Shui-bian, a candidate in support of Taiwan's independence from China,
was elected to power.

In politics the division between Mainlanders and Taiwanese remains
important, but in other realms the importance of the ethnic clash is waning. For one thing, Mainlanders are an aging population. First-generation
Mainlanders are now seventy years of age or older. They are often unable
to communicate with Taiwanese of the same age, since most Mainlanders
speak only Mandarin and, perhaps, a native dialect of their home province in China. Many elderly Taiwanese speak only Taiwanese and, if
they were educated, Japanese. Language, cultural, and political barriers
keep older Taiwanese and Mainlanders apart. Second-generation Mainlanders are a small group in Taiwan. Many Mainlander families emigrated to the United States in the 1950s, 1960s, and 1970s, partly for
fear of a Taiwanese takeover of Taiwan. Among Mainlanders who
remained in Taiwan, intermarriage with Taiwanese women was common because few Mainland women were among those who escaped to
Taiwan with the KMT. The children of these marriages often consider
themselves neither Taiwanese nor Mainlander but *xin taiwanren*—which
translates awkwardly as New Taiwan People (see Johnson 1992).

Among younger people, cultural and language barriers between Mainlanders and Taiwanese have dissolved considerably. Second-generation
Mainlanders shared the experiences of public education with Taiwanese

classmates. The KMT brought Mandarin to the tongues of all those educated after 1945. The Taiwanese language was banned from television
until the late 1980s, and Mandarin became the language of choice
among youth, as it was a mark of education and prestige. Recently
Taiwanese has made a comeback, but I seldom heard it spoken in Taipei's
bridal industry, where the primary orientation is toward "modernity"—
very much wrapped up in constructions of Westernness and interested in
avoiding parochialisms.[3] Bridal industry workers tend to be young, and
the industry's focus is on youthful modes of representation.

My use of the phrase "Taiwanese bridal photography" rather than
"Chinese bridal photography" will rile some people. Anthropologists
once convened upon Taiwan to study "China" and labeled the men and
women they encountered there as "Chinese." Since the end of martial
law, however, Taiwan's changing economic and political climate has profoundly influenced English-language writings on the island. Today few
scholars view Taiwan as exemplary of "the Chinese"; instead, most write
about Taiwan in its regional particularities and historically, politically,
and culturally complex relations with China (Murray and Hong 1991).
The present study adds to the growing body of literature that regards
Taiwan as an entity worthy of study in its own right. The convention in
the literature, however, is to account for ethnic differences in part by lim-
iting the label "Taiwanese" to only those who, in the local terminology,
call themselves *benshengren* (the people of this province), in contrast to
waishengren (people from outside the province, or Mainlanders). Therefore, when describing the island's people or history at large, authors refer
to the people "of Taiwan" or, awkwardly, "Taiwan people" or "Taiwan
history" (for an example, see Harrell and Huang 1994).

I depart from that convention here by writing of "Taiwanese bridal
photography" and "Taiwanese bridal salons." Though some bridal salon
owners identify themselves as Mainlanders, I assert that in at least this
particular realm of social life in Taiwan ethnic divisions are not salient,
and therefore the awkwardness of English-language contortions are un-
necessary. Moreover, I view the bridal photography phenomenon as having its roots in contemporary *Taiwan,* a place that is very different from,
although connected to, China. By "Taiwanese bridal photography," then,
I do not mean to invoke the Taiwanese/Mainlander divide or suggest that
Mainlanders do not participate in this phenomenon. However, I intentionally invoke a division between Taiwan and China that regards Taiwan as neither exemplary of China nor reducible to it.

PROBLEMS IN WRITING A HISTORY OF THE BRIDAL PHOTO

Bridal industry experts disagree over how the modern bridal industry came to be. Certain salons are said to be Taipei's oldest, but beyond that basic fact, the bridal industry insiders I interviewed shared no consensus on their industry's origins. Mr. Zhao, a photographer/salon owner, told me that he was the first to combine photography and dress rental under one roof, stressing that this move had launched the modern bridal industry. Mr. Lin, a salon manager, boasted that his company was the first to revolutionize the photographer-client relationship by pairing one photographer with one couple for a day-long shoot, thus enabling the photographer to evince the varied poses and expressions necessary for the large albums that are the hallmark of bridal photography today.

Mr. Zhang, a former bridal photographer who owns a commercial photography studio and teaches classes in bridal photography, insisted that the first modern bridal salon was in Taichung, in central Taiwan. Mr. Wu, the owner of the school where Mr. Zhang teaches, disagrees. He believes that Mr. T. H. Chen, a photographer/salon owner, first got the ball rolling. Mr. Chen remains one of the island's best-known bridal photographers. The elderly Mr. Xu, owner/photographer of one of Taipei's oldest (and once most successful) photo studios, agrees with Mr. Wu. Early bridal salon photographers like Mr. Chen usurped Mr. Xu's main line of business. Mr. Chen was a younger, small-time competitor of Mr. Xu, whose photo studio overflowed with customers in the 1970s and 1980s. Trying to stir up business, Mr. Chen began taking couples to a nearby park to shoot their photographs. This ingenious move first created a market for more than two photos per couple. Xu, Wu, and Chen are all somewhat well-known figures in the bridal photography industry. I located them by asking about the bridal industry's history among industry insiders.

One day midway through my field research, I attended a concert at Taipei's Chengpin bookstore, thinking it would be a break from my hectic research schedule. Noticing I was a Chinese-speaking foreigner, a woman seated in front of me turned around to greet me. She was desperately in search of an English tutor. I had a research grant and was out of the tutoring business by this time, so I offered to take her business card and put her in touch with someone else. Ever the opportunist, I told her about my research and asked if she knew anyone either recently married or in the bridal photography business. She told me that a friend of hers operates the oldest bridal salon in Taiwan. The next day, I phoned her for the friend's phone number and promptly made the call to request an interview. Christine Suzuka, hearing of my connection to a dear friend, gladly accepted. Her mother, an elderly Japanese makeup artist, hair stylist, and dressmaker, claims to have developed the concept of the modern Taiwanese bride. I tell her story in greater detail later in this chapter.

When I finally met the famous T. H. Chen for an interview, he confirmed Xu's story. He took pride in seeing himself as the creative genius behind the bridal photography industry. He also corroborated Mrs. Suzuka's story, though it seemed clear that he would not have told me about Mrs. Suzuka if I had not asked. Every history of the bridal industry I heard centered around male photographers who emerged as successful entrepreneurs as a result of an innovation. Only through a coincidental chat with a stranger at a concert did I hear about Mrs. Suzuka. The beginnings of the modern bridal industry remain uncertain to me, but clearly the telling of its history takes place through the lens of the present, where T. H. Chen's company, Sesame, is larger and better known than Mrs. Suzuka's. Mrs. Suzuka's bridal salon today is small and of marginal significance in the Taipei bridal industry. Lao Mai, Sesame, and Zhongshi are among Taipei's oldest and largest bridal salons.

My informants were interested in the history of their business for reasons different from mine. Today, competition in the Taipei bridal industry is intense. Each salon claims to have the newest trendsetting styles of dress, makeup, and photography. In this environment, bridal industry insiders place a high premium on the ability to come up with new ideas that will tap into consumer desires. They tend to look at the industry's history as a matter of which entrepreneur was the first to coin a new idea or begin a certain practice that later became standard. Industry experts' stories take the logic of success and prestige in today's bridal industry and transpose it onto the past. Focusing on the personae of creative heroes and heroines, however, their stories neglect attention to structural forces: the decreasing cost of photography relative to other wedding costs, the rise of wage labor and changing intergenerational relations within families, increases in the standard of living, and the transnational flow of visual images. These society-wide changes produced consumers and effected their demand for goods and services. Both individual creativity and structural change came to play in the making of the modern bridal industry. The history told through the lens of individual ingenuity is a project fraught with competing claims and, ultimately, not helpful in understanding why people bought into these new goods and services. My approach to bridal photography's history focuses on things—photos, gowns, hairstyles, makeup—instead of entrepreneurs.

Figure 2. This photograph is typical of old-time studio shots.
(Image courtesy of the Council for Cultural Affairs, Republic
of China, circa 1945.)

OLD WEDDING PHOTOGRAPHS

The history of bridal photography is, of course, closely tied to the history
of the camera in Taiwan. Missionaries brought cameras to China and
Taiwan not long after photographic technology was invented in Europe
in the 1840s, but it was not until the 1920s, during Japanese colonial
rule, that Japanese-trained photographers opened local photo studios
(then called *xiezhenguan*, later called *zhaoxiangguan*).[4] Wealthy clients
posed for studio portraits and commissioned large on-site group wedding

Figure 3. In contrast to old-fashioned wedding photos, modern bridal photographs portray brides and grooms as emotionally and physically intimate. (Image courtesy of Cang-ai Bridal Photography Co., 2003. Photographer: Wei Wei.)

portraits *(jiazu jiehunzhao)*. Until the late 1970s or early 1980s, professional wedding photographs typically included at most three shots: one of the couple standing side by side (as in figure 2), one of them seated, and one of the groom's extended family with bride and groom seated at front center. In stark contrast to contemporary photographs (figure 3), couples avoided smiling and touching. Interviewees expressed the view that in times past, photography served to document the marriage: these serious photographs served as proof of the couple's marriage.

Modern bridal photography is not a true descendant of the old-fashioned photo studio system of documenting weddings for the new kinship bonds they create. The work of producing photographic proof of a marriage now rests squarely with friends and relatives wielding snapshot and home video cameras. Some wealthy families hire professional photographers to shoot group photographs at wedding banquets, and an increasing number of families hire professional videographers to video parts of the wedding banquet and, occasionally, even the wedding rituals. As in contemporary weddings elsewhere (the United States and Japan, for example), those charged with taking wedding-day photos and videos in Taiwan focus on capturing particular moments such as, in the United States, the bride and groom cutting the cake or, in Taiwan, the tearful bride entering the car that will take her away from her family home and deliver her to the groom's (see Edward 1989). Weddings I attended, in fact, were quite dominated by the desire to set up particular shots. Also stressed is photographing wedding banquet guests, especially important guests (the groom's boss, for example), posed with the bride and groom or their parents. At some banquets, a lay or professional photographer is in place to shoot a quick photo of every group of guests posed with the couple as they leave the banquet.

The use and display of wedding-day photographs in the 1920s through 1970s, though, was unlike the use and display of contemporary day-of-wedding snapshots. In earlier days, photographs were very expensive. In fact, in the 1920s only elite families could afford them. For many families who commissioned wedding photos prior to the 1960s, wedding photographs were their *only* photographs and were prized possessions. As such, they were proudly displayed on the walls of the entry room in homes, where guests were greeted and entertained. The high cost of photography prohibited the circulation of copies among kin, and the photos were valued more for their display and family history functions than as objects of exchange.

Those who could afford it visited local *xiezhenguan* to commission whole-family portraits on other occasions as well. Individual photographic portraits of elderly family members became important family objects, displayed at funerals and on family ancestral altars. By the 1960s and 1970s the cost of a professional wedding portrait had become affordable for most. Photos (and their attendant technology) did not become the cheap, everyday objects they are today in Taiwan until the 1970s and 1980s. Taiwan's "economic miracle" of rapid industrialization in the 1960s and 1970s created its wide and affluent middle classes. This—coupled with technological developments that made cameras mass-produced household objects—permitted the democratization of the photograph.

Today, families store wedding-day snapshots in small books of clear plastic sleeves, provided free of charge by photo processing shops. Even working-class homes I visited had stacks and stacks of these small photo albums emblazoned with the likes of Kodak and Fuji on the covers. Well-organized people place handwritten labels on the books' spines, indicating the event or dates of the photos within; but more often families toss the books into drawers or onto shelves, storing wedding-day photographs alongside baby photos, vacation photos, graduation-day pictures, and snapshots of the family dog after a grooming. Wedding snapshots may be placed in small frames for display on a shelf or VCR alongside other family and vacation photos. (Bridal salon–produced portraits, which are *much* larger, almost always hang on bedroom walls.) The treatment of wedding-day photographs, then, has changed markedly. In contrast to the professional photos of the past, they do not necessarily receive prominent display once a wedding fades into memory. Today's bridal studio portraits, on the other hand, do not serve as evidence of the wedding in the way that wedding-day photos served in the past, yet there is a link between the two: Today's bridal portraits, like their *xiezhen-guan*-produced ancestors, hang upon household walls for many years and are the prime objects of display in relation to weddings.

THE ARRIVAL OF THE WHITE GOWN

Taipei's modern bridal salons are more than photo studios; they are also bridal-wear rental centers. And the history of bridal wear in Taiwan closely follows Taiwan's political history. In the past, most brides wore homemade *qipao* dresses of the best red fabric the family could afford. Only the super-elite, a tiny fraction of Taiwan's population, would have dressed its brides in the elaborate imperial-style crowns and gowns that are today reproduced and often worn by couples posing for bridal photos. Red (*hong*, which includes "light red" or pink) was the color associated with weddings and was used not only for the bride's dress but also for decorations and banquet foods. Although brides today almost always wear white gowns, red and pink remain the central colors in wedding decorations, invitations, and banquet items. Ironically, the color white is traditionally associated with funerals. The popularity of white bridal gowns took off after 1945, when the Nationalist Party assumed control over Taiwan upon its retrocession to China by Japan.

The white, Western bridal gown was not unknown prior to 1945, but elite Taiwanese during the Japanese colonial period were more likely to dress brides in Japanese kimono than in Western-style bridal wear. Beginning in the 1920s, the Japanese colonial regime worked to "Japanify" the Taiwanese, offering incentives to families to speak Japanese and dress like Japanese. Weddings were most likely occasions for upwardly mobile urban families to court colonial administrators by dressing couples in Japanese formal wear even while maintaining other Taiwanese wedding customs. The vast majority of Taiwanese, however, lived in the countryside and worked the land under Japan's colonial system. Countryside brides most likely continued to dress in red gowns of Taiwanese styling. Though the urban elite consisted of a very small number of people in Taiwan until more recent decades, elite wedding fashions are important to track in relation to the development of the modern bridal industry. Even in rural weddings of the past, weddings were occasions for families to demonstrate (and exaggerate) their wealth. Those wanting to put on an impressive status display looked to the practices of elite families and emulated them when possible. It is necessary, then, to understand the composition of Taiwan's elite in order to understand changes in bridal wear.

In 1945, Japan gave up colonial control of Taiwan and returned the island to China. The political transition effected a vast transformation in the elite and middle classes. The KMT had just battled Japanese forces over control of the Chinese mainland, and KMT leaders and soldiers were horrified that ethnic Chinese in Taiwan had adopted some of the ways of the enemy. Elite Taiwanese at the time had been closely associated with the Japanese colonial administration. Colonial Taiwan was an agrarian society where the vast majority of the population earned a living by farming and fishing. Most others—wealthy landowners, entrepreneurs, and Taiwanese employees of the colonial administration—had close ties with Japanese colonial officials. Many Taiwanese elite fled to Japan shortly after the retrocession; members of the urban elite who remained in Taiwan suffered greatly under KMT rule (advocates of Taiwanese independence call it the KMT "occupation," in fact) as targets of anti-"Communist" purges known today as the White Terror. The KMT placed loyal Mainlanders in all the government jobs during this time, when there were very few white-collar jobs outside the state sector, instantly creating a Mainlander-dominated urban elite. Many elite and middle-class Taiwanese were jailed as political prisoners, and thousands were killed. Mainlanders came to occupy the highest statuses in society, even as the Taiwanese majority feared and hated them. When high-profile weddings were described or pictured in newspapers, for example, they were Mainlander weddings. Mainlander-preferred bridal styles became the high-water mark in wedding fashion.

Why did Mainlanders prefer white weddings? First, the Chinese revolutionaries who overthrew the Qing dynasty in 1911 had identified certain customs related to marriage and family life as sources of Chinese weakness in the face of foreign imperialism: footbinding, concubinage, and arranged marriage.[5] The urban elite in Republican China had broken from the past by engaging in self-selection of spouses and dressing brides in white, Western-style wedding gowns. Chiang Kai-shek, the KMT war hero and president of the Republic, was Christian, and his bride wore white. Taiwan's Mainlanders brought their preference for white bridal gowns with them. Second, many Chinese cultural practices involve family, yet the Mainlanders had left their parents, grandparents, and ancestral altars back in mainland China (many soldiers left behind wives and children, too). In their view, they were awaiting "the return of the motherland" to KMT control so they could finally return home. They felt deeply dislocated not only from their families, farms, and businesses but from their cultural heritage as well. Among Christian converts in Taiwan there were many more Mainlanders than Taiwanese. Norma Diamond (1975) found that Mainlanders sought friendship in churches because they lacked the traditional Chinese paths for forming social ties. In the absence of their kinship networks, Mainlanders may have approached weddings differently than native Taiwanese. It was in this context that the white bridal gown came to the fore among Taiwan's urban sophisticates.

Another reason for the preference for Western white bridal gowns over Chinese red ones may have been U.S. military, political, and economic patronage of Chiang's Taiwan. In many realms of life in Taiwan, the policies, practices, and goods favored by Americans remain highly esteemed, but this was especially so in the 1950s, when Western bridal wear took root as a mass phenomenon in Taiwan. It is no exaggeration to say that the Republic of China on Taiwan would not exist today without the political and military support it received from the United States during the Cold War. Even today, though the United States dropped official relations with Taiwan more than thirty years ago, U.S. political commitments and arms sales to Taiwan (undergirded by American economic interests in Taiwan and in the military-industrial complex at home) serve to maintain its status as a renegade province that has evaded Communist control for over five decades.

Considering Taiwan's circumstances in the 1950s, it is understandable how a foreign object such as the white bridal gown became a local standard quite quickly. From 1950 until the mid-1980s the state and its interests had enormous influence on society in Taiwan. Martial law (involving, for example, strict censorship of media and even of personal correspondence, the closing of mountain areas where Communists might lurk, the prohibition of dance clubs) was the rule of the land. Moviegoers were required not only to view short propaganda films but also to rise and sing the national anthem before the start of each movie. State propaganda campaigns urged all citizens to focus dutifully on hard work in order to develop the nation and eventually achieve military conquest over the People's Republic. Women were discouraged from vain pursuits such as cosmetics and fashion, and families were asked to take a frugal approach to weddings so as to conserve the nation's resources for war. Yet in spite of these influences, the Western bridal gown, and the glamour today associated with it, swept into Taiwan on the same political currents produced by such grave matters as the civil war in China and the Cold War more generally. Precisely because the KMT ruled with a very heavy hand in the three decades after its arrival, Taiwan's social elite was a class intimately tied to the state. Fashion trendsetters were invariably governmental officials and their wives—precisely the members of society for whom American political patronage was most real.

The wide popularity of rented white, Western-style bridal gowns and the affordability of professional wedding portraits dovetail in the history of Taiwan—so much so that family photo collections in the 1950s seldom picture brides dressed in anything other than Western gowns. Very few families were able to afford a photograph before 1950, and after 1950 the families who were able to afford a photograph of the bride and groom were the same families likely to dress their brides in white. (Or, perhaps after 1950 people believed that the only brides worth photographing were those dressed in Western-style gowns.) My oral-history research revealed that poor families and those who were very rural continued to dress brides in homemade red gowns well beyond the 1950s. Jin-yi's mother had worn a red, homemade gown as late as 1970, in fact. In only one generation's time, her family saw styles change from a bride dressed in a hand-sewn, red Chinese-style gown with no photograph of the wedding day to that bride's daughter, in the 1990s, dressed in numerous, mass-produced rental gowns with nearly fifty huge portraits in an ornate album. Nevertheless, the mothers of most of the Taipei brides I met in the late 1990s had also worn white and been photographed as brides, though they wore fewer gowns and had far fewer photographs. And prior to the late 1980s brides rented their gowns from one business and commissioned their photographs from another.

As a result of U.S.-Taiwan trade relations, increasing numbers of brides in the United States found "Made in Taiwan" labels inside their wedding gowns in the 1970s and 1980s. Taiwanese workers' manufacture of a substantial portion of the white, Western-style gowns sold in the U.S. bridal market—women cutting, sewing, and ironing in their living rooms under a satellite factory system—was one small piece of the local economic miracle that made the blossoming of Taiwanese bridal services possible (Hsiung 1996). Thus many people in Taiwan had intimate knowledge of U.S. bridal fashions. In fact, former bridal market workers remember sweeping their living rooms multiple times each day to prevent the white fabric from becoming dirty.

The proliferation of bridal photography salons began in the late 1980s, concurrent with the end of martial law in Taiwan. Business opportunities blossomed for tapping into the demand for beauty services among Taiwan's newly rich—paralleling the start of procapitalistic economic policies in China. By the mid-1990s, Taiwanese entrepreneurs in search of cheap labor moved bridal gown production for the U.S. market to the People's Republic. Bridal gowns for Taiwan's market, however, are still produced locally.[6]

Some of the largest bridal photography salons have their own gown design and production facilities, while smaller salons buy from a handful of local bridal design and production companies. The production of gowns for Taiwan's market takes place on a much smaller scale because Taiwan's population is comparatively small, the gowns are rented (and therefore worn by numerous brides), and the styles change too rapidly to make mass production of the gowns profitable. The production of gowns for Taiwan's bridal market today has a different locus, and a different style and pace of production, than the Taiwanese-owned bridal factories in the People's Republic of China that churn out thousands of the same gown.

THE PACKAGING OF BRIDAL BEAUTY

Photography, gowns, and makeovers are the trinity of Taiwan's bridal industry today, but oral histories of the modern bridal photography, as told by industry insiders, almost always feature photographers as the ones who brought the bridal industry to its present state of success. It makes sense that Taiwan's bridal wear manufacturers are not the movers and shakers in the island's bridal industry history, since they were focused on the far larger U.S. market. Rather, a few photography entre-preneurs, it is said, began bringing gown rentals into their studios in the late 1970s. Thus began one-stop bridal shopping.

Also in the 1970s, Mrs. Suzuka was combining bridal makeovers with dress rentals. Her customers went elsewhere for their photographs. Mrs. Suzuka had moved to Taipei with her Taiwanese husband, an interna-tional merchant, in the 1960s as a young woman. Having worked as a beautician in Tokyo, she opened an elite beauty salon in Taipei, emulat-ing those she knew in Tokyo. Her initial customers were well-to-do ladies, primarily the wives of government and embassy officials. A hair wash and styling at her salon cost six times those at other salons, but increasing numbers of non-elite women came to her for wedding-day hair styling. Though there were long-standing traditions of beauty prepa-rations for brides in Taiwan, in the 1970s Taipei brides began seeking out professionalized beauty services in large numbers. On auspicious dates for weddings, Mrs. Suzuka's salon used to hair-dress dozens of young women.

Brides then, Mrs. Suzuka remembers, "were so ugly!" She remembers them wearing dirtied rental gowns of poor quality and unsophisticated design; and although many sought out professional hair stylists, few coordinated the colors of the flowers worn in their hair with those they carried in bouquets and with their lipstick color. Sensing a market for upscale bridal gowns, Mrs. Suzuka brought a white bridal gown back to Taipei from Europe and rented it out to her beauty salon customers. Soon after, she hired seamstresses to make copies from imported fabrics. Meanwhile, more and more non-elite brides whose families sought out the finest beauty services for the wedding day took advantage of Mrs. Suzuka's makeup application and color coordination services. When her two daughters finished college, she sent them overseas for training as makeup artists. One went to Japan and the other to the United States. Today the sisters run a beauty school and bridal salon—now including photography. In addition to Taipei brides, they cater to Japanese tourists wanting to be dressed up and made-over for fancy photographs that would be much more expensive in Japan.[7] The Suzukas' small bridal salon is not a major player in Taiwan's bridal market today, but Mrs. Suzuka claims that she and her daughters trained the whole first genera-tion of stylists—women who started out as hair-wash girls in her shop. I checked this fact with others and learned it was no exaggeration.

According to Mrs. Suzuka's telling, it was her sense of beauty that she developed growing up in Tokyo that made her business so popular with Taipei brides. It was not until the 1990s that other bridal business owners combined beauty services with gown/photo packages.

The importance of the mark Mrs. Suzuka made on the development of the modern bridal industry notwithstanding, I suspect that gender had a critical role in making photographers—not beauticians—the successful entrepreneurs who sought out ever-larger pieces of the bridal services market. Sesame, Zhongshi, and Lao Mai, for example, were among the largest bridal salons in Taipei in the late 1990s, and all were founded by photographers. Mrs. Suzuka may have been the only beautician-entrepreneur to have built a successful bridal beauty services and gown rental business because she was—among women working as hairdressers—uniquely situated as the wife of an international businessman. The starting point for those who made their careers as beauticians was the unskilled position of hair-washer, a job for women with little education and no capital. Photographers, in contrast, were by definition male, and men were far more likely than women to have access to family capital in the patriarchal Chinese families of the recent past. They were often the sons of photographers who were trained by their fathers and inherited their modest photo studios and equipment.

It was not until about 1990 that the most successful bridal photography salons began to incorporate hair and makeup styling into their bridal services packages. By 1996, when I arrived in Taipei, all of the more than two hundred Taipei bridal salons sold packages that included dress, beauty styling, and photography. Independent photo studios continued, though their bridal services were now limited to shooting wedding-day photos for wealthy families who hired a professional photographer in addition to the throngs of uncles and cousins wielding snapshot cameras on the wedding day. Independent beauty salons also continued, though brides tended to seek out specialized bridal beauticians called "stylists" (zaoxingshi) to produce the specialized look of a bride. However, independent bridal gown rental shops had become extinct by 1996 in Taipei. Although a few brides on both ends of the economic spectrum—the very poor and the very rich—occasionally sought bridal gowns outside the bridal photography salon system, their needs were not met by gown rental shops. Used rental gowns were periodically sold at street markets for under $10 U.S.—affordable to poorer families. There was little market for such gowns, however, and many gown rental companies preferred to sell old gowns to exporters who continued renting them to the less wealthy, less discerning brides in the People's Republic of China. Very wealthy Taipei brides occasionally sought out gowns even more unique than those available at the most exclusive bridal photography salons and commissioned custom gowns made of imported European designer fabrics. Between these two extremes, however, bridal salons served the needs of a wide spectrum of brides—from working-class to elite—with their combined gown, styling, and photography packages.

CHAPTER 2

Fantasy for Sale

The Modern Bridal Industry

It is impossible to talk about Taiwanese bridal photography without discussing competitive consumption. Though not the only driving force behind this modern cultural practice, status competition explains much about it. Brides, grooms, their families, and their guests regard the photographic displays that decorate wedding banquet entrances as indicators of wealth and prestige. Portable photo albums also make social statements about the bride and groom wherever they are put on view. As objects of competitive consumption, bridal photographs undergo what economist Juliet Schor (1998) calls "upscaling"—with each passing season the standards drift upward as couples seek to outdo the status displays put on by friends and relatives. Competition of a different sort is also played out within the bridal industry. During my mid-1990s field research, Taipei's market for bridal photography services was saturated. Too many players had joined the game. While consumers were striving to keep up with their peers, bridal salons were competing for status-conscious customers—not by cutting prices but by offering photo packages brimming with the newest fashions, stylized photographic techniques, and ever-larger photographs. In this chapter I first discuss competition in the bridal industry—among consumers and among bridal salons—and then describe the industry's workings more generally. Finally, I describe the fantasy worlds produced in bridal salons and the uses to which these fantasy images are put.

COPING WITH COMPETITION

Precisely because virtually every marrying couple in the 1990s bought and displayed bridal photographs, brides were always looking for something to make their own photographs stand out and thus gain the attention of friends and colleagues. Beginning around 1990, when bridal albums and framed enlargements became a must-have for middle-class couples, the size and number of photographs displayed at wedding banquets drifted upward yearly. For the majority of banquet guests, who cannot distinguish between last season's gown styles and the vogue of the moment, size and number of photographs are the clearest means of competition. More photographs and bigger photographs mean more money.

In 1997 Taipei, a minimal bridal package included one poster-size framed enlargement, at least thirty-six inches tall; a photo album containing at least twenty fifteen-inch-high images dry-mounted and laminated with either matte or glossy plastic inside a heavy wooden cover; a small, informal album holding the proof copies of all the photographs the couple ordered; and a box of one hundred thank-you photo cards for passing out to banquet guests (these cards also announced the name of the bridal salon). Upgraded packages could include two framed enlargements—thirty-six inches and forty-eight inches high—and thirty images in the album, or a bigger album photo size: eighteen to twenty inches in height. Package add-ons were also common. Among the newly married and to-be-married brides and grooms I knew best in Taipei in 1997, eighteen-inch-high album photos were standard. Few were content with an album of only two dozen images, and many ordered forty or more. Displaying only one framed enlargement was still acceptable, but many couples were purchasing two. I attended several wedding banquets for couples who had purchased more photographs—perhaps fifty to seventy-five images—than could fit in a single album, so two full albums were on display. As I was finishing up my field research, one salon was promoting bridal packages that included three photo albums: one large traditional album with wooden cover; one small "natal family" *(niang-jia)* book of proofs (usually kept by the couple, not the bride's natal family), and one magazinelike album with the bride as cover girl. Thus the upscaling continued.

Taiwan's most prestigious bridal salons are located in central Taipei, where rents are high and bridal packages are correspondingly expensive. Because so many Taipei couples have family roots in rural counties, it is easy to commission photography packages containing more and bigger photos at a lower price at salons near the bride's or the groom's home-town. At the time of my research, the standard photography packages in rural communities boasted more and bigger photos than those offered in the nation's capital. When the album photograph norm was eighteen inches in Taipei, it was twenty inches in Taichung—and bridal salons there were also promoting seventy-two-inch wall hangings! Bridal fashions in rural Taiwan tend to be even more ostentatious than those of Taipei. One rural bridal salon I visited was selling freestanding sculptures that creatively housed bridal photographs and plug-in framed enlargements decorated with tiny electric lights (see figures 4 and 5).

Those in the know—bridal industry workers and the status-conscious among young Taipei women in their twenties and early thirties, who see the bridal albums of many friends, coworkers, and cousins—recognize the microvariations in style that separate the cutting-edge from the trendy, the trendy from the passé, and urban elegance from uncouth countryside showiness. Brides-to-be often take the pulse of the moment, asking recently married friends about their packages, paying close attention to albums displayed at gatherings of friends and at banquets, and studying the latest bridal beauty magazines. Popular dress colors and styles change with time, and so do studio backdrops, props, poses, and photographic techniques. These young women serve as fashion arbiters, talking excitedly about photographs that offer something new and special, falling silent when photographs fail to impress. Couples who commission their photographs from Taipei's upper-echelon bridal salons seek to gain the praise of these, the most discerning observers.

Taipei bridal packages in 1997 started at about NT $25,000 (at that time, about $1,000 U.S.), though many couples felt that the cheapest packages were grossly inadequate and that NT $40,000 ($1,600 U.S.) was the least one could expect to spend. Taipei's most elite salons averaged NT $100,000 ($4,000 U.S.) per couple. Upgraded packages (and the upper-echelon salons more generally) offer more and bigger photographs, a greater selection of bridal gowns that are nearly new or show very few signs of wear, more hair and makeup style changes over the course of the photo shoot, and a trip outside the photo studio for photographs shot outdoors. Some families demand that the bride wear a brand-new gown, and salons charge extra for the first rental of a new gown.

Even individuals who are not particularly status-conscious in their everyday lives tend to engage in competitive consumption when it comes to weddings because weddings put not just individuals but whole families

Figure 4. A bridal salon has displayed this photograph in an unusual frame that doubles as a table lamp. (Image courtesy of Feichang Nan-nü Bridals, rural Taichung County, 1997.)

on display. A woman who takes no delight in status competition and prefers the simplest, least-expensive bridal package may marry a man who insists on spending more money to outdo his brother. Or a man who has no fashion sense at all may marry a woman who directs him to the most exclusive bridal salon. Even when neither bride nor groom is interested in putting on a conspicuous display, chances are good that one of them has a mother or father who will lecture the couple on the importance of presenting their families in the best light possible and implore them to have at least as many photographs as the father's best friend's son displayed a month earlier. One couple, both pursuing Ph.D.s in New England, where they were a bit insulated from the status demands of their homeland, returned to Taipei to find that the groom's mother had already selected a bridal salon and paid for their photography and gown package. The display of wealth at wedding banquets is something most families will not leave up to the whims of brides and grooms who do not themselves express enthusiasm for it.

Bridal salons have to tailor their products to meet the demands of consumers engaged in fast-paced competitive consumption, and anticipating market demand requires educated guesswork. Bridal salon managers who can predict the popular new style of the next season and provide it in a cost-efficient manner meet with success, but predicting the future is difficult. The rest must scramble to keep up with the latest twists and turns in Taipei bridal fashion trends.

Inside the bridal industry, interviewees complained of poor business conditions due to extremely high competition. Taipei bridal salons proliferated rapidly in the 1990s. Competition for customers became fierce, and a high percentage of Taipei bridal salons went out of business every year, only to be replaced by new salons whose owners hoped to tap into the approximately NT $4.5 billion ($180 million U.S.) spent annually by bridal industry consumers in the late 1990s. Some well-established bridal business owners estimated that as many as one-third of Taipei's salons go out of business or change ownership every year. Workers at many salons are routinely laid off during annual down cycles (just after the Chinese New Year and during the Ghost Month in late summer, when hungry ghosts roam the earth and meddle in human affairs). Even at the well-established salons, worker turnover is high because new salon owners lure saleswomen, stylists, photographers, and photography assistants away from their old jobs to work at new ones.

The fierce competition has forced bridal salons to come up with new backdrops, new scenes, new poses, new gowns, new props, and other

Figure 5. A framed portrait spells out "Fall in Love" in tiny lights. Salons display bridal photos in unusual ways to attract the attention of customers in search of something different. (Image courtesy of Feichang Nan-nü Bridals, rural Taichung County, 1997.)

innovations at a rapid pace to attract customers. Gown designers produce new styles every month rather than every season, for example. Sometimes bridal salons stress their novelty by pretending to change ownership. Manager Huang described how her business, which was very successful for the first few years, eventually slowed down. She remodeled the sales space, renamed the business, and reopened in the exact same location with resounding success, despite no major changes in the product.

While salon owners and photographers are constantly seeking out new marketing strategies to attract attention, they also keep a close eye on what competitors are doing and copy them; this makes it difficult to be the only salon in the city offering a particular deal or special product for more than a few weeks. When one of the top Taipei salons begins promoting something new (a new dress style, a new type of studio backdrop, a new way of displaying gowns in the store window, a new neon sign), others are quick to copy. Owners, managers, and photographers scout the offerings of superior salons in order to emulate them, and big-name salons carefully guard their plans for new marketing techniques. As soon as one salon is renamed "Paris" and looks to be enjoying success, others will be named "Milan," "Rome," "Madrid," and "Barcelona," not to mention "Paris-Taipei" and other close variations. (There were salons with all of these names in 1997.) When one salon parts company with the rest by offering shoppers European coffee drinks served in fine china cups instead of black tea served in paper cups, soon several others will be offering real fruit juices served in glassware and decorated with paper umbrellas. Among the other marketing gimmicks I observed were free honeymoon vacations with the purchase of a bridal package, foldout pages in photo albums, bridal portraits emblazoned on mirrors and clocks, and compact disks of love songs with a bridal portrait on the label.

Salon managers also look to marketing concepts outside Taipei. For instance, Manager Chen studied fashion magazines like Chinese *Elle* and *Vogue* to see what colors, fonts, and designs were being used to promote luxury brands when she wanted to replace her salon's exterior signage. She selected a Chanel advertisement that used neon green, purple, and yellow as her model. Photographers, dress buyers, and stylists also study the trends on display in fashion magazines and in local and international bridal magazines, mining them for new ideas.

The costs of labor and materials in the photo production process are easier to control than the costs relating to fashion, for there are many risks involved in attempting to supply the right styles at the right time. In the bridal photography business, keeping costs down means moving couples through the production process as smoothly and quickly as possible. At the same time, brides do not want to feel like products churned out on an assembly line; thus the bridal industry proclaims that it lavishes brides with red-carpet treatment fit for celebrities. Part of the bridal salon's product, in fact, is the bride's experience of being treated well. Plus, unhappy brides make for unattractive photographs, and unhappy customers will not refer their friends. Moving brides through the system with relative speed *and* keeping them happy is a tall order. Salons therefore take pains to retain as much control as possible even while fostering the sense that the bride is the boss, not the object, of manufacture. As a result, bridal photo albums seldom truly represent individual preferences and personalities, but brides and grooms do not often complain of having been treated as objects of manufacture. The production process goes something like this:

1. Couples visit salons in one of Taipei's bridal districts or attend a bridal fair, where numerous salons set up elaborate booths in a large exhibition hall; there they meet with saleswomen and view sample albums and gowns.

2. The bride—often accompanied by the groom, her mother, or a friend—returns to the salon to select gowns. Most brides wear one white bridal gown *(hunsha)* and two colored formal evening gowns *(wanlifu)* at their wedding banquets. Brides who have additional banquets (betrothal banquets, post-wedding banquets) require two or more additional gowns for *each* of these events. Finally, brides select gowns to wear during the photo shoot (usually different from those worn to banquets)—often two bridal gowns and three or more evening gowns. A bride whose groom has purchased a large package of photographs (requiring no fewer than six gowns) and who will be honored at two banquets (a common occurrence) thus needs to select twelve gowns. The length of time taken to select gowns varies widely. One bride reported trying on gowns and deliberating over them for six hours, with the help of her mother and her saleswoman, to make choices for her three banquets and the photo shoot. This bride described herself as "picky," however. Others needed only an hour or two. Saleswomen, here serving as dress consultants, try to speed up the process by employing maneuvers to reduce the number of gowns a bride tries on and by bringing their professional opinion to bear on the bride. For

example, after allowing a bride to try on four or five gowns, a saleswoman may ask her which she likes best so far. When the bride answers, the saleswoman announces those gowns as chosen before she pulls more gowns off the racks for the bride to try. It takes an assertive bride to wrest control over her selections back from an experienced saleswoman who wants to hurry the process so she can get back to the sales floor, where she earns her commissions. Gowns to be rented out for banquet wear are altered to fit the bride. Gowns to be worn only for photo shoots are pinned or clipped in back. All are placed on reserve for the dates in question. Generally, grooms change costume fewer times than do brides. They often wear a business suit and tie of their own for some shots and change into the bridal salon's tuxedoes for others. Grooms do not select their tuxedoes in advance; on the day of the shoot a photography assistant or stylist usually makes the selection for the groom, without consulting him.

3. Bride and groom return to the salon, often the night before the photo session, to meet with their photographer and communicate their tastes and preferences for mood, colors, and photographic style. Many salons have preprinted "communication forms" on which photographers check off each couple's favorite colors, preferred moods (*ganjue*—these include romantic, soft, cute, cool, sexy, upbeat, high fashion, and elegant), and gown colors and styles with which the photographer will coordinate backdrop and props. They also discuss sites for outdoor or on-location photos *(waipai)*. The photographer and saleswoman also advise the couple on how to prepare for the shoot (the bride should wash her hair, the groom should bring along a second pair of glasses, both should prepare for a long and tiresome day). These meetings last about an hour.

4. The couple returns early in the morning for the daylong photo shoot, beginning with the bride's three-hour makeover and hair styling. In the course of the day the couple will be worked on and assisted by at least three bridal salon workers and sometimes as many as six. The bride's hair and makeup are restyled with each dress change. A typical photo shoot day might last from 7 A.M. to 5 P.M. and can last considerably longer if the couple chooses a distant site for their on-location photographs.

5. The couple returns to the salon several days later to view the proofs, usually laid out in photo albums by saleswomen ahead of time in an effort to induce the couple to choose more photographs than their package specifies. For example, rather than grouping together all of the photos taken in the same gown, saleswomen scatter them throughout the album. Most couples want to choose at least two photos (one of the couple and one of the bride alone) of each gown and "styling." Rather than making the process easy for couples by picking out the best one or two shots in each styling for them to choose between, saleswomen and photographers will emphasize that two very similar shots have different "feelings" to boost sales. Most salons do not allow the proofs to leave the salon, and couples often labor over their selections for many hours. Saleswomen and photographers aid them, offering their expert opinions on which photographs will look best as wall hangings and thank-you cards. Photographers also advise the couple about what they can expect from cropping and retouching and explain options for special processing technologies, such as digital imaging, double exposure, and processes that print the photo within limited color ranges (in sepia tones, for example).

6. Photographers and assistants finish retouching the negatives (scratching out major imperfections) and send them out with any special processing instructions to photo labs. Upon receiving the prints, they further retouch the prints by hand, using colored paints and fine brushes. Some couples order specially painted photographs (for example, a black-and-white enlargement with colors painted on lips and eyes), which require additional hand work. Next, assistants decorate the photographs with graphic designs and text *(meigong)*, coat the photographs in plastic mounting, order the albums and affix the photographs in them, and mount enlargements in frames. Time spent on finishing work varies widely by salon and package cost. Photography assistants at Romantic Bliss Bridal Photography estimated an average of three hours of finishing work per album, figuring that some photographs require little work and others require more.

7. The couple returns to view and pick up their finished photographs.

8. The bride picks up her rental gowns and coordinated costume jewelry, packed up by saleswomen (and seamstresses; often they are one and the same), the day before the wedding.

9. The bride returns to the salon (or uses an alternate salon or stylist) for her wedding-morning makeover and styling (another three hours). The cost of this styling is generally not included in bridal packages, and brides often arrange for an alternate stylist nearer their wedding site when the wedding takes place outside Taipei.

10. The couple returns the gowns and costume jewelry to the salon within a few days of the wedding. The salon sends the gowns out for dry cleaning, and at last the process is complete.

In total, the procedure requires a minimum of thirty hours of paid human labor, and often much more. If the bride and groom's time are added, the total is at least fifty hours of labor. For some couples, the time they invest in these objects is as significant as the money they pay for them.

The competition between salons and the frenetic pace of bridal fashion write themselves on the urban landscape. Bridal salons, with their eye-catching facades, tend to coalesce into bridal districts *(hunshajie)*. Taipei has two main bridal districts, Aiguo East Road and Zhongshan North Road. Aiguo East Road is a natural spot for bridal shops because of its proximity to the scenic gardens of the Chiang Kai-Shek Memorial, once a favorite location for outdoor photo shoots, though these are now so common as to be regarded as passé. Zhongshan North Road became a bridal district only in 1994. The area attracted bridal salons very quickly, with more than seventy located there in 1997.

Each salon lines the pedestrian walkways with its wares—enormous backlit photographs of couples in bridal attire and eighteen-inch-tall sample photo albums perch on stands outside the shops. Neon lights and flashy, brightly lit storefront windows compete for attention, each shop trying to outdo its neighbors. Some salon owners have repaved the sidewalk near their storefronts with bright, Mediterranean-style tile mosaics. Others decorate the promenade with displays of plastic flowers and faux stone cupid statuettes. Every storefront has plate-glass windows facing the street, displaying lavish interiors and the newest bridal fashions to passersby. Even if many of the salons are named after European cities, the architectural styles preferred by the industry are more reminiscent of Las Vegas than Paris.

Industry insiders report that the single most important factor in attracting new customers is the shop's design. Customers look for new styles, new photo backdrops, and newness of everything they see in a store. The appearance of newness is particularly difficult to maintain in Taipei, where street-level air pollution is extremely high and dark-gray dust coats shops and homes daily. In the past, salons kept gowns in second-floor rooms, protected from dust and light, but the recent trend has been to display multiple gowns not only in windows but also along the perimeters of street-level showrooms. Many salons have installed decorative glass cases, trimmed with dark wood and ornate brass, to hold and display gowns. Saleswomen, in addition to recruiting new customers and helping brides select their gowns, wash the floors daily to prevent the gowns from being soiled.

There is greater variation in bridal salon architectural design than in the photographs the shops produce. Cinderella, for example, is a small salon on Zhongshan North Road. Inside the shop at ground level, the glossy hardwood floors stretch back through the long, narrow space and yield to a curving marble pathway. Along one wall are wooden closets with glass doors lit from inside to display white and brightly colored gowns. On the other side, display dresses hang facing out into the shop on busts. A dress on a sleek, headless, limbless mannequin faces the street. Several small, round, glass-topped tables with chairs are set up among the dress displays where saleswomen talk to prospective customers and where established customers view their photo proofs. The bases of the tables appear to be large rocks, visible through the glass tabletops. At the back of the shop is a changing area with beige velvet curtains. In the spacious dressing rooms, white, translucent light boxes serve as floors. A winding staircase leads upstairs. On the two-story expanse of wall beside the staircase is a mural of Cinderella's ball—a painting of a lavish ballroom opening up to a long, wide flight of stone steps down which the prince walks Cinderella out to her bejeweled coach. An ornate brass and crystal chandelier hangs above the mural in the winding staircase. The second-floor space contains a makeover and hair styling area, more cases of gowns, and more dressing areas.

Ostensibly, couples are shopping for specific products and services—gowns, makeovers, and photographs—not for the most intriguing salon design, but very few customers know what to look for when they shop around for a bridal package. Saleswomen, photographers, and stylists in the industry told me repeatedly that most customers do not know how to look at sample photographs to compare quality. The shop design initially lures in shoppers, and saleswomen work to form bonds with the bride-to-be once she is inside. While the bride leafs through sample albums, the saleswoman flatters her for her beauty, asks the couple questions about their backgrounds and wedding plans, and generally works to make the couple feel at ease in the salon by forging a personal connection. If the bride says she works for a bank, the saleswoman may say that her sister-in-law works for a bank, too, and talk about how demanding the work is or comment that the bride must be highly educated to hold this job. She may invite the bride to try on dresses, if that seems to interest her. Or she may ask the couple where they want to go on location for a photo shoot and suggest various exotic possibilities.

Saleswomen chat with customers for as long as possible, not raising the topic of a sale until the customers indicate that they want to see a price list or else announce that they are ready to leave. The theory behind bridal salon sales is that customers, once lured in by eye-catching designs, will select their salon based on their feelings toward salon employees. The saleswoman, who will later manage their "case," is to act like the bride's personal friend. Once they get around to talking prices and packages, the saleswoman may offer add-ons (additional boxes of thank-you card photos or a greater number of gowns to be worn during the photo shoot) and give "special" discounts on the basis of the personal relationship just formed.[1]

Many brides actively seek personal connections to the industry before they sign a contract and make a deposit on a package. One bridal magazine employee, for example, told me she had helped all her high school and college classmates select their bridal salons. Having inside knowledge of the strengths, weaknesses, and pricing of many salons, she recommended different shops based on each bride's desires. One friend wanted the salon offering the best gowns, another was more concerned with price, another more interested in quality of makeup and hair design. Having a personal contact with a salon, no matter how distant, increases a couple's hopes of getting a bargain on their photo and dress package. However, couples with personal contacts rarely receive substantial price reductions. More commonly, they are offered a free upgrade to a more expensive package or other perks (larger photos, free graphic design, more dresses) they would not have been willing to pay for in the first place.

Bridal shops know that customers who have personal connections to the salon are very likely to use it: Developing a broad network of personal connections, then, is an important sales strategy. Once while I was interviewing a salon owner, Mr. Zhuang, a representative from a business machine rental company came to the shop to collect credit card machines the shop had rented for the big bridal fair the previous weekend. He politely inquired how the fair had gone. Mr. Zhuang smiled broadly and boasted that they had signed up one hundred new customers in a single day (representing over $150,000 U.S. in new business). The gentleman politely commented that Mr. Zhuang's business was very successful. Mr. Zhuang asked, "Are you married?" "Not yet," he replied. "Come to us when you get married and we'll give you a discount!" Mr. Zhuang promised and asked, "How about your brothers and sisters?" The visitor said, "My girlfriend's brother is deciding when to get married, but I don't know if they are going to take photos." Mr. Zhuang smiled and widened his eyes in surprise, exclaiming, "Taking pictures is a sure thing! It's once in a lifetime!" He then reached behind the desk at the shop's entryway and produced a laminated brochure of price lists that resembled a restaurant menu. He opened to a page describing the NT $45,900 package. Pointing to the price, he offered a NT $10,000 discount, adding that he would throw in as many dresses as the bride would like to wear in her photos for free although the package included only two bridal gowns, three evening gowns, and Chinese and Japanese costumes. The visitor thanked the owner and said he would tell the bride of the offer.

On another occasion, I bumped into an acquaintance at a bridal fair held at a large convention center. Mei-shan and her future husband, Wei-yong, sat at a small table inside the exhibit area for the prestigiously named shop Tiffany Bridal Photography. A saleswoman I had once interviewed, Wendy (who like some other Taiwanese goes by an English name), leafed through sample bridal albums with the couple. When Wendy learned that I knew her customer, she enthusiastically invited me to sit with them and chat. Wendy listened quietly as Mei-shan and I gossiped about a mutual friend. Wendy told her of my previous research forays at Tiffany Bridal and indicated that she would extend Mei-shan and Wei-yong a special friends' discount. Later, taking out her price list, Wendy offered to sell Mei-shan and her boyfriend the mid-range NT $55,900 package for NT $40,900. Mei-shan exclaimed to me, "Wow, Bonnie, I'll have to take you out for dinner!" I smiled nervously as I noted to myself that every customer was being offered the same discount. Without asking the couple if they agreed to this package or giving them time to discuss whether or not to shop around more, Wendy began filling out an order form and writing in bits and pieces of the couple's style preferences she had gleaned during their conversation—no graphics, no Chinese costumes, a "simple and elegant" style. Doing so, Wendy demonstrated that she had listened well. She then looked to the groom for deposit money to reserve the package at the special price. The groom dutifully produced a credit card.

I told the couple I thought they would be very happy, as the quality of this salon's work was very high. I worried, however, that they had not intended to sign a contract so quickly but had planned to shop around. This was the first bridal exhibit they visited at the fair, the very first shopping they had done. They previously knew nothing of this salon, and it was only after the deal was well underway that they even came to know the shop's whereabouts. This couple lives and works in Taipei's suburbs, and the salon's central downtown location, which they would have to visit no less than six times, was not particularly convenient for them. Had it not been for my presence, perhaps Mei-shan and Wei-yong would have thanked Wendy for the information about Tiffany Bridal and visited other exhibitions.

As was the practice of all the exhibits at this particular fair (following the innovation of one salon at a fair three months earlier), once the groom's credit card purchase had cleared, the couple's names were given to a young photographer's assistant who staffed the booth's sound system. In his best television announcer's voice he read their names, announced that they had reserved their "marriage package," and offered congratulations and best wishes as about a dozen salon employees set off small plastic "champagne" bottle firecrackers—precisely the sort launched at wedding banquets upon the couple's first entry. Very frequently, as was the case for this particular couple, putting down money on a bridal photography package is the couple's first public commitment toward marriage. They had probably talked to their parents about the possibility enough to feel sure that their plans would not meet strong opposition, but they had not yet discussed dates for their betrothal and wedding ceremonies.

Bridal makeover stylists and photographers manage their customers as deftly as Wendy had managed Mei-shan and Wei-yong. Despite the fact that bridal photographs represent the couple in individualistic terms, there is little room for individuality in the photograph-producing process because couples are expected to defer to the professional expertise of stylists and photographers, whose visions strongly shape the final photographs. The couple's greatest control seems to be in choosing which salon to use, yet even that decision is highly structured by industry-wide practices of consumer manipulation. Some customers, of course, are wise to marketing tactics and assess the relative merits of different salons based on photographic or dress styles seen in sample albums. However, sample albums are regularly bought and sold between companies, and photographer turnover is high. The photographer who produced an admired sample album is quite likely not the photographer who will actually do the work. The turnover of sales staff and stylists is also very high. Women who anticipate getting married within a year or two often begin looking at the photos of friends, family, and colleagues in a more interested way, inquiring about the bride's impressions of the service and quality she received, but by the time they are ready to choose, the staff at a given salon may well have changed.

Couples are right to inquire about the skills of bridal salon staff, since bridal salon staff are very much the authors of couples' photographs. In the end, the photographs that couples display reflect in large part the modern bridal industry itself and the fantasies its workers construct for young couples.

BRIDAL FANTASY WORLDS

Bridal salon workers have three main goals in mind as they produce their images of the bride and groom. First, the bride should look as beautiful and glamorous as a professional model or celebrity. Extensive makeovers and specialized lighting bring average women surprisingly close to this ideal. Second, the couple's relationship should appear romantic. To this end, photographers set the couple up in intimate and romantic poses—displaying the couple in an embrace or picturing the groom as admiring his bride's beauty and charm. Their relationship is defined in individualistic, not familial terms, so important family members are excluded. The photographs represent the marriage as if it were about affect and personal pleasure, not about kinship and reproduction.

Finally, the couple should be made to look upwardly mobile and cosmopolitan. Clothing, backdrops, props, and poses index wealth and worldliness by placing the couple in settings ranging from the abstract spaces of MTV videos to the particularized settings of English castle ballrooms and libraries (see figures 6 and 7). Location shoots generally take place in spots suggestive of advertising photography (wind-swept beaches, fancy restaurants, designer boutiques, old-fashioned or well-known tourist sites) or other perfect, sanitized spaces such as the manicured gardens of parks (after the photographer removes any litter and sets up the photographs so the throngs of park visitors are not seen). In

Figure 6. Studio backdrops frequently place couples in "the West"; this backdrop is suggestive of a castle ballroom. (Image courtesy of the bride and groom, 2002. Photographer: Wu Yong-jie.)

Figure 7. Taipei couple dressed in "European court" attire. (Image courtesy of the bride and groom, 1996.)

recent years, "Orientalizing" scenes have become popular, too (see Said 1978). Many albums include a few shots of the couple dressed in imperial-style Chinese gowns and crowns, Japanese kimono with paper umbrella, and early-Republican-period garb (military formalwear for men and *qipao* gowns for women). These shots, too, contribute to a sense of upward mobility, in that bride and groom are pictured in so many different spaces and times that they seem to command both space and time for their own whimsical pleasure (Harvey 1989).

Other signs of upward mobility deployed in bridal photographs are graphics, which include designs as well as English, Chinese, and Japanese text placed on or around the photograph. English words, phrases, poems, and song lyrics were more popular than those in Chinese or Japanese in the early and mid-1990s. Frequently, the English text is nonsensical, misspelled, and misconceived. For example, the words "Women's Romartic [*sic*] Feelings" may be printed above a close-up of a bride's face, or "Love Tender" at the bottom of a photograph. Chinese and Japanese text printed on photographs also contains errors. The overlays of graphics are for visual effect only. To read them, as I was inclined to do, is to take them too seriously. Brides and grooms often do not even pay much attention to the Chinese-language text applied to their photographs. The presence of text makes the photographs look like advertisements or magazine layouts so the photographs and the people pictured in them look famous. The graphics tell the reader what to think about the photograph not through content (as in a caption) but by indexing a visual genre associated with fame and beauty (see figure 8).

The bridal salon workers' intention is not to produce "realistic" images that lend a sense of authenticity to the couple. Rather, like advertising company stylists and photographers, they work to create fantastical, highly perfect, and idealistic images. The fantasy worlds depicted in bridal photographs, moreover, reflect not necessarily the bride and groom's personal fantasies but rather the social fantasies the bridal industry expects all young people to share. Beauty, romance, upward mobility, and worldliness are widespread ideals, but their appearance in a bridal album does not constitute their expression by the bride and groom pictured. They are, moreover, fantasies, not social ideals toward which people work to shape lived realities.

Bridal fantasies are said to be feminine fantasies. Grooms are expected to distance themselves from the bridal fantasy project even as they engage in it for the sake of their brides. Although many brides seemed to subscribe to bridal fantasy worlds and approached their experiences at

Figure 8. "Fervent Love Soul": A sample bridal album page. (Image courtesy of Luomen Bridal Photography Co., 1997.)

bridal salons with excitement and joy, some regard the bridal photography enterprise as a social obligation entailed by weddings, family, and peer pressure. They may approach their experiences at bridal salons with skepticism and a bit of dread. A feminist activist explained to me that when she marries she will be photographed despite her distaste for the photos. She planned to tolerate the ways in which the photographs objectify women lest her peers think that her marriage was unromantic. The few young women I found who resisted the pressure to purchase and pose for bridal photographs were rare, and they explicitly talked about themselves as exceptions to a cultural rule they considered silly if not bizarre. This minority expressed distaste for the high level of artifice in bridal photography. It is precisely that high degree of artifice that makes bridal photography so attractive for the majority.

WORKING IN A FANTASY WORLD

It is fitting that bridal salon workers, the very purveyors of bridal fantasy worlds, often have a finely tuned sense of irony about bridal imagery. Many photographers I met were strongly aware of their role as producers of beauty, romance, and fantasy and talked openly about the artificiality of these constructions. Some photographers spoke of how they could make even the ugliest women look like beautiful models, though beautiful women sometimes appear less beautiful in their photos than in person. These photographers saw their work as particularly catering to unattractive and average-looking women who want to have the experience of being beautiful and photographs to record the memory.

Bridal salon photographers work daily with about-to-marry couples, creating romantic scene after romantic scene. For couples who experience the bridal photography process only once in a lifetime, the service they receive may feel personalized and special. Photographers, by contrast, come to the bridal photo shoot with a strong sense of routinization that makes some of them become jaded about romantic photography and develop a sense of humor about the photographs they produce. Photographers I met enjoyed laughing about stories of couples with less than ideal unions. I heard about one bride who had bridal photos taken twice at the same studio. Although she was not "satisfied" with the first groom and the marriage was called off, she was "satisfied" enough with the bridal shop to use their services again, the photographer joked. Photographers told me about couples who fought or refused to talk to each other; if they could not make it through a day of photo taking together, what were the chances for a lifetime of marriage? In one extreme case, while out on a location shoot, the photographer and his couple met up with a former lover of the groom who claimed to have a child by him. A fight broke out, and the couple's costumes were torn in the process.

Perhaps because they face the artifice of romantic images day in and day out and become tired of the same poses, places, and props, several photographers I knew had unusual bridal photographs of their own. For example, a photographer and a bridal shop saleswoman who married during my fieldwork took their location photos at a construction site. They assumed the same poses seen in more traditional bridal photos but used dirt, concrete sewer tunnels, and exposed steel structures as their backdrop. For one of their studio shots, the couple posed seated with the denim-clad buttocks of five photographers and assistants assembled all around them. Another photographer showed me the two very different photos he had used as the thank-you cards at his wedding banquet. One showed himself and his wife in formal bridal wear standing in front of a traffic jam of many-colored cars and motor scooters. Both bride and groom wore dark sunglasses and held one arm out straight in front of their bodies, hand flexed with palm facing the camera. Because of the photograph's shallow depth of field, the couples' hands and the traffic behind them were out of focus. The other thank-you card photo was of the couple posed against a plain studio backdrop in a more conservative pose, without sunglasses or expressive arm gestures. That photo was necessary, he said, because his father could not tolerate the "cool" photo. He kept one of each photo in his wallet, alongside a photo of his baby daughter.

The majority of Taipei bridal salons, for all their glitz and gleam, are owned by small-time entrepreneurs not unlike the thousands of "petty capitalists" who operate small businesses throughout the island (Gates 1992). Bridal salons require far greater capital investment than do roadside snack stands, of course, but many are run as family businesses, with spouses dividing up administrative tasks and employing numerous relatives as managers, sales staff, stylists, photographers, and assistants. Romantic Bliss, for example, is owned and managed by a husband-and-wife team, the Wangs. The start-up capital and fashion expertise initially came from Mrs. Wang, who had studied fashion design as a vocational high school student in the south of the island. When the beauty department was added in the early 1990s, Mrs. Wang's younger sister provided the capital and the styling expertise. Other relatives employed include another sister, who works on the sales floor, and a brother-in-law, who works as a photographer. During my field research, the couple's young son was cared for by a grandmotherly woman during the salon's busiest sales hours—noon to 10 P.M. The babysitter tended an old-fashioned dry goods shop, which also served as her living room, around the alley corner from the bright, airy modern salon. The Wangs often visited their son at the babysitter's during the day and would bring him back to the salon for a special snack and some playtime during quiet periods in sales activity. After 10 P.M., when the salon was closing, the babysitter would bring the little boy to the salon to play with the employees until his parents were ready to go home. All three in the family went to sleep after 2 A.M. most nights, rising shortly before noon most mornings.

In many respects, the owners of Romantic Bliss run the salon like other local family-owned businesses. On a designated day each month, they offer incense, fruit, and paper money to the gods to help their business prosper. When making interior design changes, the owners bring in their trusted fortune-teller and geomancer to advise on design matters. At one bridal fair, the salon had been allotted a poor spot, outside the major flows of browsing customers. The fortune-teller/geomancer visited the booth, recommended some minor design changes, and instructed the owners on where they should go to pray *(baibai)* for improved business. The owners also pay the fortune-teller to help trusted employees with personal problems as an added employees' benefit. He is credited with having solved the infertility troubles of one saleswoman by instructing her to go to a particular temple to pray. He even advised me on research troubles and told me where to pray for the successful completion of my degree.

USE OF BRIDAL PHOTOGRAPHS

What do couples do with all of these photographs? They first show them off at their wedding banquets. Couples invariably display framed enlargements at the entryway to their wedding banquet, near the red-clothed table where red envelopes of cash *(hongbao)* are collected for the bride and groom. Banquet halls and rural banquet caterers customarily provide freestanding easels to display the portraits. Sometimes, the large-as-life portraits are decorated with ribbons or flowers. On the cash-collection table are stacks of the thank-you photo cards, which are the same size as a business card. *Hongbao*-bearing guests help themselves to a card or are presented with one by a relative or friend staffing the table.

The cards sometimes serve as receipts—for example, when a friend unable to attend the banquet sends along a *hongbao* with a mutual friend. In such cases, I have seen the woman responsible for writing down gift amounts on a name register write the gift-giver's name and the cash amount on the back of a photo card for the courier/guest to hand the gift-giver later. These thank-you cards carry the bridal salon's logo (and sometimes address) so banquet guests will know the salon that provided the photos and the bride's gown.

Photo albums, too, are displayed on or near the cash-collection table at the banquet. Few guests take more than a cursory look through these albums. Friends of the bride and others who would be the most interested have most likely already seen the album. Many brides bring their albums to work to show to coworkers as soon as it is complete. Couples also show their albums to relatives and other close friends prior to the wedding. Plus, the album is often displayed before the wedding in the "new room," where the bride receives visitors before the banquet (see chapter 4). Any banquet guests who have not yet viewed the photographs may flip through the album quickly, but for the most part only friends of the bride are likely to look through the pages and talk about the photographs. Guests who stop to glance at only a photograph or two may, however, comment on the thickness of the album or the presence of two albums. Everyone understands that more photographs cost more money. Displaying more photographs suggests that the groom (and/or his family) is rich and generous toward his bride; fewer photographs suggests that he is poor or that he is stingy toward her.

After the banquet, as well, the use and display of bridal portraits are remarkably standardized. The place to hang framed enlargements is in the couple's bedroom. Many hang the huge photograph centered directly over the bed. Those who have furniture or other obstacles at the head of the bed may hang the photograph elsewhere in the bedroom—only rarely outside it. When I inquired about the bedroom as the choice location for photographs, interviewees frequently laughed. Some laughed because they understood from my question that I found this an odd practice. Others laughed because they had never considered another option; the bedroom is the only place for such a photograph. One friend, Xiao-lan, told me that her three-year-old son, while jumping on the bed he and his brother shared with his parents, took notice of the huge photograph and asked, "Who is that pretty lady with Daddy?" I asked why she put it over her bed, and Xiao-lan told me that there was nowhere else to put it. Why not put it in the living room? "That would be too embarrassing!"

she replied. Why? Because it is something "private" *(siren)*. Xiao-lan, unlike many young mothers, does not share the apartment with any extended kin (though her in-laws own her apartment and live just upstairs). Even so, she considers the living room an insufficiently private place for the portrait.

Such sentiments about the intimate, private quality of bridal photographs seems contradictory to their first use as public status displays at banquets. Not surprisingly, then, some do not regard the public display and dissemination of bridal portraits positively. One middle-aged, unmarried woman announced to her coworkers at a wedding banquet that were she to get married one day, she would not distribute the thank-you card photographs because people later throw them away or drop them on the ground. She would not want people stepping on her picture. On a separate occasion, a young woman who was to marry within the year told me she would not pass out thank-you cards at her wedding banquet because people throw them away, and she could not bear the thought of her face sitting in a trash can. Yet another young woman spoke of aggravation when a disliked coworker insisted on having a look at her photo album when she brought it to show friends at her office. Her photos, she maintained, were private and personal.

Women often told me that they planned to use the photographs to "remember" their youthful good looks once they grew old and ugly—even though the elaborate makeover and the photographer's manipulations of light and focus often result in photographs that look very little like the woman posing as bride. One woman told me she planned to deploy these symbols of lost youth and beauty for rhetorical flourish at strategic moments in arguments with her husband. The photographs stand as evidence of how much of her youthful beauty a wife loses as a result of her hard work on behalf of his family.

Grooms who deny their brides the photographs (a rarity) may unwittingly provide their wives with equally powerful claims. One woman told me that her sister's husband refused to pay for a bridal photography package when they married in the early 1990s. He considered the elaborate, expensive photographs a waste. The wife continues to mourn her lack of bridal photographs to this day, even though the couple now lives in California. Every time she gets into an argument with her husband, she reminds him that he denied her these culturally important documents of her lost youth.

CHAPTER 3

Inner and Outer Worlds in Changing Taipei

Nei zai mei is a clever saying coined in Taiwan in the mid-1990s. Translated literally, it means: a man's "inside people" (wife and children) are in America. Its cultural translation is: he enjoys the resulting freedom with a mistress.

Extramarital sex, surprisingly, serves as a useful entry point for discussion of marriage and family. National conversations about this common transgression of norms (not considered a transgression at all by quite a few men) cast light on the place of marriage and family in modern Taipei lives. *Nei zai mei* describes a man who enjoys the best of two worlds. He has fulfilled a crucial filial obligation to his parents by marrying and producing children, especially if he has a son; he has fulfilled a crucial familial obligation to his children, and to his family as a whole, by providing sufficient resources to send the children, accompanied by their mother, to the United States, where they attend schools considered superior to those in Taiwan.[1] Having placed his children on what is widely perceived to be the best possible track for a high-paying career in Taiwan, he has done his best to assure a bright future for his family and a comfortable retirement for himself, because his children (especially his sons) will be responsible for his care in his old age. And, conveniently, this situation allows him to take a mistress *(xiaolaopo)* without interference by his wife.[2]

Nei zai mei opens a window into the complexities of how familial duties are interwoven with individualistic freedoms in contemporary Taipei. Though the term "inside people" pertains only to women and children, I find it useful to expand the application of "inside"—and its opposite, "outside"—to explain the ways in which young people *(nian-qingren)* in Taipei today relate to family (inside) and the world beyond the family (outside). In other words, though "inside" is a native category, I expand on it well beyond its native uses for the purposes of my argument. To fully explain the contemporary saying *nei zai mei* and the underlying logic that ties it not only to marriage but also, strangely enough, to bridal photography, I need to first describe the historical context from which this new logic emerged.

INSIDE AND OUTSIDE IN HISTORICAL PERSPECTIVE

In imperial China, Confucian ideology stated that a proper family sent its men and boys out to study and work and kept its women and girls inside the family compound, where their sexual purity was protected from unrelated or outside men. Most Chinese families were too poor to enact Confucian ideals in daily life. The Han Chinese immigrants who settled Taiwan, moreover, were notoriously poor. Nevertheless, Confucian concepts of the proper relationship between fathers and sons, especially of sons' filial duties toward family elders, are an important part of the story of marriage and the family in post–World War II Taiwan. Parents once wielded great power over their children. The economic underpinnings of the old kinship system were overthrown when Taiwan absorbed global capitalism during the remarkably rapid development of its economy in the 1960s and 1970s, but threads of the previous era's social structure persist in kinship relations.

In the 1960s, when anthropologists Arthur and Margery Wolf conducted field research in the countryside near Taipei, Taiwan's population was largely rural and intergenerational kin ties profoundly structured most aspects of social life. Borrowing and expanding upon the concept of "inside people," one could say that the logic of the inside (i.e., family) pervaded much of life. The economy, for example, centered on family farming. Work did not draw one outside the realm of family. Those who, for various reasons, went outside the sphere of family relations were highly suspect and not trusted by others. People who moved into a new village, away from extended kin ties, were treated as outsiders by villagers for as long as three generations—when, at last, the newcomers had enough family around them to be once again firmly ensconced inside the sphere of the family. Men and women who died without living family members to care for their graves and "feed" them through ancestor worship rituals were feared as hungry ghosts (Ahern 1973; Wolf 1978).

Weddings involved the movement of a woman from outside a family to its inside space. Of course, family elders controlled this process. In what Wolf and Wolf called the "major" form of marriage evident at that time in Taiwan, the groom's family located potential brides with the help of a matchmaker or go-between *(meirenpo)* or friends and relatives. Once the bride's and the groom's families agreed upon the match and its terms (exchanges of gifts), the bride was transferred from her natal family to the groom's family on a formal wedding day. There she lived and worked as wife and daughter-in-law. The couple's children took the surname of their father, worshipped his ancestors, and stood to inherit property from their father.

"Major" marriage was the most prestigious type of marriage but also the most expensive. The groom's family had to pay a premium brideprice to the bride's parents and host a wedding banquet for kin and friends.[3] There were social costs to major marriages, too. The system put extreme stress on young daughters-in-law, and Wolf (1975) attributes the comparatively high suicide rates of Taiwanese women in the past to this form of marriage. Once young mothers produced sons for the family, they actively cultivated their sons' affection and loyalty to fortify their standing in the family by creating a strong "uterine family" within the patriarchal family system. Upon a son's marriage, the mother feared her new daughter-in-law would capture her son's loyalty and provoke the dissolution of the multigenerational family that gave the senior woman her high status and power (Cohen 1976; Wolf 1972). Both before and after marriage, a degree of sexual segregation was maintained in villages, and spousal relations were expected to be distant and cordial, not close and intimate. In many respects, marriage during this time was more about the relationship between a mother-in-law and her daughter-in-law than between spouses.

The advent of wage labor undermined parental control over the labor and lives of the younger generation by disturbing the economic underpinnings of the kinship system and opening up legitimate social spaces outside family control. Though factories at first must have raised suspicions, they quickly gained cultural esteem for the economic resources they afforded families (Kung 1983). Taiwan's incorporation of global capitalism into its fold through aggressive economic development policies in the 1960s and 1970s was by no means its first foray into global, capitalistic trade (see Shepherd 1993; Wolf 1982). What made this time period distinct, rather, was the speed of Taiwan's globalization and the island-wide expansion of its cash economy. Urban people in early-twentieth-century Taiwan—though comparatively few in number—were exploring and creating spaces outside family life, and sometimes even selecting their own spouses, long before their rural counterparts (Thornton, Chang, and Lin 1994). The cash economy and its unintended social consequences for family life, then, were not new in the 1960s and 1970s, but the scale and extent of the cash economy were.

Wage labor opportunities expanded the social realm outside family control, making the timing of marriage and the selection of a spouse more subject to youthful imagination than in the past.[4] As soon as young men found wage labor opportunities in industrializing Taiwan, they began successfully protesting marriage choices made by parents (Wolf 1972). As the countryside globalized, parental authority over sons eroded. Young people who once relied upon their fathers' capital (land rights, fishing vessels) to make a living saw new prospects for getting by—and, sometimes, for getting rich. The expanded cash economy made old agrarian ways of life less and less appealing to young men who, though now subject to exploitation by employers, could liberate themselves from control by family elders. Among their first demands was increased participation in the selection of wives.

Young men working in factories, however, seldom had opportunities to meet suitable marriage candidates on their own. Family elders continued to exert their authority, at first merely inviting prospective grooms and brides to view each other and allowing them to veto a proposed match if they so chose. Couples sometimes went on chaperoned dates during their engagement period (Wolf 1972). Over time, however, young people gained greater autonomy in the spouse selection process. In a survey of 978 women married between 1980 and 1984, 31 percent claimed that they and their husband alone had decided upon the marriage while only 13 percent reported that their parents had made the decision. A majority (56 percent) claimed that both the couple and the parents had made the decision (Thornton, Chang, and Lin 1994: 152). By the 1990s, at least in Taipei, the balance of power between parents and children had shifted such that parents' only right was one of a final veto over a chosen marriage partner.

Notably, men, not women, first initiated these changes. Observers of Chinese village life—foreign missionaries and anthropologists as well as urban Chinese intellectuals—have tended to focus on the plight of young women married off into new families, where they were subject to poor treatment and even abuse. Films such as Zhang Yi-mou's *Raise the Red Lantern* have popularized this perspective on Chinese family life for wide international audiences. It is quite clear, however, that young men also felt oppressed by the patriarchal family system.[5]

Families and factory managers gendered access to wage labor opportunities such that women's entry into the cash economy was less threatening to the old patriarchal family order than was men's. Young women went to work in factories during the last few years of youth, before parents had arranged and sealed their marriages. Women workers were typically expected to send most of their wages home to their families to pay tuition fees for their brothers' schooling and to build dowries for themselves. Companies controlled the movements of female workers by housing them in factory dormitories and paying wages too low for the women to support themselves. Though exploitative, these labor arrangements pleased families concerned about their girls being away from home and out from under the watchful eye of relatives. Had factory work become an alternative to marriage for women—allowing them to become self-supporting—it would have greatly upset the old patriarchal family system. This did not happen.[6] However, outside direct parental control, their relative freedom allowed women to entertain dreams of romance previously unthinkable, even though acting upon romantic fantasies remained difficult (Kung 1983).

Romance was not unknown in Taiwan and China prior to the modern era of the love marriage. Love stories enjoyed popularity in both literary and folk cultural traditions in premodern China (Jankowiak 1995b; Schak 1975), but romantic love was not associated with marriage until the 1960s and 1970s (happening earlier in urban centers, later in the countryside). To the contrary, romantic love was by definition something experienced by men *outside* marriage, with concubines, courtesans, and other men.[7]

The expectation today is that couples engage in free courtship (*ziyou tan lian-ai,* literally "to freely talk love") outside parental control before they marry, even if the couple is initially introduced by relatives or by professional matchmaking services contracted by their parents. Self-determined spouse selection has become a status marker, in fact. To admit to having had one's marriage arranged is to be not only old-fashioned but also backward, rural, and low-class. Modern marriages are not necessarily more romantic, loving, or passionate than those of the past. The critical difference may be, simply, that love is now "the idiom" for discussion of marriage (Rebhun 1995: 246), whereas in the recent past the idiom was family duty.

Whether or not couples feel they are in love prior to marriage is impossible for a researcher to assess accurately. Love is an internally experienced sentiment, not readily verifiable. Moreover, emotions are also asserted by individuals for reasons of status and social legitimacy (Abu-Lughod and Lutz 1990). People in Taiwan today tend to view the transformation of the marriage system from one motivated by family duty to one focused upon individual desire (see Collier 1997) as the sign par excellence of having arrived in modernity. Not long ago, though, it was perhaps just as much a matter of status for married women to talk up their dislike for their husbands. In 1950s and 1960s farming villages emotional closeness between spouses was considered unbecoming because strong horizontal relations between spouses threatened the stability of vertical relations between married sons and their parents (Wolf 1968, 1972).[8] In a remarkable transformation of the meaning of marriage, love today is fashionable in Taiwan and those who admit to marital discord and contempt are now pitied, not revered.

As I have described the history of spouse selection in post-war Taiwan, romance and courtship initially sat *outside* the realm of family as individualistic pursuits potentially dangerous to family stability and opposed by family elders. The movement of romance from outside marriage to inside was and is a source of conflict. Family elders did not simply relinquish control.[9]

The intergenerational struggle for control of the meaning of marriage comes to light especially clearly in popular romance fiction, where the romance between a young man and woman takes back seat to the drama played out between the woman and her parents (Lin 1992). The romance serves to test the strength of the parents' love for their daughter. Will they empathize with her desire for romance and demonstrate parental affection by allowing the romance to flourish? Or will they callously demand their daughter's obedience to their authority in the name of family duty? The tremendously popular work of romance novel and screenplay writer Qiong Yao focuses on just such intergenerational conflicts, dramatizing the wide gap between the domains of familial and nonfamilial (inside and outside) relationships. Qiong Yao's work also suggests that outside relationships may transform the character of inside relations—that intergenerational kin relations may be transformed if parental affection is prioritized above the logic of family duty (Lin 1992).

Weddings represent a distinct moment in the relations between inside and outside as I have developed these concepts. The bride, an outsider, is ritually incorporated into the groom's family. She becomes an insider, and the bride/groom relationship moves into the realm of the family. Yet the elaborate bridal photographs that grooms commission for their brides clearly articulate a view of the marrying couple as outside familial control. Themes of individualism and romance dominate photo albums, and bridal portraits banish the family members altogether. Why do bridal photographs emphatically represent the couple as outside the relations of family? Many young couples, women especially, talk about the photos as their last hurrah or the big finish before the freedom and individualism of youth come to an abrupt end in marriage.

THE LIVES OF SINGLE YOUNG ADULTS

Living arrangements seem to keep single young adults inside the space of the family, at least in principle. After completing schooling (vocational school or college) and two years of compulsory military service (for men), the general practice in Taipei is for young adults to live with their parents until marriage when possible. The average age of first marriage in 1997 was twenty-eight years for women and thirty-one for men for the island as a whole (Wu 1998), and Taipei residents' average age at first marriage is probably higher. It is not unusual, therefore, for young men and women to live with their families for ten years after achieving all of the markers of adult status other than marriage. Some wealthy parents provide a separate apartment (in the same building or nearby) for their grown children, and some young adults rent private or shared living spaces. But many middle-class families live together in three- or four-bed-room apartments, packed tightly with people and their possessions. A thirty-four-year-old man living with his parents is not unusual.

Cultural norms of parent-child relationships are part of what keeps families living together, but another important factor is the high cost of housing in Taipei, coupled with Taiwanese notions of frugality. Many young men and women I talked to felt strongly that it would be wasteful to pay rent when living with one's family is an option. Yet though they live with family, young adults in Taiwan have ways of avoiding home. Plus, living with their parents enables them to afford expensive consumer goods and services.[10]

The early years of working life, especially for women, are considered a time to enjoy the pleasures of consumption. Many single people have all of their housing costs paid for by their parents, leaving them a high percentage of income as disposable. One fashion magazine editor instructed me that her magazine's readership consists largely of unmarried, working women who can afford the $2,000 U.S. Chanel handbags and pricey beauty products advertised in the publication because they live with their families. Fashion and beauty-related consumption among female coworkers can be fiercely competitive—a situation advertisers exploit freely. Employers in Taiwan customarily give large bonuses at the Chinese New Year—often one or two months' salary. At the same time of year, advertisers promote expensive luxury goods such as diamond jewelry and European watches as gifts young women should give themselves as rewards for hard work.

Men experience less pressure to purchase designer wardrobes and costly consumer items; they are expected to save money for larger purchases considered necessary at the time of marriage (a bridal photography package, a car, a down payment on a home). Of course, many men indulge in consumer pleasures, and many women save money, too.

One might imagine that co-residence with parents would breed family conflict, especially knowing that the generation gap *(daigou)* is particu larly wide due to the rapid pace of change in Taiwan in the last three decades. So I was surprised by how infrequently I heard complaints of meddling parents.

Angel, a bridal gown designer, was leading a fairly typical young adult life in the late 1990s. After graduating from vocational school at nineteen, she went to work as a seamstress in a dress factory in Taipei. By age thirty, she had worked her way up the ranks to become a designer and dress factory manager. She earned around $2,000 U.S. per month and continued to live with her parents in a suburb of Taipei. She wore fashionable clothing, jewelry, and hairstyles, completely updating her wardrobe every year. Unlike most of her female friends, she even drove her own car. Angel ate most of her meals away from home (eating out cheaply is made possible by Taipei's night markets and cafeterias) and spent little time at home with her family. Her friends and coworkers knew that the best way to reach her was to call her "BB Call" (pager) when she was not at the factory because it was very difficult to find her at home. If her parents suspected that she spent so much of her time away from home with a boyfriend, they must have made a point of not asking.

Compare Angel's situation with that of my friend Alice and her sister, Gina, ages thirty-two and thirty-four, respectively. Both graduated from college at age twenty-two and have since lived in their mother's home (their father is deceased). Their brother moved out during his military service and college years, eventually settling elsewhere in Taiwan, near his father's brother. Alice and Gina then rearranged their three-bedroom apartment. Alice shared the master bedroom and bath with her mother. The siblings felt that their mother should not sleep alone, so Alice, the youngest daughter, continued sleeping by her side. Gina slept in one bedroom by herself and used the small third bedroom as a closet for her extensive designer wardrobe.

Gina worked for a multinational company as a local sale representative. Her company provided her with a car, and Gina carried a cellular phone and a pager. Alice was a customer service representative at a multinational corporation, where she earned about $1,500 U.S. a month. She, too, had a pager and a cellular phone, using them for communication with her boyfriend. He never called her directly at home or at work, as Alice hid the relationship not only from her family but from her peers at work, too. When I asked Alice if Gina had a boyfriend, she at first claimed not to know. As I pressed with more specific questions, it became clear that Alice was virtually positive that Gina had a serious boyfriend and that she had once even seen him. Similarly, Gina certainly knew that Alice had a boyfriend, but they had a tacit agreement not to discuss these secrets.

Like Angel, Gina and Alice had few financial obligations. The sisters split the utility bills and, along with their brother, contributed some money each month to an account they had set up to provide their retired mother with "spending money" to supplement her pension and savings. Alice worked late most evenings, eating dinner at restaurants and night market stalls with colleagues. Sometimes she watched television with her mother in the late evening. Whenever she was dating a boyfriend, however, she would come home late most nights after spending several hours with him—eating dinner, strolling through night markets, and lingering over tea. Alice believed that her mother probably noticed when Alice had a new boyfriend because she spent so much time away from home, but they did not talk about it. Alice would say she had been working late or been out with coworkers; more important, her mother seldom inquired about her absences from home. Although the sisters lived together, both spent so much time away from home that they often went several days at a time without seeing one another.

Home, for many young Taipei women and men, is primarily a place to sleep; it is not a place to entertain friends or dates. Cell phones and pagers enable them to carry out communications on the go. At most,

they eat dinner at home once a week. Their home lives are kept to a minimum, and time spent with family is reserved for occasional late nights
and holidays. To return to the language of inside and outside, young
adults occupy the inside space of family life every day. But the stuff of the
inner lives of young people—what they think about, who they care
about—takes place outside.

Those who live with their parents feel compelled to carry out their private lives in public spaces to avoid making their love lives known to their
families, who are apt to pry, reversing the conventional associations of
"private" and "public."[11] Young adults' living arrangements make Taipei
an extremely vibrant city. Huge numbers of people in their twenties and
thirties with large disposable incomes in Taipei spend a great deal of time
avoiding going home.[12] Hence, the city supports a robust service and
entertainment sector. In some city districts, elaborately decorated teahouses, coffee shops, bars, restaurants, spas, and KTVs (clubs offering
private karaoke rooms) can be found on every block. Night markets are
one popular form of evening entertainment. During the dinner hour,
entrepreneurs begin setting out their wares in alleyways, where they rent
space from the storekeepers who own or rent the proper storefronts.
Night market booths, always crowded, make the narrow back streets
impassable except to pedestrians. Every district has a night market,
though the goods and services offered differ. Night markets always offer
bargain-priced dinner and snack foods such as barbecued squid served
on skewers, oysters, sushi, blended fruit drinks, sugary boiled peanut
treats, and candied cherry tomatoes. Also for sale are gadgets, toys,
Chinese medicine items, Western vitamins, dieting products, pirated
movies and compact discs, video games, and fake designer goods. Many
markets also have stalls providing services like fortune-telling and foot
massage. Although entire families sometimes go out for dinner and a
stroll through a night market, the customers are primarily young adults
and teenagers, for many of whom night markets, cafés, parks, and KTVs
are the only places where they can conduct their social lives in private,
relatively speaking. On weekends, this same population prefers to leave
Taipei and visit the many tourist attractions (national parks, beaches,
hiking trails, theme parks) just outside the city.

Another notable "outside" or urban space in Taipei is the twenty-four-
hour spa or bathhouse. For a fee, one can spend an entire day and night
in a single-sex spa with exercise equipment, bathing facility, cafeteria,
and a darkened room with plush reclining chairs for sleeping and viewing
movies. In women's spas, massages, facials, eyebrow plucking, and other

beauty services are available. I am told that many men's spas sell sexual services in addition to massage treatments. On weekends women's spas are crowded with groups of friends and coworkers seeking to get out for the day.

In the late 1980s, MTV clubs popped up all over Taipei. MTVs offered private movie-viewing rooms with comfortable couches, refreshments, and movies screened on projection televisions. MTVs quickly became associated with premarital and extramarital sex and were enormously successful businesses. The movies MTVs offered were usually pirated copies, and beginning in the early 1990s the state launched strings of crackdowns on intellectual property rights infringements so as to improve its chances for membership in major international organizations. Fatal fires, too, brought public attention to the fire codes these establishments violated in order to create small, private, windowless, sound-proof, locked rooms. Most MTVs were shut down by police in the early 1990s. By 1997, a few had reopened by clearing up legal problems.

Lovers often search out private spaces outside family homes, sometimes literally outdoors. Public gardens, for example, are dotted with couples in the evenings. Taipei's ubiquitous small hotels explicitly cater to unmarried couples, with rooms by the hour and discreet service. The hotels are expensive, however, and are especially associated with older patrons and extramarital sex. The mountaintop make-out spots overlooking Taipei are so popular at night that traffic jams form on the mountain roads![13]

Keeping one's love life from family seems to be no problem for most young people in Taipei, given the many public spaces the city affords to daters, coupled with the willingness of parents and siblings to look the other way. Breakups may be more difficult to keep private. After hiding her first boyfriend from her family for two years, Alice was devastated when the relationship ended. She found herself unable to sleep, unable to concentrate, and very tearful. Trying to conceal her emotional state from her mother made it all the more unbearable. A friend in whom she confided taught her to cry in the shower, where the sound of her sobs would be masked by the sound of running water.

Alice did not tell her family about her boyfriends because she felt there was no sense in getting them involved until marriage was imminent. She meant to spare her family the worry. It is uncomfortable for parents and children to talk openly about dating, in part because despite the love marriage ideal, parents have a great deal of power in approving a match and negotiating a wedding. When a single woman or man talks to parents about a boyfriend or girlfriend, the discussion is assumed to be about marriage. Broaching the topic merely creates an opportunity for parents to voice disapproval.[14]

At the point when the topic of marriage is broached, either by the couple or by their parents, the familial and the personal must merge. Young couples begin the process of moving their relationships out of the cafés, MTVs, public gardens, mountaintop make-out spots, and love hotels into the social spaces and relations of family. A boyfriend becomes a husband, a girlfriend becomes a wife, and a love affair becomes subsumed by negotiations between families making wedding plans. The family negotiations that lead up to most weddings constitute the first merging of family and love interests in the lives of young people. Parents' roles in wedding engagements are so strong that despite the widespread expectation that young people will fall in love and choose their own spouses, marriage proposals often take a distinctly parent-centered form. Many engaged or married men and women had a difficult time answering my questions about when they had decided to get married; there had not been one particular moment when the decision was made. Judy, however, remembered immediately. One night when her boyfriend's parents were out of town and she and Yong-zhen were watching television together in the living room, he casually suggested that Judy might ask her parents how much money they would require of his family in formal engagement gifts. Neither Judy or Yong-zhen had yet met the other's parents.

One friend, Jin-ru, suffered a bad experience when, after dating for several years, she and her previous boyfriend told their parents of their plans to marry. The boyfriend's parents refused to accept Jin-ru as a bride because her family was Taiwanese. His family was Hakka.[15] Jin-ru and her boyfriend became estranged. Months later, he called and announced that his mother had lightened up and was now willing to accept her. By this time, however, Jin-ru had found a new boyfriend with whom she had already put down a deposit on a bridal photography package.

Coincidentally, in an interview with her mother I learned that Jin-ru's family had refused a daughter-in-law on similar grounds. Her father's family, the Lus, had a prohibition against taking in daughters-in-law with the surname Lin, one of the most common surnames in Taiwan. Just a few generations earlier, a Lu mother had suffered at the hands of a very disobedient (buxiao) daughter-in-law surnamed Lin. After her death, the Lu mother's ghost returned to tell her sons that the family must never take a wife with the surname Lin. Jin-ru's grandmother forgot to inform her youngest son (Jin-ru's uncle) of the family rule. Sure enough, in college he had a girlfriend named Lin whom he wanted to marry. In the end, the couple was forced to break up, and both their hearts were broken.

There is incentive for parents to avoid the appearance of meddling. Parents may fear that interfering in their children's affairs may inhibit dating and reduce their children's chances at marriage. The stereotypical Chinese mother worries most when her marriage-aged son or daughter has no marriage prospects at all, and she may network among friends, neighbors, relatives, and matchmaking services to set up blind dates. Many parents may regard silence as a small price to pay when they notice signs of romance in a son's or daughter's life. Furthermore, the right of parents to veto a match is so widely recognized that parents can afford to wait until their children make the first move toward bringing their "outside" loves within the terrain of the family. If parents cannot accept the proposed spouse, they have the power to end the relationship, because many, if not most, young people would not consider elopement. This is not to say that young people never become involved with partners whom they know their parents would refuse; they certainly do. However, forbidden relationships may be understood as such from the outset—never destined for marriage and ended, in many cases, before the pressure to get married becomes critical.

The intergenerational compromise, often unspoken, is that the older generation will stay out of the younger generation's business until marriage is likely because the younger generation agrees not to marry without parental approval. The situation is complex: A Confucian-style code of proper conduct between parents and children persists. Individuals often live inside their parents' homes for nearly three decades. And yet, they enjoy remarkable freedom.

Homosexuality provides an interesting example. Homosexual relationships that do not spill over into the domain of family are fairly well tolerated—better tolerated, I think, than in many North American families. Many in Taiwan do not regard homosexuality as a legitimate reason to avoid heterosexual marriage and refuse sexual reproduction. Anthropologist Scott Simon (2003) argues that gay men in Taiwan come under the greatest pressure to marry heterosexually only *after* "coming out." One of his interviewees reported that his mother "says that I can have as many male lovers as I want on the side, but I have to get married and have a family." The frequency of such cases belies the appearance of a marriage system that has transformed from one focused on family duty to one motivated instead by individual desire.

Sometimes parents attempt to take matters into their own hands and find a suitable spouse for a son or daughter, and some single people are happy to receive assistance in finding a spouse. By the 1990s in Taipei, though, it would have been rare for parents to expect a son or daughter to accept a parent-selected spouse without a period for getting acquainted and dating. No case was ever presented to me in that way. (However, parental involvement in matchmaking may be stronger than young couples let on.) Instead, I heard of young people who outright refused parents' help and of those who sabotaged arranged dates. When parents push matchmaking on their grown children, some will fabricate a boyfriend or girlfriend. My friend Pei-ling told me that a male friend had asked for a photograph of her so that he could pass it on to a second friend whose mother was anxious for him to marry. She obliged and, laughing, reported to me that the mother told the son that this girlfriend would not do; the mother did not like the concocted girlfriend's surname. Pei-ling's story is reminiscent of Ang Lee's film *The Wedding Banquet,* a story of a young gay man from Taiwan who creates a fake girlfriend to quell his parents' matchmaking efforts, even going so far as to marry her.

Single people boast of how easy their lives are in comparison to those of married people (see also S. Wu 1998, 1999). They have plenty of money at their disposal, plenty of free time, and few family responsibilities aside from attending weekly family dinners and annual holiday celebrations. In Taiwan's recent past, when farm life was the norm, old age was considered the best time in life. Old people were relieved from strenuous duties. Old people had the time and resources to frequent teahouses, play checkers and *majiang.* Elders held authority in families and politics. In today's consumer society, however, the people with the strongest consumptive power are in the spotlight. Married couples are expected to devote much of their resources to housing, education, and care for elderly parents. Families purchase costly items like furniture and cars and do not spend as much of their income on disposables like entertainment, eating out, fashionable clothes, and beauty services. Single people in Taipei have limited political and social power, they are underlings at work and marginalized in families, but they have high disposable incomes and strong incentives to get out of the house, away from their families, and consume goods and services. Young people I knew, moreover, often talked about marriage as if it were onerous and loathsome. Although most considered marriage inevitable, many make a point of putting it off as long as possible.

INSIDE AND OUTSIDE
IN THE CULTURAL LOGIC OF MARRIAGE

Young people I knew who were enthusiastic about dating—even those with long-term boyfriends or girlfriends whom they planned to marry one day—frequently spoke negatively about marriage. Despite the romantic bridal portraits that suggest otherwise, marriage is primarily seen not as a site of personal satisfaction and pleasure but as a family institution for organizing the labor of raising children, caring for the elderly, and performing family rituals such as attending to ancestral altars and graves, organizing weddings and funerals, and gathering kin together for holidays. Marriage as familial responsibility stands in stark contrast to the freedom of single life enjoyed in Taipei.

Both unmarried and married young people frequently expressed their attitudes about marriage in the language of "inside" and "outside," where life inside the home was constructed as inferior to life on the outside. They refer to "going out" *(chu men* or *chuqu wan)* and "staying in" *(bu chu men)* in highly patterned ways. Getting out of the house is highly valued. Young people "not yet" burdened by the responsibilities of marriage and parenthood seem to talk frequently about plans to "go out and have fun." ("Not yet" is frequently included in sentences such as this because it is assumed that all will eventually marry and accept full adult responsibility as a member of a family.) Going out includes structured activities, like going bowling with officemates or traveling to a vacation spot with friends, as well as unstructured activities, such as walking in a park with a lover or joining coworkers for dinner in a night market. The point is simply to get out of the house or, even more commonly, to delay going home.[16]

Men who by behavior or by order of birth appear too much "inside" their family are problematic candidates for marriage. I sometimes heard young women deride male peers for going home "to Mama" for dinner in the evening. Many women fear romantic involvement with men who seem too attached to home, imagining that in marriage such men will tend to "listen" to their mothers and want to remain near them. Young women also talk sometimes about avoiding men who are eldest sons because mothers are more likely to interfere in eldest sons' marriages by demanding frequent visits or even co-residence.

People express pity for those who *bu chu men,* which literally means "do not go out." Although *bu chu men* is sometimes said of young people who are shy, preoccupied with work, or particularly involved with their families, I heard it said most often of married women.[17] When young people talk incessantly about going out, they are indirectly distinguishing themselves from women who stay home to take care of family members. Yet women who are said to "not go out the door" leave their homes quite often. They shop, they do errands, and many even go to work six days a week. What they do *not* do is occupy the public spaces in Taipei dominated by young people who roam the night markets, sip cappuccinos in fancy cafés, drink in "prehistoric" beer houses, and smoke cigarettes over meals in Japanese colonial-style restaurants. In the evenings, married women purchase or prepare dinner for their families, wash clothes, clean floors, help children with school work, and watch television. Though married women are seldom trapped indoors physically, they are trapped inside metaphorically because their responsibilities leave them far less time and money for romance and leisure than their unmarried counterparts.

From my perspective, it is not marriage per se but motherhood that has this effect, but my informants seldom distinguished between marriage and parenthood. The presumption is that married women will become pregnant shortly after marriage. Of course, many women do not become pregnant within the first year of marriage—sometimes because they cannot, and sometimes because they practice birth control. Nevertheless, there is a clear pattern of couples' postponing marriage until they are ready to have children. I married before I completed graduate school and long before I planned to have children, and friends and acquaintances I met in Taiwan before 1996 found my decision to marry absolutely baffling. Sometimes when I defended my decision by explaining that my husband and I were in love, friends in Taiwan said, basically, "Right, but why get *married* if you don't have to?"

Most mothers in Taipei work hard. A service-industry working mother (such as a bridal salon saleswoman or stylist) typically leaves work promptly so she can relieve her own mother or her mother-in-law from childcare duties, and she rushes home to assemble a meal of prepared foods purchased at a cafeteria or streetside stand along the way.[18] After dinner there are always dishes to be washed, floors to be swept, laundry to be done, and children needing help with homework. Most young children sleep in their parents' beds alongside both mother and father, whole families going to sleep together late in the evening. Married couples, then, not only do not "go out and have fun," except on occasional Sunday family outings, but do not have much time alone with each other. Though not literally trapped inside, married women may be tangled inside a nexus of work and family duties.

It is widely held that the differences in lifestyle and attitude between single women and married women manifest in a woman's physical appearance. Single women are thought to dress nicely because they have more money to spend on clothes and are more interested in looking pretty to attract men. Single women are also said to wear more makeup (powder and lipstick); whereas married women, being harried by work and responsibility, lack the incentive to improve their appearance and, perhaps fearing criticism that by making up or dressing nicely they are trying to attract male attention, do not use makeup. A degrading saying has it that married women become "yellow-faced wives" *(huang-lian po)* because they fail to powder their faces and protect themselves from the sun—parallel to the American saying that married women "let themselves go." When people in Taiwan hear that a new female acquaintance is "already" married and reply with the compliment, "I couldn't tell by looking at you!" *(kan bu chu lai),* they are referencing the belief that the hardship of marriage shows up in a woman's physical appearance. Over the course of my field research I learned to politely address myself to even middle-aged women in a way that suggested they were not yet married and to react with surprise whenever I heard a woman was already married. To behave otherwise is essentially to say the woman is unattractive.[19]

While stereotypes of married women cast them as trapped "inside," burdened with heavy familial responsibilities that render them ugly, stereotypes of married men focus more on their lives outside the realm of family—especially on their extramarital sexual exploits. Married men are regarded neither as "inside people" nor as oppressed by marriage, even though the pressure to provide ample financial resources for a family falls more heavily on husbands than on wives. Men are, at least in theory, not responsible for housework, though many are happy to lend a hand as long as the older generation does not catch them defying "Chinese" family values by washing dishes. Most important, men are often expected to go out drinking, gambling, carousing with drunken KTV hostesses, visiting prostitutes, and dating young women.

In the eyes of many, male prestige is marked by a man's ability to attract and maintain a wife and one or more mistresses with his economic clout. The Taiwan media frequently report on the extramarital exploits of the rich and famous (Chang 1999). Employees gossip about the boss's extramarital affairs, and taxi drivers are quick to point out particularly good eateries with comments such as: "The noodles are excellent. The owner is rich. He has three wives!" (That is, the noodles are so delicious that the stand owner has become rich enough to have three "wives.")[20]

The popular notion that married women are stuck "inside" or bound by familial responsibilities while their husbands continue "going out to play" renders marriage unappealing from the perspective of the values dominant in the world outside family. It sounds unpalatable both to women, who fear becoming boring, ugly, and trapped, and to men, who fear being married to such a person (see Hsu 1998).

In a society where the overwhelming majority of women and men eventually marry, the rampant skepticism about achieving a satisfying marriage suggests that the transformation of marriage "from duty to desire," as anthropologist Jane Collier (1997) so eloquently puts it, is far from complete. Collier, following the historical trajectory described by Michel Foucault, argues that in Andalusia, marriages of the past were understood as a matter of duty but modern marriages are understood as a matter of desire. The difference between duty and desire is the difference between performance and heartfelt belief.[21] In the traditional or old-fashioned marriage system, satisfactory performance of duties was enough. There was no demand on desire or affect. Marriage was first and foremost about duty, not feelings. Modern marriage, because it hinges on individual desire, exacts a different kind of social control from individuals than did traditional marriages. Traditional marriage colonized behavior only, but modern marriage requires discipline of the heart. Though Taiwan's traditional marriage system exacted performance of the family duty to marry from virtually everyone, it allowed for a certain psychic freedom for spouses even as they performed their marital duties. In modern marriage, by contrast, one is supposed to *want* to perform marital duties and enjoy doing so. According to Collier's theoretical stance, the skepticism—even loathing—regarding marriage evident in Taipei today reveals that individual hearts there are not trained or disciplined to the requirements of modern marriage. Even so, people in Taiwan insist on the viability of and importance of a modern marriage system whereby spouses freely choose one another even if they do not freely choose marriage as an attractive, desirable life choice.

Two questions emerge: (1) If cultural expectations for women's happiness in marriage are so low, why do most women marry? (2) Is divorce not a possibility? I address the latter question first.

Indeed, today divorce is a real possibility for couples in Taiwan, which has the highest divorce rate among East Asian nations. The threefold increase in Taiwan's divorce rate between 1970 and 1990 (see Lee, Thornton, and Lin 1994: 259) was sharp, but in the twelve ensuing years, the divorce rate increased another fivefold. By late 2002, there was one new divorce in Taiwan for every 2.53 new marriages. This so alarmed Taiwan's legislators that they took the unusual step of mandating premarital counseling for all marrying couples ("New Law" 2003). Clearly, the late twentieth century was a time of rapid change for Taiwan's marriages. Marital behavior, however, changed more rapidly than did cultural views on marriage. Even in the midst of skyrocketing increases in divorce, the women and men who participated in my research nearly uniformly expressed the view that marriage is a "one-way trip" (see Hsu 1998). In fact, when I asked why Taiwanese bridal photographs are so much larger than those in the United States, I was told, "Chinese people regard a wedding as a big deal, as a once-in-a-life-time event." Respondents reasoned that weddings must not be a big deal for Americans, given the high U.S. divorce rate. Very few of today's Taiwan divorcees entered marriage with the view that it was dissolvable if intolerable circumstances arose. To the contrary, they married hoping that the marriage would be tolerable and believing that, if it was not, it would persist nevertheless. Given the negative outlook on marriage so many expressed to me, marriage was a frightening though inevitable life step.

It is too early to determine what factors are now leading so many couples to divorce, but extramarital affairs are one popular explanation in Taiwan. American readers might guess that because of the economic and educational opportunities women enjoy in Taiwan today, women have rejected the old marriage system whereby men were free to enjoy sexual relationships outside marriage. It is true that men's extramarital sex is less normatively accepted than it was thirty or forty years ago, when emotional distance was the norm for spousal relations. Perhaps wives in arranged marriages of the past did not mind their husbands' culturally sanctioned extramarital trysts as long as they did not drain family economic resources (see Wolf 1972; see also Stockard 1989). One imagines that the combination of women's current ability to support themselves in the capitalist economy, coupled with the new cultural environment emphasizing love before marriage, would empower wives to reject husbands' sexual and emotional disloyalty. The situation, however, is far more complex.

In interviews that took place in 1996–1997, local divorce experts argued that husbands' extramarital sex was indeed a factor in many divorces, but that it was husbands rather than wives who were initiating divorce. If divorce had to do with women's power, it was the power of mistresses to convince men to leave their marriages. Despite the fact that women could attain economic self-sufficiency, wives had many noneconomic reasons to remain married. Until the late 1990s, a primary reason was the likelihood of losing child custody in divorce. Until 1996, Taiwanese law granted automatic custody of children to the father. If the wife provided evidence of physical abuse or of the husband's extramarital affairs, the judge could make exceptions.[22] Fathers won 80 to 90 percent of child custody judgments, receiving exclusive custody without visitation rights for the mother (Liu 2001). Activists told me of mothers sneaking visits with children during recess periods at school, passing treats through schoolyard fences. Most fathers relied upon their own mothers to care for children after the divorce, and children often moved into their grandparents' homes located elsewhere on the island, which made sneaking a visit even more difficult. The child custody law enacted in 1996 required judges to place children with the parent most capable of raising them. At the time of my field research, however, local divorce experts expressed skepticism that courts would cease favoring fathers in child custody proceedings, despite the new law. It was unclear how judges would react; it was also unclear what impact, if any, the widely publicized new legislation would have upon married women and men in their handling of marital conflict.

A recent study by legal scholar Liu Hung-en (2001) documents that Taiwan's judges now tend strongly to favor placing children in custody of mothers. Liu argues that this "win" for women is problematic, however. Judges are still inclined to hand down all-or-none custody decisions, in which the noncustodial parent receives no visitation rights and is not required to pay child support. This places a "double burden" on mothers, who thus must often take full custody of children and full financial responsibility for them as well. Meanwhile, when the mother is not able to demonstrate sufficient economic resources to maintain the family independently, the father receives full custody and the mother lacks visitation rights. In other words, while the 1996 law corrected previously unequal chances at receiving child custody, the legal climate remains far from favorable for women in divorce.

There are cultural reasons, too, why women dissatisfied with marriage might avoid divorce despite improvements for women under the law. Divorced women lose the status marriage confers on women without being able to recoup the high status of a young woman who is "not yet married." Women instituted Wanqing Funü Xiehui, an organization for divorced women, to support those in this stigmatized position. Part of the stigma of divorce comes from the widely held belief that wives, not husbands, are responsible for the well-being of the marriage. If her husband has abandoned her for a mistress, a divorced woman may be blamed for failing to keep her husband's sexual attention. The other problems faced by divorced women are the same as those faced by women who never marry and become the "inside person" to a man. Let me turn, then, to the first question: Given that women's increased access to education and employment allows for female economic self-sufficiency in modern Taiwan, and given that so many young women looking at married life from the outside see it as grim, why do they get married? Ya-ling's story is illustrative.

Ya-ling, a thirty-five-year-old woman, sought support at Wanqing because her father refused to allow her to marry her older, not-college-educated boyfriend. She was convinced that this was her last chance for marriage and that if she did not marry this man, she faced a fate similar to that of divorced women. Without ties to the patriarchal family system through a husband, the social status of an older single or divorced woman is precarious. Many women fear that if they reach middle age without having located themselves inside a man's family, they will be forever trapped outside.

As Ya-ling explained her dilemma to the group of divorced and divorce-fearing married women, however, the group tended to take the side of her parents. If he's so old and uneducated, one woman asked, "Isn't it true that the only reason you want to marry him is so you can move out of your father's house?" She urged Ya-ling to endure longer to avoid the difficulties of married life. Ya-ling, sobbing into a tissue, replied that she already lived in her own apartment and that her father was denying her this last chance at normalcy. At no point did Ya-ling or anyone else mention notions such as the inviolability of love or an individual's right to self-determination. Ya-ling made it clear that she would not marry without her father's approval. Women in the group pointed out that if in the future Ya-ling became like them—wives dealing with battering and extramarital affairs—Ya-ling would have no recourse without the support of her natal family *(niangjia)*.

Unlike men, married women have "inside" access to *two* families that bestow both rights and responsibilities on them. The family a woman marries into can make many claims on her. Culturally, she bears children and performs household labor for that family. In turn, that family makes her one of its own, owing her economic support including medical care and nursing in sickness or old age. Women also maintain close ties with their natal families, both supporting them and being supported by them. Married women today give substantial financial support to aging parents, sometimes more so than their brothers, even though, according to family logic, brothers are technically obligated to support their parents while sisters are not (Lee, Thornton, and Lin 1994; Parish and Willis 1993; Tsui 1987). Parents lend support to married daughters in myriad ways, including financial assistance and child tending. The women of the support group told Ya-ling to accept her father's veto of her proposed marriage on grounds that she could not afford to forego her father's support in the future, especially in the event that her boyfriend made a bad husband.

Many families in Taiwan are not "close" in the sense of sharing personal feelings and experiences yet are tightly bound by shared responsibilities to the family and its members. All family members (but especially the men) are expected to take responsibility for the well-being of children, unmarried siblings, elderly parents, and grandparents. Older siblings, for example, contribute money to pay tuition for younger siblings. The daughters-in-law of a family may rotate the care of elderly parents. In fact, the most commonly mentioned fear concerning unmarried women is that, without children, in old age they will have no one to care for them.

Women and men who do not marry and rear children are seen as a drain on the whole family's resources. When a daughter never marries or gets divorced, she becomes a liability to the family even if she is self-supporting: Her brothers (and their sons and sons' wives) are obliged to take care of her in old age. When a son never marries, he drains the family's resources, too, by failing to provide the family with a daughter-in-law's labor in caring for the elderly and helping with holiday cooking and cleaning. Even worse, by failing to provide the family with children, a never-married son fails to provide himself with social insurance in the form of children. In old age he, too, will become the responsibility of young family members (theoretically, the wives of his brothers' sons would have to cook, clean, and care for him) if he fails to produce his own sons to bring in daughters-in-law to care for him.

The view of family as social insurance is rooted in the old agrarian society, where very few could amass enough savings to buy care for themselves in old age. Before Taiwan's "economic miracle," all but a few

Taiwanese were very poor. The situation today is quite different for those individuals who have sufficient resources. I met and heard about unmarried women in their thirties who evaded marriage-as-social-insurance but literally purchased insurance policies instead, substituting disability and life insurance policies for the children they would not bear.[23] Women may feel that they fail their end of the family contract by never marrying or ending up divorced. Parents and brothers may also accuse unmarried women of having selfishly and unfairly burdened the natal family by their actions. The purchase of insurance policies arms women not only against fears for the future but also against family members who pressure them to marry as a form of social insurance. That is, they decide to purchase insurance in cash rather than with their bodies and lives in an undesirable marriage.

Few people discuss the distinct possibility that by the time today's young women and men reach old age, patterns of family responsibility may have changed substantially. Early in the twentieth century, only 0.2 percent of the female population over age fifty had never married (Lin, Lee, and Thornton 1994: 204). Sociologists call this a universal marriage regime—not unusual for East Asia but striking in comparison to Western Europe, where, during the same time period, rates of never-marrying women ranged from 10 to 29 percent across various countries (Hajnal cited in Lin, Lee, and Thornton 1994: 206). Nonmarriage was simply not a real option in Taiwan at that time. By the late twentieth century, numbers of never-marrying women and men were on the rise, and, accordingly, they were finding ways to get by. Their very existence created opportunities for others to follow in their steps. In 1990, 3.1 percent of women over age fifty had never married—a substantial rise in nonmarriage for Taiwan, though a low number among industrialized nations (Lin, Lee, and Thornton 1994: 204). Still, large numbers of women are postponing marriage now. In 2001, 20 percent of women between the ages of thirty and thirty-four remained unmarried (Chung 2001). Perhaps a large number of these women will refuse marriage indefinitely.[24]

THE INS AND OUTS OF CHANGE: CULTURAL STEREOTYPES ABOUT MARRIAGE

In 1992, during my first visit to Taiwan, I myself was newly married and childless, and I thought my friends and acquaintances' extremely negative views on marriage were immature. Later, my own experiences of child rearing showed me that raising a family involves more hard work than I had imagined. Were friends in Taiwan right all along? I began to question the romanticization of marriage among Americans, who often cast marriage as a site of personal pleasure rather than a site for the work of family. If people in Taiwan often express distaste for the unpaid labor and burdensome duties of family life, perhaps they understood the undertaking more realistically than I did.

The views I heard expressed in Taipei, however, were not all realistic. Stereotypes about married women as housewives trapped "inside" abound. Yet survey data indicate that nearly half of married women island-wide work outside the home ("Nearly Half of Women" 1998). Indeed, many married women I met in Taipei had managed to avoid the dreaded fate of being dominated by an overbearing mother-in-law by working in the paid labor force after marriage.

Building riches is strongly valued in family life, second only to producing sons to carry on the family. Opportunities to save or earn money frequently take precedence over other values, including proper intergenerational power relations. Mothers-in-law are quick to recognize that younger women's earnings help enrich the family's coffers and provide educational and entrepreneurial opportunities for its members. The income that working wives bring their families commands respect. In fact, many men and their parents expect wives to produce income, if not in a family-owned business or at home (taking in piece work such as sewing or light industry), then in a service industry job or professional career. Moreover, in the 1990s the state was interested in tapping into the potential labor pool of housewives, because unemployment rates were so low (under 3 percent) that many industries clamored for more workers (and lobbied for relaxation of state quotas on imported foreign laborers). These facts mitigate the stereotypical images of the young daughter-in-law's sad fate.

Consciousness of change runs very high in Taiwan—so high that people say there is a "generation gap" between young people just a few years apart in age.[25] The discussion of change, though, focuses on what I am calling "outside" life, especially on modes and styles of consumption. Many people imagine families to be much more conservative than they are in practice. In fact, there are dramatic changes in "inside" life as well.

Provisioning for childcare is one place where changes in the inside realm are most apparent. Working mothers I met relied heavily on the help of their mothers-in-law, and even their own mothers, for childcare (see Bak cited in Watson 1997; Gallin 1984, 1986, 1989; Sando 1986). A typical arrangement is for infants and preschool-aged children to be in the full-time care of their paternal grandmother. In families where two generations live together or as neighbors, small children are often looked after by their mothers at night and by their grandmothers during the day. In families where grandmother and parents live far apart, however, the children commonly live with their grandmother, sleeping by her side at night and seeing their mother and father only on Sundays and during holiday visits. Even when parents reside overseas, they often send young children to Taiwan to live with grandparents until they reach school age.

The many older women caring for their grandchildren in my neighborhood often took great pride in showing off the small children, but they also complained of the hard work of chasing after toddlers and quieting fussy infants. Some grandfathers in my neighborhood could be seen pushing babies in strollers and taking preschool-aged children to the playground, but generally the work of childcare falls to "retired" women. Retirement-aged grandparents may receive regular financial support from their children regardless of childcare services they provide, but they may call these funds their "salary" or, in other cases, explicitly receive extra pay in exchange for childcare services. Some grandmothers demand pay equal to or above the rate paid in nonfamilial babysitting arrangements. When a maternal grandmother babysits for her own daughter's children, she is more likely to be compensated for her work. Maternal grandchildren are in no way her responsibility, though the family may refer to their payments not as compensation but as "help" for the maternal grandmother.

Working mothers arrange for other types of childcare, too. Institutional nursery care for infants and toddlers is neither widely available nor trusted. However, grandmother-aged women who have no grandchildren of their own who need care, and mothers of young children who need extra income, often take young children into their homes. "Full-time" childcare of this sort is twenty-four hours a day, six days per week. "Part-time" care is during working hours only (about fifty hours per week), and during my field research period part-time care cost about NT $15,000 (about $600 U.S.) per month in Taipei. This type of arrangement is considered inferior to grandmother-provided care but is common nonetheless. In such cases, the paternal grandmother is usually either working herself or is too weak or ill to care for children.

Young people—the same people who view marriage negatively— often presume that grandmothers are always delighted to take on the work of childcare. With grandmothers and babysitters performing "inside" work so young women, with greater earning potential, can work outside, it is clear that families are more complex than stereotypes voiced by young people allow. Working mothers, in fact, do not look like "inside" people at all. Structurally, they seem to occupy roles similar to fathers. If, as young people's cultural logic goes, being stuck "inside" as a housewife is an unpleasant fate, then marriage per se is not what brings on this state of oppression, because nearly half of married women work outside, in the paid labor force. Though grandmothers now do much of wives' work, there is no parallel national dialogue on the fate of over-worked grandmothers.

Household work involves more than childcare, of course. Most old women who tend their grandchildren do not clean and cook for their daughters-in-law. Young women with sufficient financial resources pur-chase the means of avoiding all household work by employing servants. Local domestic servants were difficult to find in the 1990s, when Taiwan's unemployment rate was very low. The wages that families were willing to pay were low, as was the social standing of nannies and maids. The search for household employees extended to very poor nearby coun-tries, where women willing to perform household service and childcare for low wages—by Taiwan's standards—were plentiful.

In the mid-1990s, the state yielded to popular demand for cheap house-hold, factory, and construction laborers by dramatically increasing the number of visas given to workers from the Philippines, Thailand, Vietnam, and other Southeast Asian countries. During my field work, only Filipinas were permitted to work as household servants, but the gov-ernment announced it would begin offering visas to other Southeast Asian women as well. Filipina maids (who are typically well-educated and quite fluent in English) travel to Taiwan on special work visas, which labor agents in the Philippines help them obtain for fees equal to several months' pay. Taiwan's government closely monitors the number of Southeast Asian laborers admitted to the country to prevent them from taking up illegal residence when work contracts have ended or been broken. Most impor-tantly, Filipina maids are not permitted to marry in Taiwan, and if a maid is confirmed pregnant, she is subject to immediate deportation. In 1996–1997, Filipina maids were paid just over NT $15,000 ($600 U.S.) a month for twenty-four-hour-a-day, six-days-a-week household service. They worked on one-year contracts for a maximum of two- or three-year stays in Taiwan. The demand for live-in housekeeper service was very high. Families had to meet eligibility requirements (a child under age five or a disabled or sick person in the household) and sign up on waiting lists. In 1997, families waited up to a year before procuring a maid.

The presence of Filipina maids in Taiwan households frees the wives from being stuck "inside"; wives become responsible for managing household work rather than performing it directly. In most cases, the Filipina's labor frees the young mother of the household to work full-time and earn a salary greater than the Filipina's pay. Amazingly, many Filipinas in Taiwan use the majority of their earnings to fund the raising and schooling of their own children, including the cost of hiring a nanny to care for them. Parrenas (2001) calls the successive buying out of family care work by purchasing household services from poorer women "the globalization of mothering" (see also Constable 1997 on Hong Kong).

Most families contract Filipinas to free up a wife so she can work outside the home, but there are variations. One acquaintance had for several years shared the care of her infirm mother-in-law on a weekly rotating basis with the wives of her husband's brothers. The three brothers eventually resolved to contribute NT $5,000 each every month to hire a Filipina to relieve their wives from this work, which they found unpleasant. Sometimes Filipinas are employed in wealthy households where none of the women work. There they cook, clean, and provide childcare around the clock so the women of the household can engage in philanthropic or leisure activities like shopping, playing *majiang,* and visiting the beauty spa.

Treatment of Filipina housekeepers is notoriously poor—stories of battering, sexual assault, and contract abuse abound. Even when they are not abused or victimized by their employers, Filipinas often labor under difficult circumstances. Filipina maids in my neighborhood complained of being forced to stay awake very late at night to serve drinks, snacks, and cigarettes to guests playing *majiang* or cards. Throughout the night, they had to feed infants in their care and, in the morning, rise early to prepare breakfast. Often they do not have private living quarters. Some share a room with the children of employers; others sleep on a cot in the kitchen.

Many men and women in Taiwan treat Filipinas shabbily, in part because of anxieties over the changes Taiwan's globalization processes entail for family life. Widespread stereotypes of Filipinas depict them as dishonest thieves who seduce husbands and neglect children. Mothers worry intensely about how Filipina maids may neglect or abuse their children in their absence; hence household tension runs high when parents return home from work and scrutinize their maid's every move. Sadly, the exploitative conditions of the Filipinas' contracts feed their employers' distrust. Employers recognize that the work contracts that bring Filipinas to Taiwan pay wages below market rates. Filipinas who run away from their employers can earn much better wages on the underground market (until authorities catch them), and stories regarding runaway Filipinas appear frequently in local newspapers. Fearing for their children's safety under these conditions, some parents literally lock their Filipina maids and children inside the house—rendering the Filipina women and their charges "inside people" to a degree extremely uncommon among Taiwanese housewives. One acquaintance did just this, in fact. Lily seemed to be an intelligent and kind person in other contexts, but her anxieties about the Filipina she had hired to care for her infant son led her to the cruel and dangerous practice of locking her son and his nanny inside every morning when she left for the office.

In Lily's family, the problems of the shifting grounds of inside/outside relations manifested themselves clearly. The distrusted Filipina, whom no one regarded as a family insider, was entrusted with "inside" duties. Lily's mother-in-law was a postal service employee and, wanting to capture the maximum pension benefits, did not make herself available to care for her grandson. (Without fail, however, she called every night to speak to him by telephone.) Lily wanted very much to continue working as an accounting specialist for a multinational bank. Having a live-in maid probably made Lily's life more comfortable in many ways, even as it provoked such high anxiety that she deprived her son and his nanny of the outdoors and risked their lives by confining them in a potential fire trap. Had Lily been a woman of a different class position, without a college degree, she might have earned an income by converting her living room into a small factory. Many working mothers who do not have access to an older family member to provide childcare must tend children while they sew garments or assemble factory parts at home. Lily had the means to avoid confinement "inside" by bringing an outsider into her home, but she paid a steep price to do so.

With so many young women in Taiwan employing Filipina maids, leaving children in the care of others, serving meals prepared by restaurants and street vendors, marrying later, and commanding high wages, it is often said that women's status in Taiwan has improved as a result of capitalization. The problem of "women's status" is complicated by the fact that Filipina laborers and the grandmothers whose retirement days are spent changing diapers are women, too. Rather than dividing household labor such that men and women, old and young, share in its duties more equally, in many families the low-status roles once occupied by young daughters-in-law have been delegated to foreign laborers, who are even more subject to physical, emotional, and sexual abuse than were the young daughters-in-law of the past. A daughter-in-law was at least able to spread gossip about a cruel mother-in-law and enlist the help of other village women in improving her lot (Wolf 1972). Filipinas, by contrast, can engage in everyday acts of resistance like petty theft (Scott 1985), but the only way to transform their working conditions is to run away or end their contracts and go back to the Philippines—where their families are desperately in need of money. Though grandmothers may find their care work exhausting, they at least enjoy greater protection from outright abuse by young women.

Many women in Taiwan today have more educational and work opportunities than did women in the past. If working for a boss in an office or receiving pay for repetitive sewing work at home is more tolerable than working for one's mother-in-law, then it is fair to say that most of Taiwan's young women are better off now. Old age today, however, may be less rewarding for women than in the past. Moreover, in Taipei today, the aged are often segregated inside, away from the goings-on of young people's lives outside. Maturity was once the pinnacle of a woman's power in the family and village, a time of high status and a well-deserved rest after a lifetime of physical labor, but no longer. Now many would cite young womanhood as the high point of the female life cycle, when women are considered beautiful, energetic, sexy, and high in consumptive power and style. In these respects, the high and low points for women's status over the life cycle have reversed. Do "women" enjoy greater status and power in today's Taiwan in comparison with the recent past? The critical question is: *Which* women?

Because transformations in gender roles have redistributed periods of relative power and status to earlier points in the female life cycle, the struggle to transform gender roles often takes place between women of different generations, rather than between women and men. Often it is the husband's mother, more than the husband himself, who insists on rigid gender roles in the household.

Jin-yi was a young newlywed I met one day while browsing photo studio sales material in a street market in central Taipei. She had grown up on a farm in Miaoli and met her Taipei-raised husband when he was on a sales trip there. Jin-yi works part-time as a saleswoman at a clothing stand, in addition to her full-time job as a bookkeeper for a small business. She lives with her husband's parents and four grown siblings in a small Taipei apartment made larger by an illegal rooftop structure providing additional bedroom space. I visited Jin-yi at their home on two occasions. The first time, her mother-in-law sat squarely in the center of the room in front of the television while I interviewed Jin-yi a few feet to the side. Her husband sat near us but watched a television variety show while his mother and Jin-yi competed for my attention. Jin-yi wanted to show me her honeymoon photos from a tour of Australia. Her mother-in-law wanted me to admire photos of her grandchildren by her other daughters-in-law. Jin-yi was under pressure to get pregnant, since her first wedding anniversary was rapidly approaching.

The second time I visited, Jin-yi's in-laws were out of town. Jin-yi prepared a simple meal of frozen, prepared noodle soup in the microwave. This time, she occupied the central seat in the room. She and her husband were watching a pirated videocassette of the movie *Ransom* with Chinese subtitles. I noted the change in the atmosphere of the home in the mother-in-law's absence. The couple watched a Hollywood movie instead of a local variety show, and Jin-yi frequently spoke directly to her husband this time. In his mother's absence, he now participated in our conversation, despite the dramatic action on the television screen. Several times Jin-yi ordered him to bring something from their upstairs bedroom to show me, and when we had finished eating, she asked him to help her with the dishes. In fact, he cleared and washed the dishes by himself. When he scurried out of the room with the bowls and other items, I commented on how nice it is that her husband is willing to wash dishes. She agreed, saying that he is very willing to help around the house; but she warned me, "Do not tell my mother-in-law," who would get angry if she heard her son had washed a few bowls and chopsticks.

I heard about mothers' disapproval of married sons doing household work many times and saw it played out in television shows. The same theme occasionally surfaced in connection with bridal photographs in which the groom posed in a subservient position in relationship to the bride; the groom's mother or grandmother took offense at these photographs because they seemed to "reverse" gender roles. Mothers, it is said, try to protect their sons from changes in gender roles that seem to undermine male prestige and predominance. At the same time, many mothers urge their daughters to exploit the shifting terrain of gender roles, advising them to find progressive husbands who are comparatively independent of their mothers and seem least likely to take mistresses in the future. With the battle of the sexes taking place across generational lines in Taipei today, mothers' differing views on gender when it comes to their sons and daughters seems to be a Taiwanese double standard.

Historians who study changes in family life associated with the

Industrial Revolution in England and the United States describe a process similar to what I have described here for Taiwan, although the particular contours of the transformation differ substantially. One common feature is a growing separation between spheres of family and production, as wage labor becomes more widespread and the importance of family farming diminishes. Another is young adults' decreasing dependence on their parents, resulting in reduced parental control over spouse selection (Cancian 1987; Engels 1985; Stone 1997). The concepts of "inside" and "outside" lend a useful framework for thinking about the particular family practices that, at least for now, have taken shape. The influence of outside spheres in young people's everyday lives has expanded exponentially relative to the inside sphere of family.

Available ethnographic depictions of village life just prior to the rapid acceleration of Taiwan's globalization emphasize the domination of the young by the old in a way of life where the reach of families was extensive. By the end of the twentieth century, an informal intergenerational compromise was forged. Creatively making use of communications technology and public spaces, young adults managed to conduct much of their lives outside even while living at home. Older generations were not entirely marginalized in this process, however. With young people virtually evacuating the inside sphere of the family until the point of marriage, their parents and grandparents consolidated control of this space. This is where parallels to British and American families' experiences of industrial capitalism diminish.

Because marriage remains a critically important step in the life course in the eyes of most people in Taiwan, the freedom that youth and young adults experience in the outside sphere is necessarily viewed as temporary. Marriage marks the transition between a life dominated by the styles, viewpoints, and practices of the outside world and a life that is at least partially dominated by the styles, viewpoints, and practices of the inside world. Hence, weddings create not only a set of rights and responsibilities between two individuals and two families; they also mark the movement of young people away from the outside and toward the inside. The significance of the transition, many believe, is more profound for women than men. I have argued that single young women and men who spoke to me about marriage seemed to hold unrealistically negative expectations about women's necessary seclusion inside marriage. The view that married men live far less restricted lives may be exaggerated, too. The saying *nei zai mei,* after all, implies that before a man's inside people leave for America, they exert powerful claims on him.

The cacophony of beliefs and practices around the institution of marriage in Taiwan today includes cultural ideas with roots in different historical periods and political economies. Deeply rooted beliefs in strong intergenerational ties of work and mutual support coexist with deeply felt desires for individual freedoms and pleasures; inside and outside worlds have tremendous potential for conflict. Segregating the two works well most of the time, although this compromise necessarily produces points of tension. Extramarital affairs—the subject of a great deal of controversy in both public and private forums—are one point of tension. Should "inside" relationships constrain not just women's but also men's outside lives after marriage? Weddings are another point of tension today; weddings cause inside and outside worlds to collide. When couples who have courted outside the spaces and cultural logic of family announce their plans to marry, the process of turning their outside relationship into an inside, marital relationship begins.

It is tempting to read bridal photographs as reflective of a much-changed social universe where marriage has become a site of desire and pleasure more than of duty, and where emotional ties between spouses are more significant than family ties between generations. The situation is much more complex than this, however, and far more interesting. Intergenerational ties, differences, and struggles remained central to the experience of marriage in 1990s Taipei, while bridal portraits intentionally obliterated intergenerational ties in their representations of marriage. In doing so, they painted a fantasy world made fantastic precisely by its opposition to brides' fears and expectations for marriage. And yet, the fantasy worlds pictured in bridal photographs have at least some basis in the outside world that young adults experience before marriage. Given the widely held opinion that young women's experiences on the outside are the high point of their lives, bridal photographs exaggerate the beauty, romance, and individualistic pleasures of outside lives just before they abruptly end. Bridal photos help young women go "in" with a blast.

CHAPTER 4

Family Wedding Rites and Banquets

Mr. Xu, one of Taiwan's oldest wedding photographers and the founder of a once-booming but now outdated photography studio, lamented that Taiwan's young people do not value Chinese traditions the way Japanese value theirs. In Japan, he noted, couples still dress up in Japanese costume as part of their weddings; in Taiwan couples wear only Western attire.[1] I reminded him that since the early 1990s it has been popular for couples in Taiwan to dress up in imperial-style crowns and gowns for their photo albums. Yes, he said, but they do so only for fun, not because they value Chinese traditions.

Mr. Xu was absolutely right. Not only do couples say that they dress up in the Chinese costumes just "for fun," but they also sometimes strike irreverent poses in them—with tongues sticking out or eyes crossed. Such photos are taken not only *for* fun but sometimes also to *make* fun of old China, old Taiwan, and old approaches to marriage (see figure 9). Dressing up for a photo or two in the Chinese *qipao* gown and military garb of the early Republican period (circa 1920), in Japanese kimono, in medieval European court costume, or in modern athletic attire is just as popular. And couples and their photographers do not treat the imperial crown costumes with any greater reverence than they do these other "fun" get-ups. I even heard of a Taiwan Independence Movement activist who, in his bridal album, wears the costume and political symbol of his party's archenemy—an early KMT military uniform. The bridal industry and the couples who partake of it demonstrate a Disney-esque approach

Figure 9. Photographs of couples in non-Western costumes are often said to be "just for fun." This bridal salon advertising image makes light of the past by combining Chinese-style costumes with a fun pose. (Image courtesy of Cang-ai Bridal Photography Co., 2003. Photographer: Chen Chong-ping.)

to culture when it comes to these exotic dress forms. Their photo albums romp through time and across space in pursuit of fun; the industry reduces culture and even politics to costumes donned and removed at will.[2]

Although some—such as the older photographer just quoted—might take offense at the exoticization of Chinese costumes alongside Japanese kimono and medieval European costumes, there is in fact a basis for treating all of these costumes alike as foreign, touristy kitsch. Only a minute, elite class of pre-Japanese colonial Taiwan would have had the means to provide brides with Chinese gowns and crowns of the sort available today for bridal photo shoots.[3] Virtually every Taiwanese bride and groom I met came from a family who had been poor rural farmers or middle-class merchants just one or two generations back. Most of my young informants' mothers had worn white Western-style gowns. Their grandmothers had worn homemade *qipao* dresses of the finest fabric they could afford, *if* they had weddings at all. Marriages among the very poor were frequently not marked by the ceremonial transfer of the bride from one family home to another. In some parts of Taiwan, especially the north, "major" marriages, resulting in ceremonies like those described later in this chapter, were few. In many cases, the bride had been adopted into her mother-in-law's family as a small child and raised as a sister to the groom until their marriage, when their parents provided them with a private bedroom and expected them to develop sexual relations and produce grandsons for the family. Other marriage contracts required the son of a very poor family to marry into his bride's family, taking up uxorilocal residence with her parents and agreeing to give some or all of his children their mother's surname. The past that is invoked by the wearing of imperial-style wedding costumes today, then, has nothing to do with the ancestral experiences of the vast majority of couples.

Sometimes bridal photographs of the late 1990s involved more realistic representations of the past, with couples dressed in outdated Western-style white gowns and dark suits. In 1997, a few of Taipei's most expensive bridal salons were producing black-and-white photographs parodying Taiwan's earliest wedding photographs, of the 1940s and 1950s. The couple stands side by side without touching each other. They face the camera straight on, with deadpan facial expressions.[4] Sometimes a stretch of burlap is used as a backdrop. Occasionally the bride and groom are barefoot, suggesting, perhaps, that either they could not afford to rent shoes to accompany their bridal attire or that they had to walk through flooded, muddy rice fields on the wedding day. By poking fun at old styles and ways of life, especially the lack of affection between bride and groom, these photos assert the difference between the present cohort of newlyweds and those of the past. However, these photos depicting bride and groom in Western-style wedding attire have a stronger connection to Taiwan's lived past than do the Chinese imperial costume shots, which index contemporary "historical" soap operas. In either case, young people do not seek to honor the past and uphold traditions in their photographic representations of themselves. The photographs plant the couples firmly in the outside realm beyond the reach of the family. By making fun of tradition and old-fashioned approaches to marriage, couples photographically position themselves as modern, individualistic, and upwardly mobile.

If bridal photos picture couples in the realm outside family, weddings do just the opposite. Young couples are not as free from the older generation and the familial constraints associated with the past as the fantasy worlds captured in their bridal photo albums assert. The past, it turns out, is alive and well in the present. Nowhere is this fact clearer than in weddings.

CEREMONY AS OLD PEOPLE'S BUSINESS

Despite Mr. Xu's concern about young people's lack of respect for Chinese traditions, in practice, present-day betrothal *(dinghun)* and wedding *(jiehun)* ceremonies contain many of the features that scholars describe for Taiwan's past (see Freedman 1970; Wolf 1972; see also Ebrey 1993 on ancient China). On the surface, however, it looks as though everything has changed. In addition to old-fashioned betrothal and wedding ceremonies that take place in private homes and include only a small number of guests, there are now public ceremonies that are anything but traditional in Taiwan. Few older Taiwanese see these relatively public mini-ceremonies as the real thing.

The most public representations of weddings—bridal photography and the mini–wedding ceremonies sometimes performed at the start of wedding banquets—suggest what many people call the Westernization *(xifanghua)* of weddings. The attire has origins in Victorian England, and the structure of the mini-ceremony is more similar to those led by religious officials in contemporary Chicago than to traditional Chinese or Taiwanese wedding rites. These mini-ceremonies are considered supplemental, not necessary, components of weddings but were increasing in popularity in the late 1990s. The couple walks down a red-carpeted aisle to Mendelssohn's ubiquitous "Wedding March," piped in over a public address system. Guests armed with firecrackers in tiny plastic "champagne" bottles and cans of "silly string" bombard bride and groom with noise, paper streamers, and explosions of color. At the front of the room, parents and other important guests stand on a stage, and the men take turns making short speeches. Sometimes the bride and groom sign an unofficial wedding certificate and bow to their parents, their grandparents, and each other. Banquet guests seated at their tables, meanwhile, chat among themselves and pay little attention to the ceremony, attesting to its lack of significance. Many families invite virtually everyone they know to the wedding banquet, so these mini-ceremonies have far more witnesses than do the family ceremonies that usually take place at home in advance of the wedding banquet.

Couples are married in the eyes of the law only when they register their marriage at city hall. Beyond that single fact, there is a great deal of diversity among weddings in Taiwan. Some couples have no ceremony beyond the presentation of photo identification and the signing of forms with city officials as witnesses, perhaps exchanging rings right there in city hall. These couples may or may not have a wedding banquet, depending on personal and family circumstances. A wedding banquet may occur many months after the marriage registration; it is regarded as a wedding banquet regardless of its timing. When there is no banquet, friends and family often say it is a pity and may gossip about the reason for the failure to invite guests for a celebration. When there is a banquet, few guests are likely to know specific details about the legal and ceremonial proceedings that occurred (or did not) beforehand. The legal marriage may have occurred weeks or months before, or it might not have yet occurred. If there were family wedding rites, they may have happened on another day or that very morning. The wedding banquet, in other words, is quite distinct from the act of getting married. It is, however, the public face of the wedding.

Most couples I met registered their marriages in city hall, underwent old-fashioned betrothal and wedding rites, and invited guests to one or more wedding banquets. Yet many brides and grooms, like most young people, profess to know very little about wedding customs—just as older folks disclaim knowledge about bridal salons and photography. Betrothal and wedding ceremonies—like all rituals that involve ancestors—are the older generations' terrain. The ceremonies are "old people's business" *(laoren de shiqing)* and bridal photography is "young people's business." The old people's business, moreover, is complex—involving a series of rituals that take place over time and in multiple places.

Writing a century ago, Arnold Van Gennep (1960) remarked that in many societies betrothal and wedding rituals are repeated over time to accomplish the striking change in status entailed for the spouse who leaves one family, clan, lineage, or village and becomes a member of a new one. The complexity of weddings, he argued, reflects the major social drama involved, for marriage is a rite of passage second only in severity and importance to birth and death. According to this classic anthropological understanding of weddings, customary wedding rituals should have lost much of their cultural meaning in modern times. Why would people in late-twentieth-century Taipei have wanted or needed rituals that treated marrying couples, especially brides, as if they were living in the agrarian society of the past? When Margery Wolf (1972) conducted research in a Taiwanese village in the 1960s, weddings were seen as traumatic for brides, who were taken away from their families to live among a new family and experience sexual initiation with a strange man. Today, women are much older and more experienced when they marry, and they are already familiar with the outside world as well as with their grooms. Today's women also retain close ties to natal kin after marriage; in many cases a woman's ties to her parents and siblings become stronger after marriage. A married woman who once avoided her mother for much of the week may now rely on her for childcare while she is at work. She and her married siblings may get together more often, with their own children, and share more intimate details of their lives than they did as single adults focused on activities outside family life. The dramatic "rites of separation" of the past described by historians and ethnographers do not seem to fit with the contemporary context. Why do they persist?

One answer might be that wedding ceremonies today are more focused on the drama of a woman's incorporation into a new family than on her separation from her natal kin. Yet even a woman's transition into a new family is not nearly as remarkable as it was forty years ago. Even if she moves into her in-laws' home, she will most likely continue working outside, and her mother-in-law's control over her as a household laborer will be less significant than it would have been in earlier times. Changed courtship practices and present-day expectations of spousal relations as already emotionally and sexually intimate by the time of the wedding surely lessen the personal trauma of the wedding night as well. Van Gennep's theory of wedding rites fails to explain why the old-timers' rituals persist despite the vast transformations in the social context in which these rites now take place.

Weddings, then and now, are not merely rites of familial separation and incorporation for the bride but also rites of passage through which both bride and groom become adults (though until they produce a child, the process of becoming a full-fledged adult is considered incomplete). Weddings move both men and women from the "outside" realm to the "inside," and ceremonies orchestrated and controlled by family elders without regard for the bride and groom's individual tastes, preferences, and values make good sense as initiation into the adult world of selfless performance of familial responsibilities.

"Inside" status and its responsibilities, however, fall more heavily upon married women than married men. Hence weddings serve as rites of separation from youth and rites of incorporation into adulthood for women much more so than for men, to continue Van Gennep's terminology. Traditional marriage ceremonies accomplish this only to a point, however, because their focus is on the movement of the bride from one family to another. The modern bridal industry steps in with its own rituals—makeovers and photo shoots—to bring weddings up to date with contemporary experiences of what it means to get married.

Though a foreigner, I was not much worse off in my knowledge about weddings than many local people my age, who had gathered what they knew about Chinese weddings primarily from television and movies. Several factors conspire to prevent young people from knowing much about actual weddings. First, the ceremonies are small family affairs organized and orchestrated by parents and grandparents. Attendance at ceremonies is usually limited to a dozen or so who are close to the couple and their families. The guests are not seated in rows as a formal audience, as one expects at an American wedding. Rather, they mill around casually before and after each ritual activity, gathering to view and photograph particular moments, such as when the couple bows to the groom's parents. Depending on one's position in the family, it is possible to reach marriageable age with little or no experience of betrothal and wedding ceremonies. For example, a first-born child may attend an aunt and uncle's ceremony as a small child. With all aunts and uncles married and no older siblings, the next wedding ceremony such a person attends is likely his or her own. Some young people do get invited to intimate friends' ceremonies and so experience wedding rituals this way. Their friends' family ceremonies, however, may not be like their own. Wedding ceremonies vary widely across Taiwan, and every region and family has its own wedding customs. Young people expect to follow the customs their *own* parents and grandparents require, regardless of what their friends' families did.

Second, the dictates of fertility and luck exclude certain categories of persons from betrothal and marriage ceremonies, even though all are welcome at banquets. Those born in a tiger year are banned from all wedding ceremonies except when they are the bride or groom, or a parent or grandparent of the bride or groom. Some families enforce this rule strictly while others are more lax. One tiger friend of mine told me that she had twice violated the rule by visiting her girlfriends in the "new room" (see later in this chapter) prior to the banquet. Both friends later suffered miscarriages, and my friend now believes in the custom's efficacy. Others excluded from wedding ceremonies include those who were themselves married very recently and those mourning the death of a parent or grandparent.

Third, the timing and location of betrothal and wedding ceremonies limit their attendance. Astrology dictates the exact timing of these ceremonies, and many families prefer to follow astrological counsel even if the ceremony must take place during hours when most adults work. Frequently, the location is also not conducive to guest attendance. In Taipei, where at least 40 percent of the population consists of recent migrants (Speare, Lin, and Tsay 1988: 63), brides' and grooms' parents frequently live elsewhere on the island. In such cases, the marriage ceremony normally takes place outside Taipei—making it inconvenient for Taipei friends to attend. When weddings require both time off from work and travel to family homes in the countryside, even young family members—aunts, uncles, cousins—may not attend their relatives' ceremonies. For these reasons, retirees and housewives make up the bulk of relatives in attendance—substantiating the notion that weddings are indeed old people's business.

As a middle-class American accustomed to relying on manuals, magazines, and newspaper advice columns for guidance on matters of ritual and etiquette (e.g., see Ehrenreich and English 1978; Elias 1978), I assumed wedding manuals would be the best place to start my research on wedding rites. Commercially produced books on ritual are available in bookstores, and each edition of the bridal fashion magazines (most prominently *Xin Xinniang* and *Weiwei Xinniang*) contains a short section on basic wedding customs and gifts. To my disappointment, recently married brides and bridal industry workers insisted that few families rely on written guides in planning their traditional wedding ceremonies. Brides consulted bridal magazines primarily for fashion, not ritual, guidance. Most brides and grooms leave the ceremony preparations up to their parents; the parents, in turn, consult with elder kin, friends who have recently put on a wedding for their children, and paid fortune-tellers.[5] Written sources serve as poor guides in part because the overarching principle for wedding rituals in Taiwan is that they should involve customs *particular* to the families involved and their specific native places or hometowns. How, then, was I to begin making sense of it all?

Aware that the bridal magazine guides to wedding rituals could provide only a basic orientation, I nevertheless looked to them for a starting point. Though they too reference the notion that every family has its own customs, the guides suggest that wedding rites are more standardized than they are in practice: The families begin by negotiating transfers of money and expensive goods (bride-price and dowry) with the help of a go-between *(meiren)* and agreeing on dates for the betrothal and marriage ceremonies with the help of a fortune-teller or astrological calendar. At the betrothal, the bride serves tea to a group of men sent by the groom's side and receives from them red envelopes of cash *(hongbao)*. The groom's side delivers a sum of money to the bride's side (the "large bride-price"), and the bride's side returns a portion of the money (the "small bride-price") to the groom's side. At the betrothal, the groom's side also provides gifts of foodstuffs, including boxes of cakes or cookies known as *xibing*. Afterward, the bride and groom distribute the cakes or cookies to the bride's family and friends by visiting their homes or workplaces. At the marriage ceremony, the groom's side sends a car to take the bride from her family; the rented car's make and year may be negotiated by the families beforehand. The bride and groom bow to her parents and grandparents and thank them for raising her, and the groom's side lights firecrackers. The groom's side then delivers her to the groom's family home and ancestral altar, where the couple bows to the parents, grandparents, and tablets representing dead ancestors. Later, guests gather at a wedding banquet to celebrate the marriage.

Layered on top of this simplified, normative structure are dozens of practices—varying widely across regions and families—that many young people refer to as superstitions *(mixin)*. One such practice is the exchange of the bride and groom's "eight characters" *(bazi)* during marriage negotiations. Each person has eight characters representing his or her exact time and date of birth. Fortune-tellers read these to ascertain a person's fate and to determine a couple's compatibility.[6] What families do with the eight characters of a proposed spouse varies greatly. Some may take the eight characters of both bride and groom to a trusted fortune-teller. Others may do as Margery Wolf's rural informants did in the 1960s: place the eight characters near the family altar and watch around the house for signs of heavenly disapproval. Others may do nothing. As one mother of three married sons told me, with her eldest son's marriage she was very strict about following such customs, but by the time her youngest son married she followed few customs because she felt less anxious and more experienced concerning weddings. Though she did not mention it, I know that when her youngest son married she already had a grandson. Perhaps with one grandson already in preschool she had the luxury of worrying less about her youngest son's wedding.

Just about everyone I met timed marriage rituals according to astrological calculations for fertility and prosperity. For some families, it is enough to consult a mass-produced astrological calendar that specifies generic dates broadly appropriate for marriage ceremonies. Other families leave the betrothal and wedding dates up to a fortune-teller, who looks at the couple's combined eight characters and finds a date and time perfectly suited to improve the couple's fate. In such cases, the most fortuitous date is occasionally much sooner or later than the couple had hoped to marry. Very often, fortune has it that the best time for a marriage is at six in the morning. Young people refer to parents who insist on precisely timed wedding ceremonies regardless of considerations of convenience as conservative (baoshou). For a 6 A.M. entry to the groom's family home, the bride has to arrange for her makeover and hairstyling to take place at one or two in the morning (and handsomely compensate the stylist for working in the middle of the night).

Astrological calendars allow few or no good days for weddings in some months, producing interesting consequences. Couples and their families may agree on a general time frame for the wedding (say, May or June) and find that only one, or even none, of the dates the fortune-teller recommends falls on a weekend. Competition for banquet halls on lucky wedding days can be fierce, and the most popular spots book long in advance. When a lucky weekend day for a wedding rolls around, everyone in Taipei knows it. Firecrackers, set off outside the homes of both bride and groom, can be heard in every part of the city. Wedding rush-hour traffic forms as a high percentage of people attend at least one wedding banquet on those lucky days.

Although young people I met sometimes labeled beliefs about marriage ritual as "old people's superstitions," they too observed the astrological calendar. The seventh month of the lunar year, known as Ghost Month, is so dangerous to couples that few are even willing to have their bridal photos taken then. In recent years, salons have advertised special discounts on photo packages of glamour shots for young women and girls to lure in non-wedding business during Ghost Month. The preferred time of year for weddings is just before the Chinese New Year holiday, and bridal shops are extremely busy during that time. There is a saying—*you qian, mei qian, qu ge laopo guonian*—which, in rhyme, says, "Rich or poor, marry a wife to celebrate the New Year." Immediately after the New Year, however, the industry again experiences a downtime because couples inclined to marry have rushed to do so before the holiday. Some shops close up for a month and lay off workers. Others advertise special prices to induce business in the hope of keeping experienced photographers, stylists, and saleswomen in their employ.

Beyond concern over the eight characters and a fortune-teller's read on the fate of the couple, families may place a lot of importance on getting all of the acts that comprise betrothal and marriage rituals just right. Because these vary by region, families need to negotiate them in advance. For example, it is a widespread view that something should be held above the bride's head when she goes outside on the wedding day to protect her (and her fertility) from negative heavenly forces. In a single week I attended one wedding where an umbrella was held over the bride's head and another where a flat disc printed with a Taoist design was used. Sometimes, the object held above the bride is a rice-sorting pan. At the second wedding banquet that week, I asked my friends Xin-de and Yu-ling, sitting to my right, why an umbrella was used in one wedding and a Taoist symbol in the other. They told me, in no uncertain terms, that the bride in the first wedding was pregnant or thought she might be pregnant. The bride's head is always covered by some object, preferably one with this Taoist symbol, they said. But if she is pregnant and the symbol is used, she will miscarry, so it is better to use an umbrella. Xin-de and Yu-ling had met and courted in Taipei, but she hailed from central Taiwan and he from the south. After their wedding, they had moved into his family home in the countryside outside Tainan. When I reported this interesting "fact" to Mei-hua, a single woman who had grown up in Taipei and was sitting to my left, she leaned over me to question Xin-de and Yu-ling. She had seen umbrellas used at her brothers' weddings and was sure the brides were not suspected to be pregnant. Soon the whole table of ten banquet guests erupted in animated debate over the meaning of the object held over a bride's head. In the end, all concluded that there must be regional differences. In the north, an umbrella is customary, whether or not the bride is pregnant. In parts of the south, the Taoist symbol, preferred over umbrellas, is reserved for brides who are certain they are not pregnant.[7] Considering the confusion and heated debate among this group of friends, who had no personal ties to the bride whose wedding I had attended earlier that week, one can imagine that planning and performance of wedding rites are fertile ground for misunderstandings and conflict between the bride's and the groom's parents if they are from different parts of Taiwan.

At one wedding ceremony, I joined the bride's side in what an aunt described to me as a traditional meal marking the moment when the bride is taken away from her parents. While the six men from the groom's side sat in the living room, the bride, Florence, and her relatives sat down to a meal they called *jiemei zhou,* or "sisters' table," even though Florence had no sisters. Her mother had prepared special foods with Taiwanese names that suggested luck, prosperity, and fertility. She fed bites of each dish to the bride one at a time, reciting the name of the dish as she placed a morsel in her daughter's mouth, being careful not to disturb her lipstick. The tone was somber, as this was to be the mother's last time taking care of her daughter. The bride and groom then thanked her parents and grandparents for raising her well. Florence bid them farewell tearfully, careful not to use the everyday expression for good-bye that means "see you again"—which on the occasion of a wedding connotes that the bride might end up divorced and return home. In the rush of camera-bearing uncles, a videographer, and a few aunts and friends all trying to see the bride leave, I missed observing which relative had the task of spilling a cup of water to signify that their daughter should not return home as a divorcee, just as spilled water does not return to the cup. The rented, decorated black Cadillac drove off as the deafening blast of firecrackers prompted on-lookers like me away from the scene. The crying bride dropped a paper fan out of the window as her car pulled away.[8] Upstairs, Florence's relatives, one of her childhood friends, and I cheerfully sat down to finish the elaborate meal.

The ritual drama about the bride's departure was striking, for Florence's parents had purchased a flat for the newlyweds right across the street, in the same apartment complex. The car carrying the bride drove around town for about twenty minutes before taking her to the new apartment, where the groom's family awaited her. Curious why a car was used to transport her across the street and why the bride was driven around for twenty minutes, I asked Florence's aunt. She said it would have been too embarrassing to the groom's family for the couple to proceed directly across the street. The close distance between the couple's new home and the bride's natal flat was, perhaps, too much like the uxorilocal marriages of the past, where the poor parents of a groom agreed to marry their son off into a bride's family and the couple's children took their mother's surname. Much about this wedding was unusual, though.

For instance, the six men from the groom's side typically take the bride to the groom's parents' home, not to the couple's private flat. Also, the couple traveled to his family's home in the countryside a few days after the wedding and bowed to his ancestors only then. They hosted a rural banquet for his family's kin and friends, too.

The following week, when I told my friends at the bridal magazine about Florence's wedding, none had heard of the sisters' table custom, though everything else about the wedding—including the twenty-minute drive around the block—sounded familiar. My bridal salon friends had never heard of a sisters' table either, despite their similarly high level of familiarity with weddings. None, however, were surprised to hear of an unfamiliar wedding custom. They reminded me: "Every place has its own customs." It is telling that bridal magazine and bridal salon workers—employees in institutions that work to regiment and standardize weddings through commodification of the Bride—accept the nonstandardization of wedding ceremonies so readily.

The notion that wedding ceremonies are so rife with regional variation and particular family customs that they defy standardization is curious when compared with neighboring countries Japan and Korea. In those countries, wedding ceremonies used to take place in family homes. Today, however, Japanese and Korean weddings take place in commercial wedding halls and have been routinized and standardized by wedding industry employees, who direct the ceremonies as well as the banquets (see Edwards 1989; Goldstein-Gidoni 1997; Kendall 1996). Why has Taiwan bucked this regional trend?

The particularism and regionalism of weddings in contemporary Taiwan are also curious in comparison to changes in other realms of life. In the last half-century, high-speed transportation systems, newspapers (along with high levels of literacy), telephones, television, the Internet, and centrally organized systems of government and retailing have brought once-disparate communities into close engagement. A centralized system of government, national mass media commanding island-wide attention, and national chain stores providing the same goods and services throughout Taiwan are now strong, active forces of standardization. In 1997, there were very few national bridal photography chains, but highly mobile dress designers, salon managers, photographers, and stylists were so skilled at emulating the work of their competitors that the bridal industry was quite standardized. Why did wedding ceremonies remain an outpost of the regionalism and particularism of the old days?

When a family wants to celebrate a member's birthday, for example, they know just what to do, and they know all their friends and neighbors do the same thing: go to the bakery and buy a birthday cake, pre-decorated with mass-produced plastic signs that say, in English or Chinese, "Happy Birthday." Just about every bakery in Taiwan provides the same tiny plastic forks and Styrofoam plates for serving birthday cake.[9] University graduation ceremonies, similarly, are highly regimented. The graduates all know to rent the same gowns and caps, which are like those worn for commencement ceremonies in the United States. The parents, whether Kaohsiung pig farmers or Taipei CEOs, all know to bring a camera and photograph the graduate. All take the film to the local quick photo-processing shop and get back their photos in small mass-produced photo albums with a plastic sleeve for each photo and the logo of a multinational film company imprinted on the cover. Similarly, when a couple decides to marry, they know that the first thing to do is to select a bridal salon and reserve a date for the photo shoot, regardless of their Taiwanese places of origin, class status, or family name.

When it comes to planning wedding ceremonies, however, the rules are less clear. There is no equivalent to the bakery, the graduation gown rental business, the photo processing shop. Variation in wedding customs is, in fact, often a *problem* for brides, grooms, bridal shop workers, parents, and grandparents, who have grown accustomed to standardization in other realms of life. It is tempting to think that weddings are slow to change simply because the family elders who orchestrate them refuse change and reject standardization, but this is not the case. Ritual supply stores provide the older generation with many of the items used in weddings. In previous times, live pigs and handmade noodles were part of the customary betrothal gifts. Today, ritual supply stores provide commercially packaged hams and noodles in pink or red wrappers, carried and displayed on rented pink or red trays.[10] Also available are red velvet-lined boxes with glass tops for the presentation of cash and jewelry to the bride's family. The older generation's acceptance of standardization in wedding customs shows up most clearly in the bride's parents' propensity for specifying the exact brand name of engagement cakes they require of the groom's side.

Every wedding seems to make use of the same factory-produced red stickers in the shape of a double happiness character, decorating doors and the couple's new furniture, appliances, and other gifts. Bridal salons, as part of their package deals, provide the couple with the standard decoration for the wedding car (a red wreath around Caucasian-looking dolls dressed in white gown and tuxedo) and a preprinted red book for logging gifts to the couple at the banquet. Banquet foods, too, are subject to the standardizing forces of the banquet industry. Urban families host banquets in restaurants and hotels. In rural communities, they hire professional banquet caterers to set up a tent, bring in tables and chairs, and cook and serve the meal. In both contexts, the same dishes are popular, and rice wine is the standard drink. Yet, unlike Japan and Korea, families in Taiwan have not moved their family wedding rites out of homes and into commercial wedding halls where they are structured and standardized according to "professional" interests. Rather, ceremonies are informally put together, subject to regional variation, and rife with special family traditions.

Even popular media representations of weddings fail to serve as a strong force toward standardization in wedding ceremonies. Many popular serial dramas take place in historical settings—constructing images of past weddings, not contemporary ones. Popular media depictions of contemporary weddings tend to portray public ceremonies that focus on bride and groom more than on their families—like the mini-ceremonies sometimes performed at the start of wedding banquets or the Sunday morning church weddings that the Christian population (4.5 percent) holds ("Taiwan, Facts and Figures" 1999). And yet banquet and church-based ceremonies do not displace family wedding rites in most cases; they merely supplement them.

Family wedding rites are not mere survivals from a premodern past when regional variation was strong. They are very much of the present. Centripetal forces toward standardization of family wedding rites are weak in the absence of a centralized organization or authority guiding the practice of family wedding rites, and centrifugal forces toward differentiation are also strong.[11] Indeed, people in Taipei *expect* family wedding rites to differ from region to region, family to family. Parents and grandparents who do not remember particular customs themselves may ask aunts, cousins, or fortune-tellers to teach them some when planning a child's wedding. It seems likely to me that families who have no knowledge of particular customs might even invent new traditions to make their weddings special (see Hobsbawm and Ranger 1992). This has an important parallel in Taiwanese tourism. In contemporary Taipei, where 7–11 chain stores grace nearly every street-front block and life is predictably routinized, standardized, nationalized, and even globalized in many ways, consumers seek out occasional amusement in particularistic regional customs and goods. When visiting scenic areas or places of historical interest, tourists eagerly consume the foods and handicrafts *spe-*

cific to the area. Global capitalism tends toward both the demise of old ways of life and nostalgia for the same (see Rosaldo 1989: ch. 3; Wilk 1995). Of course, tourists' pursuit of the authentically local takes a rather standardized form: most visitors to a local tourist spot purchase identical "traditional" snacks from vendors who sell mass quantities produced specifically for the tourist market. In the realm of weddings, there is no vendor promoting or packaging particularistic family wedding customs to family elders grasping for something unusual. My point is simply that regional variation is not merely a holdover from the past but is also an invention of the present.

Regional and family differences in wedding customs are, on the one hand, a source of pleasure but, on the other hand, a source of conflict between bride and groom's families as they plan for and execute betrothal and wedding ceremonies. When bridal salon saleswomen advise Taipei brides and grooms about wedding planning, their first word of advice is often that every family has its own customs and that the two sides must clearly communicate their expectations. A common set of understandings and expectations cannot be assumed. If the bride's side from the north holds an umbrella over the bride's head when she marries a man from the south, his parents might conclude she is pregnant. If the bride's family had not notified the groom's side of their intention to perform their sisters' table custom, the groom's side could have taken offense at not being invited to the table to eat.

The function of the go-between has been transformed from matchmaking to coping with the widely differing regional cultural backgrounds of Taipei couples. *Meiren* still can carry the meaning "matchmaker," and the term is even used by commercial dating services. In most of the weddings I observed, however, the *meiren* was not the one who introduced the couple. In fact, the man or woman responsible for introducing the couple—often a coworker or school friend of either bride or groom—commonly holds a special place as the *jieshaoren* (introducer) in the wedding. He or she is perhaps invited to give a speech at the banquet but seldom serves as the go-between for the families. Sometimes, families appoint a go-between to play a largely symbolic role. In other cases, after the bride and groom have announced their intentions to marry and found approval among parents, the go-between assists the families in marriage negotiations over matters such as bride-price and engagement cakes. People told me that a go-between should be older, be happily married, have sons, be rich, and (ideally) hold a U.S. green card—the hope being that her high status would confer luck on the couple. Often, the go-between is an aunt or great-aunt of the bride or groom.[12] In practice, families may negotiate aspects of the wedding without a go-between to initiate the discussion, and when the go-between is a rich relative who lives overseas, her role may be entirely honorific. Thus the go-between is seldom truly a matchmaker, but the role persists, in part because finding an appropriate spouse is only one small step in the process of getting two families to agree to the terms of a marriage.

MARRIAGE NEGOTIATIONS AND TRANSFERS

Bride-price *(pinjin)* presented by the groom's side at the betrothal includes a sum of cash and various foodstuffs for the bride's parents, gold jewelry and a set of pink or red clothes for the bride, and engagement cakes for the bride's side to distribute to friends and family. When the groom's family provides a good bride-price, the bride's family is expected to provide a substantial dowry *(jiazhuang)* of furniture, appliances, and other items for the couple. Foremost among difficult negotiating points is the bride-price, particularly the cash and the cakes, and the term *pinjin* is often used to refer to the cash only.

Parents seeking to undermine their son or daughter's choice of spouse may refuse to negotiate reasonably on bride-price, thereby putting an end to the relationship. Because the bride-price can be seen as a reflection of the bride's worth and her family's status relative to the groom and his family, parents who feel their daughter is too good for her boyfriend (because of her higher level of education, for example) may demand an outrageous sum of money. Similarly, parents who feel their son is too good for his girlfriend may offer only a small sum.

The stories I heard about unsuccessful bride-price negotiations, however, might be a form of urban mythology among young people who are keenly aware that their parents hold much power over the fate of their romantic relationships. Parents who are intent on preventing a marriage need never enter bride-price negotiations at all.[13] One mother, Mrs. Li, opined that these days families do not fight as much over bride-price as they did in the old days when she was married because today people are more educated and open-minded. She went along with the bride-price demands for her daughters-in-law, she said, because the young women bring money into the family now as wage earners.[14] Nonetheless, marriage negotiations may bring families from disparate parts of Taiwan, and sometimes from disparate socioeconomic positions, together. There are bound to be differences of opinion. What is a small sum to one family may be a huge sum to another.

Mrs. Chen, Florence's mother, told me she had asked a bride-price of NT $100,000 (about $4,000 U.S.) for her daughter because that was the amount her older son's bride's parents had requested. And, she added, it is a nice even number. I knew her daughter-in-law was very young and lacking in educational credentials, in contrast to her daughter, who was about thirty years old and held a master's degree from a British university. The money, Mrs. Chen claimed, was not at all important to her and her husband. She felt, however, that a bride's parents must ask for a large enough sum so the bundle of cash *looks* good in the red velvet presentation box. The custom she and her husband followed in this case was for the "large bride-price," which the groom's side presents at the betrothal ceremony, to be twice the amount of the "small bride-price," which the bride's side returns to the groom's side at the close of the ceremony, along with half of the trays of other gifts.

The groom, David, later told me he experienced Mr. and Mrs. Chen's demand for the NT $100,000 large bride-price as a hardship. Already in his mid-forties and a youngest son whose parents had both passed on, David was a well-paid attorney and paid all the wedding expenses himself rather than burdening his brothers with them. He had paid for many expensive items selected by the bride, including a bridal package at one of the more expensive salons, a diamond ring from Tiffany, a Tiffany watch, and over two hundred boxes of the most expensive brand of engagement cakes.

The dowry Mr. and Mrs. Chen gave the couple at the time of the wedding, though, involved even greater sums of money. Her parents provided the down payment on a newly renovated apartment—even providing money for Florence and David to select bedroom furnishings. Although the bride's parents certainly kept up their side of the deal in outlays of cash, it seemed to me that they had forced the groom to go to great lengths to keep pace with their expectations. (Banks promote "wedding loans" for just such purposes.) David, I suspect, was especially accommodating because he wanted to get married quickly. He had just suffered the death of his mother and wanted to marry within one hundred days *(bai rizi nei)* as an act of devotion to her. It was said that she would worry less about him in her death if he were married. Some young people will not marry within a year—or three years, depending on regional custom—of a parent's death unless they marry within that first hundred-day period.

In another interesting case, a young Chinese Australian man made the error of announcing to his Taiwanese prospective in-laws that he came from a rich family. He had meant to indicate that they "have money" *(you qian)*, which, to him, meant something like "not poor" but translated into Chinese as "rich." The bride's father, himself a very wealthy man, demanded a bride-price of NT $1 million ($250,000 U.S. at that time), a Mercedes-Benz automobile, and nearly $25,000 U.S. worth of engagement cakes. After consulting with the young man's father, the couple explained to the bride's father that his family was not *that* rich. Her father abandoned the demand for the cash and the car, but he insisted on the cakes.

ENGAGEMENT CAKES

Engagement or betrothal cakes are another common source of conflict between families.[15] Presented to the bride's side at the betrothal ceremony, the engagement cakes are even more loaded with meaning than the cash in the red box. Mrs. Li, sixty years old, told me the story of her marriage and its unforgettable engagement cakes. She grew up in Keelung, a port city in northern Taiwan, the daughter of a bourgeois urban mother who had married uxorilocally. (Her mother's family must have been well-to-do in order to afford a uxorilocal marriage for their daughter.) Though she had only completed primary school, this was considered a good education by the standards of the 1940s, when Taiwan was a very poor and rural country. She held a job at the telegraph office, where she fell in love with her future husband. He, too, was unusually well educated for the times and could read some Chinese, Japanese, and a little English. He came from an extremely poor farm family but was educated because a wealthy uncle had taken him in as a child. His parents, however, were ignorant of city life and so far below Mrs. Li's parents in status that they had no concept of the status distinctions important among the urban middle class. Unsurprisingly, her parents did not approve of the match.

Before the couple tried to initiate marriage negotiations, however, Mr. Li was imprisoned for alleged connections to Communists. He stayed in the Green Island prison for several years during Taiwan's White Terror period, when anxious KMT government leaders took many middle-class Taiwanese men as political prisoners to prevent the formation of an independence movement. Mrs. Li's parents took the opportunity to have her introduced to more suitable men. She refused them all, even though she was quickly approaching an unmarriageable age. By the time Mr. Li returned from prison, her parents feared that if they did not accept Mr. Li as her groom, their daughter would never marry.

Her parents requested a specific number of engagement cakes, according to their custom, to distribute to family and friends. Today, brides' families in Taipei specify the brand and type of cake or cookie they want. In those days, however, there were no brand-name cakes, and brides' families specified the weight of the cakes as an indicator of their value. Oil was expensive; the heavier the cake, the more oil it contained. Hence the weight of the cake was an important bargaining point between families. The groom's family, according to Mrs. Li, was so ignorant and backward that they did not know the custom of weighing the cakes. On the betrothal day, they delivered the lightest, cheapest cakes to her family. The cakes, distributed to the bride's family's widest social network, were a horrible embarrassment for her. The quality and number of cakes indicate the value of the bride, and in Mrs. Li's case, she was made to look like a country bumpkin. Four decades later, the cheap cakes remain the worst embarrassment of her life.

Similar conflicts arise today around engagement cakes. For example, in Tainan county in the south of Taiwan, the custom is for the bride's side to demand huge quantities of cakes, thousands of them. While some are distributed, many are just thrown away. Tainan families are interested only in the quantity, not the quality, of the cakes, informants told me. By contrast, quality is the central concern about engagement cakes in Taipei, where the cakes are to be eaten, so the number of requested cakes is comparatively low. When a woman from Tainan wants to marry a man from Taipei, the families are fortunate if they have a go-between or other knowledgeable friend who advises them of this regional difference. Otherwise, the bride's side may request upward of one thousand cakes and the groom's side may quickly calculate that one thousand Taipei-type cakes would cost at least NT $200,000. Given that very few families know one thousand people to whom to give cakes, the groom's side might be offended.

The domination of the Taipei engagement cake market by a handful of designer brands adds a degree of specificity to marriage negotiations. If the bride's family requests one hundred large boxes of Yi-mei cakes, the groom's side knows it cannot make substitutions without prior approval. Even if the groom's side is from southern Taiwan, they can deal with a Yi-mei branch store in Kaohsiung. People who are recently married or who have recently negotiated a marriage for a child are frequently well versed in the exact cost of each brand of cake and its distinctive package design. Each elaborately decorated red and pink cake box comes in its own fancy shopping bag with company logo. Engagement cakes also come in "Japanese" and "Western" cookie varieties, with each cookie individually vacuum-packed.

Among the gifts exchanged at the betrothal ceremony are new outfits for the bride and groom to wear when they distribute boxes of engagement cakes to the bride's friends and family. Again, customs vary considerably, but the outfits are often said to entail items from head to toe. In brand-name-conscious Taipei, this may include Italian designer shoes, French designer suits, and Swiss designer watches. Jewelry is also sometimes requested according to designer brands, and Euro-American-style diamond engagement rings are increasingly included. The South African diamond company DeBeer's has advertised heavily in the region in an attempt to make engagement diamonds customary in marital transfers. Flipping through the glossy bridal fashion magazines found on any Taipei newsstand, it is easy to discern which components of weddings are subject to brand-name competition and which are not (and are therefore absent from magazines). Bridal salons, engagement cakes, jewelry, furniture, and banquet halls all figure prominently. Customary gifts less beholden to name brands include noodles, hams, potted plants (with coins placed upon the soil), and other relatively inexpensive items.

POWER RITUALS

Among the most interesting ritual acts commonly performed at betrothal ceremonies is the couple's exchange of rings. Although diamond rings such as those presented at the proposal by many American grooms are increasingly popular in Taiwan, ring exchange lacks the particular symbolism it carries in the United States. Betrothal or wedding rings are not worn on any particular finger or hand to convey a woman or man's marital status. Some Taiwanese recognize the "ring finger" (as it is called in the United States) as the preferred finger for wearing rings but not as reserved for wedding rings specifically. Rings given at the time of the betrothal are often not worn daily afterward. Gold in the form of rings, bracelets, necklaces, and earrings are all customary gifts presented to a bride, and many brides—especially those marrying into rural families—wear dozens of pieces of gold jewelry on the wedding day. Married women keep these as their personal property and wear them for special occasions.

In one case I learned of, a group of coworkers wanted to give a special gift to a bride who was marrying an American and moving with him to Houston. Because she was not having a proper Taiwanese wedding, bridal photo album, or banquet, the friends decided to give her a special present, instead of the customary red envelope of cash. To commemorate both her wedding and their friendship, they selected a diamond ring that, to my American eyes, looked like a conventional engagement ring. These women associated diamond rings with weddings and wanted their friend to have one in the absence of such items presented by the groom's family. (Why this American did not give the bride a ring himself is another matter!) The ring, as this case makes clear, is not a sentimentalized, personal gift from man to woman in Taiwan. The groom's mother may select and purchase rings and other jewelry for the bride herself. Weighted down with dozens of pieces of gold jewelry at the wedding, the bride demonstrates the wealth of the groom's family.

The presentation of the ring at engagement ceremonies in a rural village of the 1960s was described by Margery Wolf thus: On the betrothal day, the groom goes about work as usual while a party of at least six from the groom's side plus the go-between bring gifts and engagement cakes to the bride's home. The bride serves them sweet tea, receives red envelopes of cash in return, and then leaves the room so the two sides can talk. The go-between formally asks both sides if they agree to the marriage. When they agree, Wolf (1972: 125) says, the bride

> is seated by the go-between on a stool, facing the door of her father's house with her back to his ancestral altar. . . . The central act of the engagement, that is, the point after which the girl is irrevocably engaged, is both symbolically and tangibly the beginning of the struggle between mother-in-law and daughter-in-law. The mother-in-law attempts to place a gold ring on her daughter-in-law's finger, and the girl attempts to prevent her from getting it over her middle knuckle. If the girl fails, she will be dominated by her mother-in-law all her life.

Today, this ritual—then performed in the groom's absence—has changed in telling ways, though it remains a central act in betrothal ceremonies and is much talked about in society at large. In engagements today, the groom tries to place the ring on the bride's finger. Although *popo/xifu guanxi,* or mother-in-law/daughter-in-law relations, remain a culturally recognized trouble zone, even more contested in today's marriages is husband/wife relations—particularly when it comes to men's extramarital affairs.

On Florence and David's betrothal day, David, dressed in his best suit and a brand-new Italian silk tie, arrived at the bride's home with six representatives of his family bearing trays full of gifts. The go-between, Florence's aunt, was already at the bride's house. A handful of Florence's extended relatives, two friends, and one anthropologist were also in attendance; our only ritual function was to pose for photographs and be an audience to the central acts of serving tea and presenting gifts. Florence's brother's wife had cleaned the living room, washed the tea cups, and prepared the tea while Mr. and Mrs. Chen, Florence's parents, nervously awaited the start of events. She scurried off to her room before the formal events began. Recently married herself, she was ritually excluded from the events of the day. Florence's brother, too, was absent. Florence wore a red, formal gown with an off-the-shoulders neckline and tightly fitted bodice. The floor-length skirt puffed out around her for a couple of feet in each direction because of the hooped slip she wore beneath it. She wore red lace gloves to match the gown. Her hair was pinned up and decorated with red flowers, her naturally freckled skin covered over by thick foundation for a perfectly fair, unblemished complexion. False lashes graced her eyelids. She had had her makeover at the bridal salon early that morning.[16]

Immobilized by her costume, Florence could barely move her body to serve the tea, let alone prepare it. She struggled to fit her puffed-out gown into the small space between the living room couch and coffee table, bending down to serve tea off a tray to the groom's party. While the groom and his men sipped tea, the red velvet box of cash and jewelry was taken from the gift trays displayed prominently on the living room floor just beneath the Chens' large-screen television. Mrs. Chen removed the gold jewelry from the box and placed a necklace around her daughter's neck, to join the three other gold necklaces Florence already wore. In preparation for the ring ceremony, she tied two rings to a tiny white lace pillow of the sort ring bearers sometimes carry in American weddings. Then Mrs. Chen returned the box of cash to the living room as the bride collected the empty tea cups, now stuffed with red envelopes of cash.

Next, the groom's uncle posed beside Mr. Chen in front of the Chen family ancestral altar while on-lookers competed over prime spots for shooting photos. Each man held one side of the red velvet box containing cash for the bride-price and assorted gold jewelry for the bride. Smiling, Mr. Chen accepted the box. Later he would take the "large bride-price" from the box and return the "small bride-price" to the groom's group, along with half the trays of gifts they had brought and a few trays of other items, such as a new outfit for the groom and potted plants with coins on top of the soil prepared by the bride's side for the groom's.

Finally, Florence sat on a low stool with her back toward the ancestral altar. The go-between handed the ring pillow to the groom. David took the ring and tried to place it on Florence's finger. She kept her finger bent to prevent him from pushing the ring past her knuckle. He struggled a bit, trying to get the ring properly on her finger, and told her that he could not get it all the way down because her finger was bent. Finally, he let Florence finish putting the ring on herself. All the bride's female relatives and friends burst out laughing.

Next, David took the seat on the low stool with his back to the altar. Florence took his ring off the tiny pillow and moved to put the ring on the groom's finger. He held his finger out straight. She looked at him and asked, "Is it really okay to put the ring all the way down?" Puzzled, David said, "Okay." This sent the women in the room into hysterical laughter, because this signified that he would be controlled by his wife for the rest of his life, especially since Florence had prevented him from putting the ring on her, so she would not be controlled by him. Later one of the bride's old aunts made a point of telling me that David, because he is a tiger, had never before attended a wedding. Neither first-hand experience nor years of television watching nor guidance by relatives (in the absence of his parents) had taught him the ring custom.

The groom and his posse went back to the living room while Florence was instructed to rub wine into a cooked chicken in the dining room. The bride looked unsure about how to perform this task, and one of her girlfriends coached her to just "massage" it. The bride removed her rings and the lace gloves and gave the chicken a quick massage. Her mother then took two longan fruits—round fruits about one inch in diameter—from a display on the altar and instructed the bride to eat them. With her back to the living room so the groom's men could not see, she peeled the fruits and ate them quickly. The bride explained to her friends and me that the name for these fruits *(longyan)* sounds like "eyes" and that by eating these "eyes," she would prevent the groom from looking at other girls. Again, we laughed at the groom's expense.

Later, when I mentioned the eating of the eyes to bridal industry friends, they had heard of the custom but were aghast that the bride and her mother had dared to do it. If the groom's family had discovered it, my friends said, they would have been extremely angry. A more common practice is for the bride to wait until the wedding night, when she can surreptitiously place her shoes on top of her new husband's shoes in order to get the upper hand in the marriage.

Among culturally recognized power struggles between women and men in marriage is the husband's willingness to perform household and child care labor, to listen to his wife's opinions about important matters, to let her control the family's finances, and to refrain from taking mistresses. The wife's willingness to maintain positive relations with the husband's parents and willingness to be a dutiful mother and wife are also potential arenas for dispute. The betrothal ceremony's ring exchange is said to predict who will prevail in the marital power struggles to come. Unlike Wolf's description, where the mother-in-law and daughter-in-law engage in a real struggle over moving the ring past the knuckle (one of my older informants recalls that sly mothers-in-law used to buy very large rings that could be slipped down easily), most couples today expect that neither party will try to force the ring all the way down the finger.

FERTILITY RITUALS AND THE NEW ROOM

Another major theme in betrothal and wedding rites is the continuation of the groom's family line through the bride's production of sons. The older generations often take these aspects of wedding rituals very seriously. Some younger people I interviewed viewed their parents' and grandparents' concerns about fertility rituals as superstition, but some brides and grooms shared the older generation's concerns about fertility for their own reasons. With so many women postponing marriage until reaching their mid-thirties, infertility is getting increasing media and medical attention in Taiwan. In the late 1990s, thirty-five was generally regarded as the latest "safe" age for a woman to have a first baby, and quite a few women wait until what feels to them like the last possible moment to get married and still allow time for reproduction. So, whether brides and grooms go along with rites designed to protect fertility out of respect for their parents or out of their own fears, fertility rites remain a critical component of marriage rituals.

On the wedding day (usually at least several weeks after the betrothal), the bride retreats to her "new room" *(xinfang)* upon arriving at the groom's home and bowing to his ancestors. Even when the couple will not be residing with the groom's family after marriage, a room is set up for them as their "new room" for the day. There may be a pair of the groom's trousers draped over two chairs in the room so that later, when the bride and groom sit down, they each sit on a leg of the trousers to enhance fertility. Other rites are more involved. The couple's bed—as well as the sheets, pillows, and bedspread—should be new. And sure enough, most bridal magazines contain a section on bedding design with advertising from bedding manufacturers, because the expectation that a couple will select new bedding is so high. Astrological considerations determine when the new bed may be moved from the store into the new room, and no one may sleep upon the bed until the wedding. The night before the wedding, in some families, the groom sleeps on the bed for the first time in the company of a young boy. Some time on or before the wedding day, a little boy is invited to jump on the bed. Round items like oranges may be included in the boy's romp on the bed.[17] No one else should use the bed until the bride and groom get in bed on the wedding night.

The new room also serves as a place where the bride is semisecluded between the wedding ceremony (usually held in the morning) and the banquet (sometimes at lunchtime but frequently at dinnertime). Florence spent her first hour in seclusion on the telephone with her brother's wife, across the street, who was coaching her on how to repair the false eyelashes that were messed up by her tears when she bid her parents goodbye. Later in the day, a florist visited Florence in her new room, after it was made certain he was not born in a tiger year, to discuss floral arrangements for the banquet. The groom's family members may not enter the room, though the bride's friends and the groom himself—in weddings I observed—were welcome. Wolf writes that the wedding day, and perhaps the two days following it, was a transition time for the bride when she was not yet expected to begin performing household labor under her mother-in-law's direction (1972: 137–40). Wolf describes the bride's terror upon entering her new life as a daughter-in-law and her fear of her first sexual encounter on the wedding night. The room was to serve as her refuge and private space in the strange house. The groom, too, kept out of the room except at night, when the couple was expected to engage in sexual intercourse. With the dramatic changes in courtship, premarital sex, and intergenerational power relations that have taken place in Taiwan in the past thirty years, most brides are less frightened than in the past. Most know their grooms well, and many have had sexual experience before the wedding night. Furthermore, today's brides are older and have had contact with the world outside their families through school and work, so the need for a place of refuge seems much diminished. Nevertheless, new room practices persist, though shortened in duration.

WEDDING BANQUETS

As guests arrive at the banquet, those associated with the bride first visit her in the new room. At countryside banquets that take place under a tent adjacent to the groom's family home, the new room is in the groom's family's home. When the banquet takes place in a restaurant or hotel, as is usually the case in city weddings, the facility provides a private room for the bride, and she receives her visitors there. Wedding banquets are usually sponsored by the groom's side, and among the bride's relatives only the closest are invited. But friends of both the bride and the groom are widely invited. The bride's friends usually make a point of arriving early to see the bride before the start of the banquet.

The arriving guests stop at a table near the entryway to present red envelopes of cash to one or two family members, who open the envelopes, count the money, and log the name of the gift giver and the amount given in a logbook. Guests give varying amounts of money, depending on their relationship to the groom and his family. The groom's cousins give less than his uncles. The groom's father's boss gives more than the groom's father's underlings. The neighbor whose son was married the year before gives a sum slightly higher than the one the groom's father gave at the neighbor's son's banquet. The banquet sponsors keep the gift log so that they know how much money to give when it is their turn to reciprocate (and to check to see whether gifts given in previous weddings were properly reciprocated).

The cash collected is usually enough to pay the banquet bill and is sometimes substantially more. When it exceeds the cost of the banquet, the banquet sponsors—usually the groom's parents—keep the money. Sometimes they make a gift of the excess cash to the newlyweds, but I stress *sometimes*. The gift money, in a way, is recompense for all the red envelopes the groom's parents paid out in the past and all they will pay out when they attend future wedding banquets. Hence the money that comes in at their son's wedding is theirs to keep. Guests who are close to the bride may present their red envelopes directly to her in the new room, so she can keep the money for herself and for the nuclear family *(xiaojia-ting)* she will establish as a branch of the groom's father's family line. This, and other money provided by her parents, is called her *sifangqian*, or "private money" (see Cohen 1976: 178–91; Gates 1992).

Sometimes marrying couples sponsor banquets themselves, however. In those cases, the banquet gift proceeds are theirs to keep. When the groom is financially better off than his parents, for example, he may sponsor the wedding banquet himself. He may even give the excess money to his parents to help them recoup any expenses they incurred for the betrothal ceremony. Most commonly, however, the groom's parents sponsor a banquet on the wedding day at a location convenient to their home. Couples often invite all of their friends and coworkers to banquets held in distant counties with the understanding that very few will attend. The situation can be somewhat awkward. Invited guests are obliged to give red envelopes of cash even if they do not attend the banquet. Wedding invitations (which are always a shade of red) are called "red bombs" because the receiver is obliged to provide a cash wedding gift.[18] When a couple invites Taipei guests to a distant banquet, they may fear that their red bomb is an imposition, since many of the invitees will not come; on the other hand, failure to invite virtually everyone the couple knows can be even more embarrassing. Couples who work for large companies or otherwise have substantial numbers of Taipei guests on their "must invite" lists sometimes sponsor their own banquets in the city shortly after their out-of-town wedding-day banquets. With men and women in the 1990s marrying at increasingly older ages, gift exchange networks were forming among young people independent of the gift exchanges the older generation conducts when their children marry. The trend toward couples sponsoring additional banquets is an outgrowth of young couples' changed life circumstances at the time of marriage.

The vast sums of money exchanged among networks of kin, coworkers, and friends is one reason why many people consider it a real pity when individuals never marry or when they marry but do not have a wedding banquet. Virtually all adults take part in wedding gift exchanges. To never marry or, worse, to have a son who never marries is to fail to collect one's share.

At banquets held after the wedding day, brides do not necessarily wear white bridal gowns; they usually wear bright-colored formal gowns rented from bridal salons. Rather than wearing three different gowns, they often wear only two. At one such banquet I attended, the bride wore only one dress. Though she had worn the typical rental gowns at her first banquet, at this one she wore a purchased white formal dress and a feather boa. Post-wedding banquets are in other respects similar to wedding-day banquets and are called by the same names, *xiyan* and *xijiu*. Red envelopes are collected, bridal albums and framed enlargements are displayed, and meals of ten to twenty courses are served. The couple and their parents visit each table for toasts of rice wine. At city banquets sponsored by the couple, many guests may not even realize that the wedding itself took place the previous week.

There are other kinds of wedding-related banquets as well. Wealthy families often put on banquets to celebrate the marriage of a daughter, either at the time of the engagement or the day after the wedding, depending upon regional customs. Hosting a banquet for one's daughter is expensive because the guests do not indirectly pay for the banquet with gifts. Mr. and Mrs. Chen, for example, hosted an engagement banquet on the afternoon of Florence's betrothal ceremony. Their three hundred guests did not give red envelopes upon their arrival, because guests at engagement banquets do not give gifts but instead receive them. Each guest (or pair of guests when two attended together) received a beautifully wrapped box of designer engagement cakes in a high-class tote bag, paid for by David.

Though wedding-day banquet features—such as the display of photographs, the giving of *hongbao,* the bride's changes of gowns, formal toasting, and an elaborate meal—occur in both city and country weddings, there are other, striking differences. At countryside weddings held outdoors, it is standard practice for the banquet sponsor to hire an entertainment troupe providing humor, karaoke equipment for guest performances, and singing and dancing girls. Often the entertainment troupe includes an emcee who introduces the bride, groom, and their families to the crowd and peppers the evening with ribald humor—joking, for example, about what the newlyweds will do in their new room that night. Many rural entertainment troupes provide striptease dancers who strip down to a tiny bikini and sometimes perform bare-breasted. At one rural wedding banquet I attended, a female impersonator stripped down to a bikini over the course of several dance numbers.

Taipei city weddings I attended, however, rarely included any entertainment at all. I frequently heard banquet guests complain of how terribly boring wedding banquets are in Taipei, where the meals are long (dish after dish is presented to the tables for about two hours) and guests who share a table often do not know one another. City banquets were perfect opportunities for me to interview the other guests at my table because all were held captive there for a couple of hours, and my tablemates usually welcomed my willingness to initiate conversation at the table as a way to alleviate the boredom. Especially at city banquets, the bride's changes of clothes help to mark time through the seemingly endless meals of expensive dishes. When the bride changes into her second gown and visits the tables to toast the guests, the banquet is about halfway over. When she dons her third gown and the couple stands near the doorway—the bride holding a tray of candies and cigarettes—guests know the last dish of oranges or other round sweet items is coming, signaling that they may bid the couple and their family good-bye at last.

Wedding banquets—urban and rural—can involve heavy, competitive drinking. Bottles of rice wine are provided, and men seated at each table organize and lead the drinking—filling drinkers' cups and toasting one another, calling "Bottoms up!" *(ganbei)*. Depending on with whom one is seated, the extent of drinking varies dramatically. Though women are often invited to drink, too, men generally do not pressure them to drink unless a woman shows willingness to participate. It is standard practice for the groom's friends and male relatives to try to get him very drunk by toasting him repeatedly and asking him to drink large cups or even pitchers full of rice wine. Moreover, the couple and the groom's parents always visit each table at a banquet for a formal toast. Even small banquets have ten tables (seating about one hundred people), and it is common for banquets to include twenty, thirty, or more tables. Twenty shots of rice wine are sure to get the couple quite drunk, so couples arrange for the caterer to substitute tea that matches the color of rice wine for at least the bride, and often for the groom, too.

Drunken male friends of the groom may initiate a custom called *naofang* (literally "harassing the new room") at the end of the banquet. "Old people" know to leave the couple and their young friends alone at this time, when for the first time on the wedding day members of the younger generation take center stage. Smoking, drinking, and laughing, their friends make demands *(yaoqiu)* of the couple. For example, one group of friends told the couple to stand atop a banquet table and kiss for two full minutes while the friends timed the kiss. When the groom's buddies accompany the couple back to the new room, they require the couple to engage in even more intimate acts. People told me that *naofang* rites stem from a time when bride and groom were sexually inexperienced and too embarrassed to touch each other; therefore others prodded them into sexual contact. Today *naofang* is usually a rather mild post-wedding hazing ritual focused more on the groom than on the bride, and no one I talked to pretended that *naofang* activities are to ease the couple into sexual contact. *Naofang* is clearly for the amusement of the friends, and brides and grooms who greatly fear the embarrassment tell their friends beforehand not to harass them too hard, or to focus the harassment only on the groom.

These sexualized hazing activities do not take place at every banquet. If the groom's friends are quiet, shy, or serious types, they may do no more than to have him drink a full glass when he comes around to their table for a toast. And with the population of young people in Taiwan so mobile, some grooms have few friends in attendance at their wedding banquets (unless they sponsor a post-wedding banquet in the city). For example, a young man who leaves his home in the south after high school for military service and college may work in Taipei for ten years before marrying in his mid-thirties. When he returns to the south for his wedding, only his closest Taipei friends are likely to make the trip down for his banquet, where they join his remaining childhood friends. For Xin-de and Yu-ling's rural wedding, which I attended, a closely knit group of college friends from Taipei chartered a bus to take them south. Anxious to get back on the bus right after the banquet, the groom's friends conducted a mini-hazing session right at the entry to the banquet tent once all the older guests had gone. When the women whipped out their lipsticks to refresh their lip color after the meal, one of the men asked to borrow a lipstick from a friend of the bride. The groom's friends drew all over one another's faces in hot-pink lipstick, preparing to approach the couple, who were still bidding farewell to guests at the tent entryway. Kissing the groom and rubbing their lipstick-smeared faces on him, they also drew on the couple's faces and demanded that they pass a candy from mouth to mouth.

Firecrackers, silly string, heavy drinking, strippers, and ribald humor create a carnival-like atmosphere at some rural wedding banquets. *Renao,* literally "hot and noisy," is the ideal. It seems that sponsors of urban banquets and the hotel and restaurant staff seek to mute the carnival atmosphere expected at country weddings (though sometimes rowdy male guests manage to whoop it up anyway), while the entertainment troupes at country weddings work to create a rowdy environment even when guests are not in the mood. Some Taipei informants told me city weddings seek to be more refined and elegant, with boredom as the unfortunate cost.[19]

Though young people create much of the drunken rowdiness, young brides I knew in Taipei often expressed preference for an elegant wedding banquet. They saw rowdy wedding banquets as "traditional" and preferred by old people. The entertainment troupes, however, are by no means traditional in the sense of having historical roots. They play pop music on electric synthesizers. The strippers strip out of Las Vegas–style costumes and down to string bikinis. The older people who are almost always the hosts of such banquets want to meet or exceed the expectations of guests and create as much "heat and noise" as possible to celebrate the occasion. Though city wedding banquets are usually less rowdy, even their hosts call attention to themselves by setting off loud firecrackers and inviting throngs of guests, who create traffic jams in the vicinity of banquet halls. Whether they spend their money on boisterous entertainment troupes or elegant shark fin soup, families see weddings as an opportunity to build status. Competitive consumption is the name of the game when it comes to banquets.

The prestige associated with the banquet hall in the city or the entertainment troupe in the countryside, the number and quality of dishes, the style and quality of the bride's gowns, the quantity of gold jewelry worn by the bride, and the size and beauty of the photographic displays are all key foci for status display and building at weddings. Notice that the bride's body is the subject of three of these five focal points. She seems to enjoy terrific prestige on this "once in a lifetime" day when she is a momentary celebrity. The kind of prestige she enjoys, however, is not translatable to power. Though the bride is the centerpiece of the wedding day, she is not an agent of it. Like a celebrity, she is an object. Her job is to assume the role of the bride—that is, appear beautiful and demure. If she smiles, graciously accepts compliments on her beauty and well-wishes for her marriage, eats almost nothing, and keeps her head lowered a bit when on view, she has played her role well. Her primary task is to serve as visual object.[20] There is fairly little she must actively do, though just getting through the day in the elaborate, heavy, and constraining gown while trying to hide discomfort and appear happy can leave a bride exhausted.

The bride is guided through the day's happenings by those in charge, the go-between and the parents. Although today the bride and groom have a good deal of input into the most important aspects of their wedding—whom they will marry and when in their lives they will get married—the rituals are by and large left up to parents. Thus, casting the bride as a celebrity with high prestige and low power works well.

EXCEPTIONAL WEDDINGS

Though the normative map for weddings leaves room for a great deal of variation, some weddings are off the map entirely. Generally, couples have weddings that do not fit cultural expectations for one of two reasons: the parents do not agree to their chosen union, or the couple strongly dislikes local wedding customs and expresses their individuality by blatantly defying them, even in the face of their families' protests.

Couples who marry without their families' consent seem to be rare, and those who do so seldom flout their disobedience by putting on wedding banquets, but there are exceptions. I heard about one such wedding where a local bride married a foreign man and held a small but very conventional banquet even in her parents' absence. The banquet was the gossip of the month in her office. Another late-1990s wedding was the gossip of the nation and was highlighted in the mass media: the union of Hsu You-sheng, an author, to his male partner, an American. The men put on a large banquet, and Chen Shui-bian (then mayor of Taipei, now president of the Republic of China) was among their honored guests. These are truly exceptional cases. Couples in nonconformist relationships sometimes commission the same kind of photo albums and wall hangings, even in the absence of a wedding or banquet. Though some couples reject conservative family expectations about how marriage ought to *be*, they do not necessarily defy cultural notions about how wedding celebrations ought to *look*. In other words, they may reject the substance of conventional marriage yet embrace its conventional cultural representations.

Others are rebellious in the opposite way; they choose partners acceptable to their families but do not accept their families' views on how weddings ought to look. Ruth, a fundamentalist Christian, told me how her small church wedding had scandalized both sides of the couple's family. Both bride and groom were not only very religious but also highly opinionated about weddings. In stark contrast to nearly every other couple I talked to, Ruth and Peter insisted on having control over their wedding ceremony. The groom, an architect, insisted on decorating the church himself. He was so concerned that they should marry in a beautiful space that the couple attended a different church, with a more elaborate and special chapel, for the month before their wedding (while still attending services at their own church) and attended premarriage counseling in both churches so they could marry in the prettier place. He rented tall potted trees to line the walkway instead of the typical pink ribbons and flowers. Everyone was shocked by the unconventional trees and by the money and effort he had devoted to decorating the church hall. For her part, Ruth refused to have photographs taken at a bridal salon out of strong distaste for the artifice of typical bridal photos, though she eventually gave in to her parents' pressure that she rent an expensive white gown (she wanted a simple white cotton gown) and have a professional makeover. During the makeover she repeatedly reminded the stylist not to use too much makeup, and she outright refused to wear false eyelashes despite the stylist's urging. For their small banquet, Ruth bought a black velvet gown. She loved the gown, but her grandmother was very upset by the dark color. Again, Ruth agreed to conform. She selected a red gown instead, but she wore only one gown, not the customary three. After the wedding, Ruth made a small photo album out of four-by-six-inch prints taken by a professional photographer at the church on the wedding day and included in the album copies of the wedding program and the words to hymns sung during the ceremony. Ruth and Peter stressed to me that in contrast to the experiences of everyone else they knew, their wedding—and their photo album—was personalized to their own tastes. Many Christian couples have a short church ceremony but also perform the customary Chinese rites at home, including bowing to the ancestors. This couple, however, was apparently influenced by their extensive experience living abroad and their involvement in evangelical Christianity.

I often asked informants about exceptions to wedding norms, and in response one friend introduced me to a former coworker, an advertising executive named Susan. Susan had participated in a corporate-sponsored group wedding, which took place at half time during a professional basketball game, with the ten couples dressed in T-shirts and shorts. Taiwan's fledging professional basketball league had staged the group wedding as a promotional event. For their participation the couples received watches, household goods, and other gifts from the sponsors. The gifts, it seems, were the main reason why Susan and her husband got married this way. He had read about the basketball wedding in the local edition of GQ magazine and said "Let's do it" by way of proposing. They had no other ceremonies and no banquet despite pressure from friends. They also skipped having professional bridal photos taken and, instead, hung a framed movie poster above their bed. When I asked how her parents felt about the nontraditional wedding, Susan smiled, saying that her father was just relieved she did not marry her previous boyfriend, with whom she had lived for five years. This story was unusual in every respect, but most telling is how the sponsors of the basketball wedding turned the cultural notion of weddings as media events on its head. Instead of couples, families, and the wedding industry appropriating the symbols of media events to promote the importance of the wedding, the basketball league had appropriated the symbol of the wedding to promote basketball.

The Taipei city government periodically sponsors mass wedding ceremonies and puts the symbols of weddings to promotional uses, too. The city government staged a mass wedding the day before the opening of the Peitou mass-transit line. Construction problems had delayed the project and increased its cost exponentially. The public was grumbling about the result: a much delayed opening day and much higher ticket prices than initially projected. The city apparently sought to drown out the grumbling with the roar of firecrackers and joy of a gigantic wedding, offering a NT $10,000 *hongbao* wedding gift (then about $400 U.S.) each to eighty-eight couples.

When I contacted city officials in advance of the wedding, I was led to believe that city-sponsored mass weddings were a form of philanthropy directed at poor couples, who could not otherwise afford a festive wedding.[21] The brides and grooms, however, arrived in rented Cadillacs and Mercedes decorated with red ribbons and wedding wreaths. Every bride was dressed to the nines in white bridal wear, and each one I saw appeared to have had a professional makeover. When I inquired among the crowd of couples, I learned that indeed many of them were having customary wedding rites at home with wedding banquets to follow and had squeezed attendance at the midday mass wedding rite between customary events. They participated not for lack of other ways to celebrate their marriage but for the fun of being involved in a major media event and the NT $10,000 *hongbao*.

The couples gathered at the second-to-last train stop and rode to the terminal at New Peitou Park aboard train cars decorated with pink ribbons and flowers. They then processed through the terminal on red carpet runners and stood before a stage set up in the park in the blistering March sun. Throngs of relatives and other onlookers stood beneath sun umbrellas and purchased cold drinks from the 7–11 convenience store booth set up in a prominent spot where its logo would appear in news photographs of the mass of couples. Hordes of photographers and media camera crews documented the event. Among the famous people presiding at the wedding were the first popularly elected mayor of Taipei, Chen Shui-bian, and the Mandarin pop rock star Zhou Hua-jian, who performed two love ballads and offered his well wishes to more than 150 newlyweds.

The city's use of a mass wedding to promote a troubled mass-transit system simultaneously performs two symbolic tasks. First, by tying the positive connotations of a wedding to the train line, city officials attempted to improve public attitude about the project and bolster support for the mayor. Second, the mass-transit mass wedding had the unintended effect of furthering the cultural association of weddings with media events. It was an actual media event because of the large number of couples and the presence of the mayor and a pop rock star, but it simultaneously worked to make brides (and to a lesser extent grooms, too) into celebrities for the day. Of course, the country's vast bridal industry is founded on the principle that every bride should be treated as a celebrity for the day, but only rarely does a common bride brush so close to real fame.

CONCLUSIONS

Young and old have, rather respectfully, carved out their own domains within weddings. The planning and practicing of wedding ceremonies remain squarely in the hands of the parental generation, at least for now. Brides and grooms agree to perform the rites under the direction of the older generation, but couples (and their young bridal photographers) control the public representation of their marriages in their pre-wedding-day bridal photographs on proud display at banquets.

Many older Taiwanese would have wanted me to write more about the ritual practices they find important and meaningful; an entire book could be written on the subject. The younger couples with whom I spent more of my research time, however, maintained a distance from these ritual practices by denying understanding of them and labeling them "old people's business." By defining the ceremonies as the terrain of parents and grandparents, marrying couples maintain respect for their elders while expressing their differences from the older generation elsewhere, at the bridal salons.

The fundamentalist Christian couple, Ruth and Peter, are extremely rare. They rejected the bridal industry ideology that posits the photograph as the repository for youthful values, like individuality, associated with the world outside family control. They also rejected the idea that formal wedding rites are a repository for the customs and values of the older generations. Ruth and Peter wanted control over their wedding *and* its public representation. Their families were dismayed, and even their Christian friends were shocked.

The double lives that young people carry out when conducting their private lives in spaces outside family control carry over into weddings as well. It seems only right, to young and old alike, that parents control wedding ceremonies and couples control photographs. Allotting each generation its own domain suggests that they agree to disagree on core values. Yet in their wedding ceremonies young couples tacitly agree with elders that weddings are, at least in part, about the bride entering a new family—not just about the personal ties between her and the groom. In interviews, many women and men contrasted themselves with Americans, who, they imagined, think only of romance and not of the larger kin ties created by marriage. Weddings bring couples into the fold of the "inside," into the family responsibilities of full adulthood. The photographs, shot before wedding ceremonies commence, serve to celebrate (and document) the last youthful indulgence of the couples, most especially the women, in the freedom of the space outside family.

Considering how thoroughly other aspects of life are standardized in Taiwan, it is remarkable that wedding ceremonies have remained largely in family homes rather than moving into commercial wedding halls, as they have in Japan and Korea. The lack of standardization and lack of professionals involved in formal wedding ceremonies contribute to keeping them the domain of the older generation. Young people are comfortable with the process of shopping around for the best bridal salon and analyzing the minute differences between the styles they offer, but the commercially uncharted terrain of wedding ceremonies leaves even practiced consumers uncertain about how to proceed.

Banquets serve as a middle ground between young and old, where everyone's interests converge in the name of showing off to family and friends by means of expensive dishes, free-flowing wine, an elaborately decorated bride, and the display of costly bridal portraits. Even though the parents sometimes complain of money wasted on luxurious photographs, few hesitate to brag about the portraits' great expense and beauty. Parents not only allow the display of youthful bridal albums containing images that sometimes poke fun at the older generation at the banquets that they sponsor, but they also often expect or demand the display of photos. In the rare cases I found of couples who did not want to buy and display bridal salon photos of themselves, it usually turned out that the couple's parents had pressured them into buying a bridal photography package for fear of loss of face. Some parents even insist that the bride wear brand-new gowns (rented at a higher price) though she herself may be content with previously worn gowns to save money. The bride's beauty reflects on not only her own status but that of the groom and both families as well. If her gown is shabby, her makeup imperfect, her jewelry too sparse, or her photos too unattractive, this speaks poorly of the parents at the banquet.

Whether or not she enjoys it, the bride is the celebrity of the day, and its visual focus. The role is high in prestige but low in agency—a contradictory status that makes sense on the wedding day, when the families are in charge. Their task is to move a woman ritually from one family to another. She is the focus of the day because the wedding is *about* her, not of her. She plays the role by downplaying her individual thoughts and feelings as much as possible, and her immobilizing costume helps her accomplish this. Although bridal photography certainly takes the notion of the bride as a visual object from weddings (rather than vice versa), the bride's treatment at her wedding and at the bridal salon differ dramatically. At the wedding, the bride—primarily through her beauty and comportment—confers prestige on the family. She is a means to an end, not an end unto herself.

In his book on modern Greek Cypriot weddings, Argyrou (1996) argues that weddings are no longer rites of passage for bride and groom because Greek Cypriot couples today are already self-supporting, sexually experienced adults when they marry. He contends that today weddings are "rites of [social] distinction" in that their ritual function is not to change the status of bride and groom from child to married adult but to advance the families' class standing. I might have reached the same conclusion about Taiwanese weddings had I not focused my research efforts on the preparations for weddings that take place in bridal photography salons, where, as I argue in the following chapters, modern rites of passage for bride and groom occur.

While many parents and grandparents take pains to provide their children with the proper rituals for their marriage, many brides and grooms I met seemed unenthusiastic about the formal ritual process but went through with it primarily out of respect for the older generations. When I asked some of my college-educated Taipei friends if they envisioned providing the same types of ceremonies for their own children at marriage, they said probably not, since they would not know how to put on the ceremonies and would not believe in the efficacy of the rituals enough to expend time and effort to learn them in their full complexity.

I found, however, that brides (and, to a lesser extent, grooms) place a great deal of importance on their photographic portraits and that their personal experiences at bridal salons in selecting gowns, being made up, and being photographed in themselves constitute a rite of passage that is meaningful in the context of modern Taiwanese brides' lives. On the wedding day, the products of the bridal industry—gowns, makeup, portraits—participate in the wedding-as-rite-of-distinction in that they mark class distinctions. Sophisticated banquet guests know how to tell the work of an elite bridal salon from that of a banal one, even though all the salons engage in a singular project of portraying bride and groom as modern, wealthy, and worldly. But the consumption of bridal services, I argue in chapters 5 and 6, is more than an effort by men and women to express status distinctions.

The space of the bridal salon serves as an alter ego to the space of wedding ceremonies. One is the ritual domain of the older generations, the other is the ritual domain of the younger. The cultural worlds represented therein are nearly inverse images. Each side has trouble understanding the importance and meaning of the other's activities, and both sides generally agree to stay out of each other's business.

CHAPTER 5

Making Up the Bride

Brides wear a sort of mask painted right onto their skin, glued to their eyelashes, carved out of their eyebrows with razor blades. Bridal make-overs turn women into brides, transforming everyday women with their individual characteristics into generic look-alike beauties in three hours' time. Meticulous hairstyling sculpts hair into perfectly shaped curls, aided with hair extensions and gluelike hairspray. Bridal stylists *(zao-xingshi)* target not only hair and face but also breasts and hips in their labors, outfitting brides with breast padding and hip-exaggerating gowns. Stylists' work involves laborious, transformative processes that bring women's bodies into compliance with the beauty standards of the mass media, many specifically emulating images of white women's bod-ies produced and circulated by interests in Hollywood, New York, London, and Paris. After her makeover, a bride's closest friends and rel-atives often can no longer recognize her with ease.

Why does this happen, not just occasionally but virtually universally among brides who undergo a proper wedding? The question plagued *me,* but it hardly occurred to people I knew in Taipei—making the mystery all the more compelling. When a belief or practice is so taken for granted or naturalized that it is not discussed, questioned, and debated, that belief or practice can be called hegemonic. Of course, many beliefs and practices are of a hegemonic nature. If societies were to question and debate absolutely everything, they might grind to a halt. Societies need some operational assumptions to make cultural life possible. In the past, many anthropologists regarded beliefs and practices that the people under study take for granted to be simply their "culture." Labeling them "hegemonic" marks a shift in the conceptualization of culture that points toward the connections among culture, power, and history (see Comaroff and Comaroff 1991; Dirks, Eley, and Ortner 1994). The inquiry is no longer "What is Taiwanese culture?" but rather "How did this specific cultural practice of bridal makeovers come to be?" and "Why is it taken for granted?"

To begin with, I interviewed brides, stylists, bridal magazine editors, and the friends and family members of brides. I tried to question the bridal makeover practice in terms that I thought people would really understand. Makeovers are costly. Most brides are made over twice— once on the day of the photo shoot and once on the day of the wedding. Brides who have more than one wedding banquet (for example, an engagement banquet, or one wedding banquet outside Taipei near the groom's family home and one in Taipei for the couple's colleagues and friends) undergo a makeover for each banquet as well. The cost of the first makeover is included in the bridal photography package, and each additional makeover was $80 U.S. or more. People in Taipei today are always talking about how busy they are, how little time they have. At three hours per makeover plus travel time to and from the salon (or exorbitant extra fees to bring a stylist on site for the wedding), couples invest a good deal of time in brides' makeovers. Given their great expense, I asked, why do brides have professional makeovers?

Baffled by my questioning of the obvious, people responded with equally inexplicable answers. Everyone agreed that bridal makeup is necessary. Even those who regarded the standard highly made-up bridal look as unattractive believed it necessary. Furthermore, brides and their families believed that only professionally trained, experienced stylists were capable of making over a bride. Individuals did not question the required outlays of money and time because they had no choice in the matter. Still, how did professional bridal makeovers become obligatory? Many answered my question with the pat statement that "girls love beauty" (nühaizi ai piaoliang). The essentializing notion that all females are the same in this regard is interesting in and of itself, but it is simply not true. Not all "girls" love beauty, and even brides who would characterize themselves as loving beauty do not regard the standard bridal look as beautiful. More than a few brides told me that they find that look downright ugly on the wedding day, even though the same heavy makeup makes for beautiful photographs. These brides underwent wedding-day makeovers not for the love of beauty but because of pressure to conform. Furthermore, one of the reasons women cite for reliance upon professional stylists is that they do not make up on a regular basis and never learned makeup application skills. If women adore "beauty" so much, why not learn to wield a wand of mascara and apply eye shadow?

Young brides and stylists sometimes claimed today's bridal styling has roots in Chinese customs and traditions *(fengsu xiguan)*. In discussions with older women, however, I learned that very little of the styling I observed in bridal salons was experienced by the mothers and grandmothers of today's brides at their own weddings. Old women frequently brushed off my questions about beauty, saying that in the old days people were simply too poor to care about attractiveness, let alone allocate precious resources to the purchase of expensive, imported beauty products.[1] Almost no one wore makeup in the 1940s, when my older informants married. China and Japan were at war. American forces bombed Taiwan in the early 1940s. In the late 1940s, KMT forces terrorized the population. Childhood mortality was high, and marriages were dominated by the interests of elders, not youth. Older women whom I interviewed believed that their mothers and grandmothers similarly did not emphasize beauty, which they saw as a luxury of more recent times. Furthermore, according to the model of the Chinese family developed by Margery and Arthur Wolf, good looks were not a central consideration in marital arrangements in the 1950s and 1960s; rather, mothers-in-law sought hard-working, strong, and not-too-attractive women to marry their sons, so they would provide the household with high-quality labor but would not challenge the mothers' position of power by charming their sons into allegiance to their wives. Even then, though, imported luxury goods like soaps and powders were available in Taiwan via Shanghai.[2] Such products were extremely expensive, and only the elite (first Japanese and, later, KMT officials) could afford them. Middle-class brides did, however, undergo some inexpensive beauty treatments, including a trip to the hairdresser to have their hair, then worn unpinned in short styles, curled.[3]

Another old beauty practice is *wanlian*, literally "pulling the face" but also referred to in English as "face peeling." Today, *wanlian* is a skill practiced by few.[4] In times past, however, a bride might have gone to the market and paid a small fee for the service, or had a female relative peel her face for her. As face peeling is practiced today, the practitioner first dusts her client's face with powder, then pulls taut pieces of coarse string between her fingers, twisting them together as she moves them rapidly over the woman's face. The strings pull the tiny hairs out of the woman's skin, removing the top layer of skin cells at the same time. The purpose of face peeling is (and was) to lighten the face by removing all traces of dark facial hair. The process is painful. Young women usually had their face peeled for the first time as brides-to-be, undergoing the procedure a few days in advance to allow the red, splotchy skin to heal before the wedding.[5]

The face peeling and hairdressing practices of the past suggest that the association between brides and beauty is not new, but the past sheds little light on the present. To dig more deeply into the practice of bridal styling, I explored the details of the practice by observing makeovers in progress, attending beauty school classes, hiring a stylist to teach me how to style brides, and undergoing bridal styling myself.

THEORETICAL PERSPECTIVES ON BEAUTY PRACTICES

Examination of the minutiae of everyday bodily practices allows us to better understand the contours of power and the persistence of culture.[6] Second-wave feminist theorists from Simone de Beauvoir (1952) on have argued that sexism colonizes the female body through beauty practices that, quite literally, restrict physical freedom (e.g., footbinding and high-heeled shoes) to boost attractiveness. Feminists have also argued that the resources girls and women are expected to devote to beauty keep too many from investing themselves in other important matters. In other words, the fastidious attention to appearance that beauty norms require of women helps to undergird structures of male dominance.[7]

More recently, scholarly and popular critics alike have argued that second-wave feminism did not articulate sufficiently complex views of gender politics—did not, for example, understand the ways women wield beauty practices as tools to cultivate power. The work of creating beauty—dieting, exercising, making up, sculpting hair—can be seen as the work of creating wealth and power, not as diversions from such pursuits. In her study of women who elected to undergo cosmetic surgery, for example, Kathy Davis (1995) concludes that cosmetic surgery is a cogent means women use to reshape their lives by transforming their bodies. In other words, women may be agents of the power of beauty, not victims of it.

The relationship between power and agency in beauty practices is undertheorized, however, in formulations such as Davis's, which emphasize agency. Susan Bordo (1997) argues that human action is driven by desire, and desire is always already embedded in cultural norms and social realities. Many women who undergo breast augmentation, lipo-suction, and rhinoplasty respond to accusations of endangering their health for the sake of men with "I'm doing it for me." They imagine that "me" as "a pure and precious inner space, an 'authentic' and personal reference point untouched by external values and demands" (Bordo 1997: 32). Davis's study misses the problem that women elect cosmetic surgery under conditions and contexts not of their own making. Women who engage in beauty practices and services are not cultural "dopes" complacent in their own subjugation. Indeed, they creatively harness cos-metic surgery and other beauty practices as paths to power. Yet celebra-tion of women's agency under the surgeon's knife seems to miss a critical point: The pursuit of status and power through dangerous and disabling beauty practices might better be understood as the "weapons of the weak" in the absence of less problematic means.[8]

Bordo argues further that consumer culture is the driving force behind the popularization of dangerous beauty practices such as cosmetic sur-gery and self-starvation (see also Hansen and Reed 1986). Consumer capitalism "cannot allow equilibrium or stasis in human desire. Thus, we are not permitted to feel satisfied with ourselves and we are 'empowered' only and always through fantasies of what we *could* be" (1997: 51). With standards of beauty set according to the looks of youth, women are assured that only early death permits the escape of loss of beauty in the absence of consumer beauty products and services. Beauty industry workers—from executives who create cosmetic ads and dentists who bleach teeth to aestheticians who "pop" pimples—actively promulgate a "pedagogy of defect," writes Bordo. In advertisements as well as per-sonal consultations, they teach consumers how to investigate their bodies for "defects" in need of beauty treatments to remove hair, reduce pores, and vanish cellulite.[9]

Beauty and fashion magazines are notorious for what Naomi Wolf calls the "visual censorship" of natural physical features common among women, such as the pores of the skin, the unadorned lip, and the fat deposits of the hips. These same European and U.S. beauty magazines are consulted by bridal stylists and photographers as inspiration for their work in Taiwan. Wolf's research reveals instances of advertisers with-drawing their business from magazines featuring models who, for exam-ple, do not wear enough makeup to suit the cosmetic companies' tastes. The result is made-up, thin models with airbrushed features and an ever-higher bar for what counts as "normal" or acceptable in women's ap-pearances. Natural features of older women (wrinkles, sagging breasts) are vanquished, if not by cosmetic surgery then by computerized editing of photographs. Wolf argues that young women need access to the sight of real aging bodies in order to counter the despair many feel over their imperfect bodies when commercially produced images are their only referent (1991: 81–83).[10]

When women such as Davis's informants say that they feel "trapped" in a body that does not reflect their inner selves, their statements contain many cultural ideas in need of further investigation. The high value placed on artificially constructed images of the body is only one of the referents we need to consider. Perhaps even more important is the historically and culturally specific concept of the interiority of a soul or mind paired with a distinct, external body (Bordo 1993; Butler 1990; Martin 1987). Western dualistic constructs setting apart mind and body are gendered such that men are associated with the mind and rationality and women with the body and corporeal irrationality (Bordo 1993; see also Grosz 1994). The body, therefore, becomes a particular problem for women wanting to distance themselves from irrationality, emotionalism, and sexuality. Control over the body can become an obsession for women, resulting in eating or "body image" disorders. Female fat or flab, for example, is often read as evidence of a woman's lack of moral stature, her lack of self-control. Female hunger is associated with sexual hunger and impropriety. Much as Victorian physiognomy regarded the face as a "window on the soul," contemporary attitudes about the body (particularly female bodies) take the body as reflective of moral character (Bordo 1993; Brumberg 1997; Finkelstein 1991; Gilman 1998).[11]

Although the ultimate effect is that women suffer from body image problems in much higher numbers than do men, Bordo does not attribute this to the actions of men dominating women as such. Rather, gender here works on a symbolic level, not an institutional one (Scott 1988). When women pursuing beauty claim to do so not for men but for themselves, they are right. Men in general do not themselves compel women to engage in beautifying practices. To the contrary, some men find women's preoccupation with appearance perplexing if not downright annoying (Beausoleil 1994: 42; Wolf 1991: 169). Examination of beauty practices, then, leads to a nuanced understanding of sexism where power lies not in the hands of men so much as in the cultural worlds that shape both men and women.

Among body parts considered "defective" in the United States are those that mark nonwhiteness or immigrant status. Bridal stylists in Taipei similarly target facial features and body parts that, to them, mark

Chinese bodies as inferior to those they see in the mass media.[12] U.S. beauty standards tend to normalize Anglo-Saxon physical features and proclaim all other types as defective. For example, preferences for thin noses, light-colored eyes, and bouncy hair have been historically problematic for Blacks in the United States (Haiken 1997; hooks 1992; Peiss 1998). Those whose features fail to conform to Anglo-Saxon-based norms often deploy beauty technologies to minimize signs of race, class, and age associated with low-status groups because physical differences are often turned into justifications for discrimination. Cultural stereotypes caricature key features and associate them with undesirable personal qualities. Kaw (1994: 244) reports that her Asian American informants looked to eyelid surgery (blepharoplasty) to address "the psychological pain of feeling inadequate" in the United States, where "small" and "slanted" eyes are often thought to reflect "a 'dull,' 'passive' personality, a 'closed' mind, and a 'lack of spirit' in the person." Hence physical "divergence" from the "norm" is construed as not merely physical but also *moral* failure (see also Furman 1997; Gates 1985).

Fixing one's racialized "defects," however, is also problematic. Those who undergo cosmetic surgery or hair relaxing to erase features associated with minority ethnic groups in the United States face criticism for betraying their groups by normalizing their bodies to the appearance standards of those who dominate them. Some see such beauty practices as acts of colonization of the body, whether they apply to women or men. The way an African American wears her or his hair has not only beauty significance but connotations for political alignments as well (Rooks 1996). Asian Americans have raised similar concerns about the devaluation of Asian facial features that has led increasing numbers of Asians both in the United States and abroad to undergo plastic surgery to create eyelid folds and a more prominent nose (Chapkis 1986; Haiken 1997; Kaw 1994). The refusal of normalizing beauty practices, then, becomes a political act. The politics of beauty can be contradictory, however. Haiken (1997) points out that while Michael Jackson's cosmetic surgeries are seen as demonstrating his betrayal of African Americans, Barbra Streisand has been criticized for *failing* to tame her Jewish nose (see also Furman 1997).

TAIWANESE BRIDAL BEAUTY IN ITS OWN CONTEXT

The literature on beauty in the United States clearly points toward connections among valued looks, cultural practices such as consumerism, and structures of power. Several continuities between bridal styling in 1990s Taiwan and beauty practices in the United States are immediately apparent. First, stylists subject only brides to extensive beautifying efforts, not grooms. In fact, brides submit to standards of beauty that apply to very few other categories of women in Taiwan. Are brides agents or victims of beauty, or both? Second, stylists mold brides according to criteria of beauty set by foreign standards. Do stylists racialize brides through their efforts to improve upon their looks? Third, stylists mold brides according to standards of beauty set by women who are not only Caucasian but whose images are altered by makeup and hair stylists, photographers, and airbrush artists, not to mention the aestheticians, personal trainers, nutritionists, and surgeons who work on the women's bodies before the photo shoots. Does bridal styling promulgate the "pedagogy of defect" through which the emulated images came to exist in the first place? The answers to these questions are more complex than the literature on beauty in the United States leads one to expect at first blush.

Gender, power, and beauty come together in brides to render them the objects of much visual attention but little actual power during the period when they are made-up. However, brides are made-up for only short periods of time. Once returned to everyday appearances, the women may be able to capitalize on their beautiful photographs and public appearances as passive, beautiful brides, thus realizing the power of beauty only later. Though the physical confinement and discomforts are brief, the resulting effects on status and power may last longer. Though beauty of the type demanded of brides is a preoccupation of the bridal industry, it is not necessarily a preoccupation for most women except during the brief period in their lives before and after their weddings.

Stylists' work clearly has something to do with race, but the precise relationship between beauty and race relations in Taiwanese bridal photography is not clear-cut. In the course of my fieldwork, women, men, and even children told me that Westerners (xifangren) have more attractive skin, noses, eyes, eyelids, eyelashes, cheekbones, chins, hair, breasts, and hips.[13] Though they said "Westerners," what they clearly meant was white Westerners, using "Westerner" in a way that assumes nonwhite Westerners are not really Western. These physical features—like Italian clothing, French handbags, German automobiles, and American graduate degrees—index wealth and worldly sophistication. Taiwan has only a small number of European, Australian, and American expatriates in residence, so notions of Western good looks come primarily through mass media.[14] When confronted with actual Westerners in the flesh, people often point out that such bodies are unattractively fat, grossly tall, disgustingly hairy, or offensively smelly.[15] For most people in Taiwan, direct interaction with the white Other is not a daily occurrence, though indirect interaction through consumption of foreign advertisements and goods transpires daily. Consuming images of white Westerners is different from being consumed *by* them. To the extent that people in Taiwan experience global capitalism as something that they wish to absorb rather than something foisted upon them, their appropriations of images of white women may be seen as colonizing those images, not only as being colonized by them. (Of course, not all people in Taiwan are equally well positioned vis-à-vis global capital and its transnational cultural currents. Those who are elderly, aboriginal, or poor may tend to see things differently.)

Finally, it is apparent to all involved that creating bridal beauty is no simple task. The task is so very complex that brides rely on professional stylists to raise them to the standards set by models and celebrities, who are also professionally beautified. On a day-to-day basis, only lipstick, powder, and foundation makeup are widely used, and most women use only lipstick. Practical and convenient hairstyles predominate. The difference between bridal beauty and everyday looks is extreme. The rarefaction of brides as beauties may put such great social distance between bridal beauty and everyday femininity that the gap between them becomes a space in which women can critically contemplate mass-media-inspired visions of physical beauty. Experiencing first-hand what goes into bridal beautification, women regard mass media beauty standards as so alien as to be inapplicable to everyday life.

Styling is a rare experience for women who are not professional entertainers or models, and, for brides, the transformation from woman to bride achieved through bridal styling is not merely a means to an end. The "once in a lifetime" experience is something of an end in and of itself, a rite of passage that many brides may quietly experience as more meaning-laden than the formal wedding ceremonies orchestrated by family elders.

BEAUTY PREPARATIONS FOR STYLING

Included often in marital transfers today is a *wanlian hongbao*—a red envelope of money to pay for a face peeling prior to the wedding—given to the bride by the groom's side. None of the young brides I knew, however, had their faces peeled by a traditional practitioner. Many went to a modern beauty salon for a facial treatment consisting of cosmetic cleansers, steam, masques, skin bleaching, massage, and the removal of pimples and facial hair. One young woman told me that "of course" brides have a modern facial prior to their wedding because they want to have a "new face" to begin their "new life" in a "new family." Despite this lovely phrasing, having a prewedding facial is by no means universal. When I asked another bride why she had skipped a facial, she joked that she would save the cash for when she was married, old, and more in need of beauty treatments than she was then.

Taipei and other urban centers in Taiwan offer a vast array of facial cleansing, repairing, whitening, and anti-aging treatments based on modern cosmetic preparations and technologies. Many of the salons are local operations, though some of the more elite salons are owned by European and Japanese beauty companies. Among the services they offer are invasive skin-improving techniques that remove layers of the skin until pockmarks, scars, and other imperfections are less visible.[16] Some of these businesses advertise specifically to brides, offering one-time and series programs for lightening the skin and clearing the face of freckles, acne, and blotches. Japanese-owned Sogo department store aesthetic salons boast an expensive bridal package—fourteen-, thirty-, sixty-, or ninety-day treatment programs that can cost more than the bridal dress and photo packages themselves. Their logo: "For a lifetime of happiness, prepare to be most beautiful."

The message is that consumers must spare no expense in making the bride the most beautiful she can be because her wedding is such an important event and her beauty on that day is indicative of her future well-being. Indeed, aesthetic salons promise dramatic results as well as a relaxing, pampering, and even homoerotic experience for the bride as her body is gently tended to by female aestheticians. The largest bridal shops offer facial treatments as part of their beauty departments. Many salesladies, in their role as wedding consultants, advise brides to have a facial prior to their photo session even in smaller shops, which do not themselves offer facial treatment services. I often heard it said that a facial (*zuolian*, literally "doing the face," or *pifu baoyang*, "skin maintenance") prepares the skin so that foundation makeup will better adhere to the face. Some women also feel it necessary to have a facial afterward to cleanse the skin of residual makeup lest it cause acne. Hearing about the "need" for facial treatments to make the foundation "stick" to the skin and, again later, to remove the dirty residue left by makeup, I came to see bridal facials as antipollution rituals (see Douglas 1966). Facial treatments ritually prepare the face for the "once in a lifetime" process it will soon experience, as if skin and makeup somehow naturally repel each other, and facial treatments later rid the face of the "dirt" left from makeup to cleanse away its degrading, sexualizing aspects because heavy makeup carries associations of promiscuity (discussed later in this chapter).

Beauty salons offer an array of beauty services, from slimming machines to eyebrow tattooing, from skin whitening to treatments that claim to eliminate conspicuous pores from the nose. Those not content with the techniques of beauty salons may visit cosmetic surgeons for surgical treatments that provide double eyelids *(shuang yanpi)*, cheekbone and chin bone implants, larger breasts, higher nipples (for sagging breasts), face lifts, liposuction, varicose vein removal, and hymen repair surgeries. None of these surgeries are particularly associated with brides, though they are, like skin whitening and body slimming, available to women who feel particularly anxious about their appearances prior to playing the role of bride/visual object. The most common prebridal beauty preparation is dieting. In the old days, plumpness was considered attractive as a mark of wealth. Today, thin is in (see Lin 1996, 1998).

ONCE-IN-A-LIFETIME STYLE

Bridal styling takes place at unbearably early hours because the time-consuming process must be completed before normal working hours begin so the photo shoot can end before evening. Stylists often require brides to be in the styling chair by 6 A.M. On the day of the shoot, a couple (and their anthropologist) must first find the before-hours entrance to the bridal shop. Searching for side doors and crouching beneath security gates underscore what an unreasonably early hour it is. The only people on the streets are older people in pajamas out for their morning *tai-qi* exercises in the pre-rush-hour freshest air of the day. Also out and about is the occasional young person, still half-drunk from partying, stumbling home in hip club wear from Taipei's all-night discos. Workers in the bridal industry as well as customers (particularly grooms) often complained to me that Chinese weddings are too complicated, too troublesome. They add loss of sleep and long, boring hours of styling to the high price tag of bridal photo packages on the list of "once in a lifetime" sacrifices made for weddings.

After greeting the bride and commenting on the early hour, stylists get to work. Larger bridal salons have separate beauty departments set up much like hair salons, with a row of client chairs facing mirrors along a wall. Others have small styling sections right up at the front window, where passersby can see the stylist primp brides during costume changes later in the day. In either case, the work of styling is usually not hidden from view as an unsightly, secretive affair but is visually highlighted with mirrors and lighting where visitors to the shop can see and imagine themselves the recipients of such luxurious attention. By contrast, in the United States cosmetics are usually applied in private or in "near secret" because women make up to become socially presentable; the unmade-up face is, in some contexts, considered an impolite sight (see Beausoleil 1994; Chapkis 1986).[17] Though bridal styling's purpose is to make a plain woman into a beautiful bride, there is no presumption that the unmade-up face is unpresentable or defective.

Stylists often meet the bride for the first time just moments before going to work on her hair and face, which requires intimate physical contact between the stylist and her client.[18] Stylists do not see a need to get to know their clients personally. Their quiet style of work contrasts markedly with that of bridal salon photographers and saleswomen, who receive explicit direction to get to know their clients personally, thereby fostering many and varied photographs to capture the bride's personality and individual tastes, and so increasing sales. Stylists, by contrast, allow brides only limited influence over their bridal stylings. Instead, stylists use their own tastes and professional opinions to design makeup and hair-stylings that coordinate with the half-dozen or so gowns selected by the bride. The stylist's read on the "feeling" of each gown (and her knowl-edge of the photographer's preferences for backdrops that coordinate with particular gowns) guides her selection of eye and lip colors, hair-style, and costume jewelry. At the comparatively upscale salons, stylists change the bride's hair and makeup six or more times per photo shoot, once for each change in gown. At less expensive Taipei salons, stylists perform fewer and less complete changes, altering only lip color and accessories for each gown change, for example. The more complete the style changes, the fewer brides a stylist can work on in one day.

The bride sits facing a mirror at a styling station, where supplies are kept on hand. Very often, the bride sees herself surrounded by reflections of the model brides featured in large photographs hanging on the wall behind her. The stylist sets the bride's hair in rows of rollers. She sits on a stool at the bride's side, her thigh and hip pressed against the bride's thigh so that although they face each other, the bride's face is as close to the stylist's as possible. Next, the stylist washes the bride's face, deftly wiping cotton pads across the bride's skin. Applying heavy moisturizing lotion, the stylist prepares the skin so the foundation makeup will stay on throughout the long day of posing, costume changes, and bright lights. Silently assessing the bride's face (sometimes complimenting her fair skin), the stylist takes out her single-edge razor blade and begins shaving and shaping the bride's eyebrows.

EYEBROWS

The stylist fashions the bride's eyebrows into perfect and symmetrical shapes, carving away hair where there should be none and imagining how she will later fill in, with eyebrow pencil, the areas where the bride's own brows are insufficient. Often a bride's brows also require length trimming so the hairs do not stand up from the face. For some of the women I interviewed, the first time (or only time) they experienced the odd sensations of eyebrow shaping was the day of their photo shoot.

One friend, Nai-jin, reported that the razor blade held close to her eyes frightened her, making her very nervous for the five minutes or so that this unfamiliar woman carved out and snipped away at her eyebrows. As she sat in the styling chair Nai-jin found herself wondering if the stylist had ever cut someone and worrying that the stylist, whose hands held her face and whose breath brushed her cheek, would notice her nervousness and become uneasy herself, making a slip of the hand more likely. Prior to my turn in the styling chair I also worried about the blade and the threat of a botched eyebrow shaping. I recall looking back at the stylist as she intensely focused her gaze on my eyebrows at close distance; her eyes seemed to cross. As she chiseled away my eyebrow hair, millimeter by millimeter, I heard the strange sound of the dry blade raking across my brow and decided I had best close my eyes. I found the stylist's hands reassuringly controlled, the blade painless in contrast to the eyebrow tweezing my mother had insisted I have before my own wedding.

For stylists, eyebrow shaping is one of the most difficult parts of the makeover process. Eyebrows are considered a most important, expressive part of a woman's face. Chinese physiognomy (*mianxiang*—fortune-telling by facial features) is popular in Taiwan. Face fortune-tellers regard the eyebrows as a major element in predicting one's personality and fate. One popular physiognomy guide provides assessments of thirty different eyebrow types, focusing on eyebrow shape, length and density of eyebrow hairs, and placement of the brows on the face (Cai 1995). Another piece on popular physiognomy—a handout on cosmetics from a fortune-telling fair held at a department store—proclaims that eyebrows are the number one facial feature for predicting personal relationships. Female eyebrows that are too thick and too dark give others an unfriendly feeling. Eyebrows that are too close together represent an unlucky family life of many hardships and little happiness. Eyebrows should be long and curve downward, representing a fate of abundant and deep love. Eyebrows should not curve downward too much, however, as this leads to excesses of love and hatred. Very straight eyebrows connote a woman who is too practical, giving others an icy feeling (Wu 1996).

The Chinese saying *meimu chuanqing* refers to communicating romantic feelings with the eyebrows. In Taiwan eyebrows can play a "window to the soul" role similar to the one eyes play in my Euro-American settings. Eyebrows, however, are easily shaped with razor blades and cosmetic pencils to encourage a happy family life. Many old women in Taipei have had their thinning eyebrows tattooed, probably for the same reasons. The tattoos, over time, turn from black to dark purple, making them easy to spot. I found that relatively few younger women bother to shape their eyebrows, though. (Men, I observed, are even less inclined to shape their eyebrows, with the exception of shaving away brow hairs over the nose. These hairs threaten to bring on financial misfortune.)

If everyone believed in physiognomy, of course, women would all want the same long, downward-curved-but-not-*too*-curvy eyebrows with plenty of space between them. Virtually all brides receive these eyebrows. In everyday life the wide range of eyebrow shapes suggests that many people do not worry enough about physiognomy to keep their eyebrows under constant control. The only time a stylist would create a differently shaped eyebrow is for theatrical purposes—to make an actor or actress look sinister, icy, or shy. Stylists themselves do not necessarily subscribe to physiognomy beliefs, but physiognomy perspectives on facial features generally assign good luck to traits that are considered normal or handsome and bad luck to traits that are not.[19] Brides, whether they care for the typical beautiful-bride look or not, usually allow the stylist to "style" their faces according to the stylists' sense of what is proper and attractive. Facing strong social pressures to be beautiful, brides are expected to suspend their day-to-day agency over their bodies and give themselves over to professional stylists to sculpt their appearance. (Note, however, that stylists usually leave grooms' eyebrows alone.)

AGENCY AND THE CONSTRUCTION OF THE STYLIST

Although photographers ask brides and grooms about their preferences for the look of their photos, brides are seldom asked about their preferences for the look of their makeup in any but the most general ways. (Every bride and stylist I met in Taipei expressed preference for makeup that is "not too thick, more natural.") If ever a bride protests some aspect of the stylist's makeup work, she is told that the lighting used in the photo studio is not like everyday light and that the stylist's techniques are specifically tailored to make brides look their best in the photos. This statement is enough to silence most brides. The stylists' tight control over the makeover process is legitimated by their claim to knowledge that lay people lack. Referred to by the honorific terms "teacher" *(laoshi)* or "master of styling" *(zaoxingshi)*, deferred to by other salon employees (except photographers), and dressed in personalized stylish clothes in contrast to saleswomen's uniforms, stylists present themselves as respected professionals. Clients know they should not question the stylist's judgment too blatantly.[20]

Some brides told me that though they did not like the styling they received, they never spoke their preferences for fear of insulting the stylist by questioning her authority. On the day of Xiao-lan's photo shoot, she told the stylist she did not want to wear false eyelashes. The stylist insisted, telling her that if she did not wear the false eyelashes the quality of the photos would suffer terribly. Xiao-lan was too embarrassed to refuse in the face of the stylist's strong insistence. The eyelashes, however, irritated her so much that she could not fully open her eyes. Finally the photographer ordered the stylist to remove the false lashes, which she did obediently.

Sometimes silent power struggles ensue, the bride using her body to communicate dissatisfaction without forcing the stylist to lose face in a direct confrontation. Stylists busily ignore these cues and do as they please, or they might ask what is wrong in such a way that forces the bride to either overstep her bounds and insult the stylist or concede in submission that everything is fine. Once I observed a strong-willed bride and her stylist engage in a daylong power struggle. During one costume and style change the bride expressed her dislike of a lip color by commenting, unsolicited, "It's dark." The stylist said, "Oh no, it's just right for your dress." A few minutes later, boxed lunches were served, and they paused for a break. After lunch, the bride returned for makeup retouching, and the stylist asked accusingly, "Did you wipe off your lipstick or eat it off?" The stylist, who had made a point of instructing the bride to drink her tea through a straw, seemed to disbelieve that so much lipstick had come off without purposeful wiping. She silently repainted the bride's lips, starting the slow process over from scratch, in the same dark color.

Although stylists have firm opinions about proper eyebrows, eyelashes, and foundation, some are less firm about eye shadow and lip colors. On these aspects they may ask the bride for her preferences, but brides often invite the stylist to select a "natural" color because she is more knowledgeable. By choosing this bridal salon in the first place the bride has implicitly expressed her approval of the styling done there and, generally, on the day of the shoot makes herself passive. Some brides find the process of being transformed relaxing and fun; others told me they were sometimes frustrated with the process but decided to go along with it in hope that the stylist knew best how to produce beautiful photographs.

I found brides were more often critical of their wedding-day makeup than that for photo shoots. Xiao-lan told me she hated her wedding-day makeup terribly and was embarrassed to be seen with such a hideous makeover. Five years later, this former bride reasoned that her stylist only knew how to do photo-shoot makeup, which is too heavy (nong) under normal lighting conditions. I asked her why she did not wash it off. She laughed at my question. She could not wash it off because there was no way she could have reapplied it herself. She did not know how, and she believed it would have been so socially unacceptable to go to her wedding without formal bridal makeup that the embarrassment of the unattractive makeover was preferable to going without formal makeup at all.

BRIDAL BEAUTY VERSUS EVERYDAY LOOKS

Many women stressed that they knew very little about makeup and therefore did not consider making themselves up for either the photo shoot or the wedding. I repeatedly heard women say, "We Chinese are not like American girls, who learn how to make up from an early age." Several told me that in Taiwan students are too busy studying for college entrance examinations to learn how to apply makeup. Furthermore, they argued, most women have no opportunity to make up since they did not attend formal balls, as (they presumed) I did back home in the United States. A beauty editor for an international fashion magazine complained to me that she was the only woman at her college who wore makeup and that this showed that women in Taiwan were "not yet" educated about beauty. Women I observed in shops, banks, and on the street seldom wore cosmetics other than red lip color and sometimes powder to lighten the skin and prevent oily shine.

Many young women I interviewed were critical of the few women whose daily makeup involved more than lipstick and powder. Makeup as dramatic as brides wear is extremely rare in everyday settings like offices, restaurants, shopping districts, and temples; it is seen only on brides, models, entertainers, men's club hostesses, and sex workers.[21] Although the prevailing opinion is that a bride wears specialized makeup because she is the "star" (mingxing) of the wedding day, the connection between weddings and sexuality also helps to make sense of why brides wear makeup associated with sex. At a wedding banquet, the bride and the female entertainers (such as the strip dancers described in chapter 4) are normally the only people among the hundred or more present who are wearing eye makeup. As commented earlier, at rural weddings the bride and groom are commonly the subject of the entertainment troupe host's ribald jokes about what the couple will do that night in their new room.

Bridal costuming also connotes sexuality. Bridal gowns often have open or off-the-shoulder necklines, lace backs, and tightly fitted bodices revealing the curves of breasts enlarged with padding—styles not considered appropriate for respectable women in everyday life. A woman dressed in comparable styles who is not a bride would be presumed promiscuous. The Westernness of makeup, hair, and gown styles seems to make sense in this context, as Western women are presumed to be promiscuous by local standards. Of course, fashion models and celebrities also—when on the job—wear makeup of the sort worn by brides and men's entertainment industry workers. Such women, when they do not pose for or play overtly sexual roles, constitute an elite sector of the broader class of entertainers, but they share with lower-status entertainers the role of visual object, pleasing men and women with their beauty and charm.

Local constructions of Western femininity as more sexually open (unrestrained by familial obligations and pressures) derive in part from media images of foreign women, including fashion and cosmetics advertising. In Taiwan's media market, both foreign-produced and locally produced advertising associate beauty products with sex. Most frequently, overtly sexualizing advertising images picture Caucasian models. Underwear and lingerie advertising, for example, always features Caucasians. When I inquired about this fact among magazine editors and modeling agency executives, they gave me two explanations. First, local women do not have sufficiently curvaceous bodies—their chests and buttocks are flat, their hips small. Second, local models either refuse to pose in lingerie or else charge rates four times higher than their usual rates. Four times the local rate is what foreign models earn, and their images sell more products. For the United States, Wolf (1991) argues that beauty industry advertising conveys the message that if you look beautiful like this, you will experience more and better sex. The same type of ad strategy in Taiwan carries additional layers of meaning because of the use of sexual imagery and Caucasian female bodies of the curvaceous sort that Taiwanese consider Western. The ads seem to say that if you buy this beauty product, you will mark yourself as modern, participate in a cosmopolitan culture of beauty and sex, and experience cosmopolitan (not just parochial) sexual pleasures. But in the 1990s, for everyday use, making up one's face to norms set by beauty magazines and advertising transgressed the limits of sexual propriety. Pursuit of everyday beauty in Taiwan took certain forms accordingly. Skin cleansers, moisturizers, toners, and bleaching agents were the most popular beauty goods sold at cosmetic counters. Worries about body shape *(shencai)* ran very high and were the subject of many conversations between female friends. Cosmetic surgery was rumored to be quite common (particularly for creating double eyelids). With the exception of lipstick use, beauty practices that were invisible were preferred.

Interestingly, the popularity of foreign models in ad campaigns (not just for lingerie but for all fashion and beauty commodities) is *not* imposed by American and European multinationals. Editors at the Taiwan edition of a major fashion magazine told me they were under strict orders from Paris to rely primarily on local models, even though experience taught the local editors that when they put a foreigner's face on the cover, far more magazine copies sell than when they use a local model. The irrational business thinking in Paris is explained by the huge wall hanging that decorates the entryway to the Taiwan branch office. Displayed are magazine covers from more than twenty countries, boasting the magazine's international coverage. Magazine executives, it seems, think of their work around the world as locally rooted in each of these many nations, despite the simple fact that, at least in Taiwan, this means selling fewer magazines. Locally owned magazines suffer from no such globalizing aspirations and frequently display white models.[22] In fact, I seldom heard anyone speak of beauty in relation to questions of ethnic or national pride ("Chinese women should have Chinese beauty standards") except the employees of this foreign-owned magazine.[23]

FOUNDATION FOR A NEW FACE

Once the eyebrows are perfectly shaped, the stylist selects a foundation makeup. My beauty school tutor, Christine, taught me to look at the bride's chest just beneath her shirt when determining her skin color—not her face, darkened by a lifetime's exposure to the sun. In practice, however, I suspect that most stylists use the same light foundation color on all but the darkest brides. A stylist who confronts a client with particularly reddish or yellowish skin tones may use color-correcting makeup beneath the foundation. For example, red and green, as opposite colors on the spectrum, work to cancel each other out. Therefore green makeup applied over ruddy cheeks or red, inflamed skin makes it easier for foundation to cover these color imperfections.

Even more than the eyebrows, fair skin is the primary marker of beauty in Taiwan, so to say "Your skin is so fair" is to say "You are beautiful." Fair skin has been the beauty ideal for Chinese women since ancient times. Fairness once connoted wealth—the leisure to remain indoors and avoid work in the fields. Today in Taiwan, women rich and poor take pains to avoid the sun.[74] Women (street sweepers, gardeners, farmers) who perform outdoor labor typically wear wide-rimmed hats with scarves hanging down to cover their faces and necks, and long sleeves, gloves, long pants, and covered shoes, even in extreme heat. In the south of Taiwan, many women who work out of doors completely veil themselves to prevent tanning, leaving only an opening for their eyes. Many women who work indoors leave arms, legs, and head uncovered but carry parasols when walking outdoors even for a block's distance. Women who go out in the sun without proper covering receive critical looks from strangers. Sometimes old women urged me to take cover during my first trip to Taiwan, when I was too embarrassed to carry a parasol.

I found the preference for fair skin personally significant as it helped me relativize the loathing of fair skin in the United States, where tanned skin is in vogue. Growing up in Chicago with very fair skin and freckles, I hated my skin. I was so desperate for a tan as a teenager that I would sit out in the sun and suffer burn after burn. Only after I traveled to Taiwan as a young adult was I able to understand fully how foolish I had been to risk skin cancer and suffer blistering burns in obeisance to my society's standards of beauty when my skin simply could not conform. In Taipei, women (from bank tellers to bridal salon owners) frequently admired my fair skin and complained that theirs was too dark. I took pains to tell them that in America my skin is considered very undesirable, in hope of relativizing their beauty standards for them. Instead, they laughed at how stupid Americans are for not knowing that their white skin is the most beautiful.

I was continually amazed at how rarely I saw women with dark, tanned skin. Occasionally I saw darkly tanned women on crowded Taipei buses only to discover that they were Chinese American visitors. In the summertime, parents often scold young girls for playing outdoors in bright daylight as the fun of outdoor play outweighs the little girls' desire for fair skin. For rebellious women, refusing to carry a parasol serves as a form of cultural resistance. I recall once accompanying a feminist Taiwanese friend who defiantly walked about without the protection of a flowered parasol on an oppressively bright, hot afternoon. As I walked beside her, I felt the sharp sting of the sun on my skin but was too embarrassed to take out my "sun umbrella" for protection and conform to the highly feminized mode of comportment that is holding a parasol.

Boys and men, by contrast, carry sun umbrellas only when walking with women or babies for whom they provide shade. Boys and young men enjoy spending long hours playing basketball on unshaded outdoor courts. On men, darkly tanned skin represents masculinity and freedom. High school boys who study for their college entry exams all summer appear feminized in contrast to vocational school boys their age who play outdoors, developing deep tans. One bridal salon manager's husband smiled when I inquired about his darkening skin. His wife, who often commented that I made her look inferior because of my fair skin, boasted that he went swimming every morning in the summertime (his status as the boss allows him this leisure). And yet, dark skin, though it is masculinizing, can index low-class status, too. The darkest-skinned people in Taiwan (except for the rare expatriate executive, embassy official, or university student of African descent) are the Thai and Filipino male construction workers, who labor shirtless six days a week. Darkness is tough and masculine; fairness is soft, sweet, feminine, and upwardly mobile.

Multinational cosmetic companies unabashedly exploit culturally contingent beauty ideals. The very same companies that push self-tanning lotions in the United States promote whitening lotions in East Asia. For sale in Taiwan are two very different types of whiteners. One type is sunscreen—no different from sunscreens sold in the United States, but advertisements in Taiwan promote them as skin lighteners. The second type chemically slows or stops melanin production by interfering with melanin-producing cells. These products are very costly when offered by multinational luxury cosmetic companies like Christian Dior and Estée Lauder. Shiseido's line of whitening products costs upward of NT $2,500 ($100 U.S.) for a one-to-three-month supply. A French cosmetics executive working in Taipei told me that his company refuses to develop its own line of melanin-inhibitors despite what he knows to be the strong market for them in Taiwan, Hong Kong, Korea, Japan, Singapore, and Malaysia. The CEO of his company worries that melanin-inhibitors are excessively invasive, altering the human body's natural system of protecting the skin from cancer-causing ultraviolet light. Inhibiting melanin production may prove life-threatening, particularly if women who use such products feel emboldened to go outdoors without sun protection because they have a chemical means of preventing tanning. His concern, of course, is about future lawsuits of the sort filed against silicon breast implant manufacturers.

This same cosmetics executive laughed when telling me that recently his company had had to airlift additional supplies of self-tanning lotions from France to Taiwan. Knowing that some women in Hong Kong use self-tanning lotions on their legs in lieu of wearing panty hose in the summer, even while using whitening lotions on their upper bodies, he had imported self-tanning products to Taiwan to test the market for them. The supplies sold out so rapidly that the company's headquarters accused him of diverting the products back to Europe to cheat the company of money. Although he had no hard data on who purchased the self-tanners, he had heard the products were bought by men. Actually, this is not so surprising. Men who hold office jobs and work long hours indoors do not have much opportunity to tan themselves and combat the effeminate look their occupations produce. Certainly not all men in Taipei have dark skin (and I am sure there are plenty who prefer to be fairer skinned to show they do not perform outdoor labor), but tanned skin has become one more fashionable habit of masculinity, in addition to smoking, drinking, and betel nut chewing. Even as gendered power structures in families and workplaces are blurring, gender is written in increasingly dramatic terms right on the skin. The contrast of male and female skin tones in bridal photographs is often extreme.

Brides should be fair *(bai)* in color but not stark white. Bridal stylists, of course, use foundation to bolster the bride's femininity by lightening and perfecting her skin. Applied layer upon layer, the thickness and coverage of these foundations are comparable to theatrical makeup. To provide total coverage of the bride's natural complexion, stylists make hundreds of quick dabs to the face, covering even lips, brows, and eyelids, and applying multiple layers of coverage with the already heavy foundation makeup. Those who have dark freckles or acne-darkened cheeks (both of which are very common) require more foundation. The makeup covers over such imperfections entirely; not a single blemish is evident when the stylist's work is complete. Photographic lighting and focusing techniques completely erase the appearance of makeup-covered lumps and bumps.

After the foundation is applied, stylists use dark brown and stark white highlighting cosmetics to make the bride's face appear more "three-dimensional" *(liti)*. Along with double eyelids and round eyes, three-dimensionality of the face is coded as Western. Even in Taiwan today, Caucasians are sometimes referred to by the nickname "big nose" *(da bizi)*. Although in the recent past, the Westerner's big or high *(gao)* nose was a symbol of imperialistic ugliness (e.g., Dikötter 1998), today in Taiwan many people prefer the look of a "higher" nose, deeper-set eyes, and more prominent cheekbones and chin bones than most Chinese people have. Stylists and lay people in Taiwan complained to me that Chinese faces are not as good-looking as Western ones because they are too flat. One mother, admiring my son's nose, remarked to her sister-in-law that her baby girl was so pitiful *(kelian)* because her nose was too flat. The girl's aunt agreed, saying, "She barely has a nose at all."

Cosmetic techniques for making a face look more three-dimensional are based on the observation that dark objects appear to be farther away than light objects on a two-dimensional plane such as a painting or photograph. Stylists put white highlighter along the bridge of the nose and dark brown makeup on both sides of the nose so it appears to protrude. For the many brides with round faces, dark brown makeup applied in front of the ears is supposed to make the face more oval or egg-shaped. Similarly, dark brown placed underneath the chin and white applied on the chin is meant to make the chin more prominent. Stylists also put white highlights on the skin just below the eyes and dark highlights in the upper inside corners of the eyes, where many Caucasians have a prominent nose bone. These practices were not foreign to me; as a teenager I learned the opposite technique from a fashion magazine—to put white highlights on the side of the nose and in the corners of the eye sockets so the nose appears to protrude *less*.

All of these highlights are blended into the foundation and appear in the photographs only as light effects, indiscernible as makeup per se. Loose powder is powder-puffed onto the face until the foundation makeup loses its shine. The desired finish is a perfectly matte, absolutely even skin tone with no sign of freckles, moles, or blemishes.

PAINTED EYES

Next come the eyebrows again. Soft eyebrow pencil in black or dark brown is meticulously applied onto a tiny, stiff brush and then applied to what little eyebrow hair remains after the shaving. Stylists draw the outlines of the brows with pencil and then carefully blend the lines. While working on the eyes and lips, the stylist holds her face only inches away from the bride's face, and the stylist's arm brushes against the bride's chest and shoulder.

When I had my makeup done the day of my photo shoot, I found the stylist's work on my eyelids extremely uncomfortable. Every time she paused to refuel the colors on her brush, I shifted about in my seat. As I had seen stylists do to other brides, my stylist labored over my eye makeup for a very long time—probably fifteen minutes on just my eyelids and lashes. She spread powdered eye shadows in various shades of blue over each of my eyelids and painted a fine dark line of at least five layers right at the point where my upper eyelashes rise from the skin of my eyelids. Applying eyeliner and shadow, the stylist instructed me to open my eyes, close my eyes, open, close, open, close, until my eyelids felt remarkably heavy, wet, and tired. My eyelids felt so heavy I was afraid I would not be able to open them widely for the photos. I mentioned this to the stylist, who told me they would feel better in a little while and, without pause, resumed her work, whispering open, close, up, and down commands to me, her lips just inches away from my beleaguered eyelids.

My eyelids, however tired, were spared the slivers of clear tape usually applied to brides' eyes beneath the many layers of eye shadow and liners. The slivers of tape create the appearance of eyelid folds or "double eyelids." I attended a beauty school lesson to learn more about eyelid "improving" techniques and was shocked that the teacher had enough material to last two and a half hours. The lesson analyzed five types of eyelids, hierarchized from most to least beautiful. An eye that stands out a bit from the eye socket, has thick lashes that curl upward, and has an eyelid fold that runs all the way across the lid was presented as the apex of beauty. In the middle range were eyelids whose crease runs only part of the way across the lid. The least desirable eye types have "single eyelids" that do not crease and have short, sparse eyelashes that do not curl up. Using tape (concealed by eye shadow), a stylist can move the four lower types of eyelids up at least one level in the hierarchy, sometimes two. One must pay close attention to the eyelid—determining its shape

Figure 10. Stylists create custom eyelashes, one lash at a time. (Image courtesy of Cang-ai Bridal Photography Co., 2003. Photographer: Chen Chong-ping.)

and degree of elasticity—when deciding what shape slivers to cut out from a strip of tape using fine, sharp scissors.

Eyelash curlers, false lashes, and mascara application correct *(xiu)* insufficient lashes. All but one of the 1990s brides I met wore false eyelashes in their portrait photos (as in figure 10), and most wore them on their wedding day as well. The false eyelashes in use in Taipei come in many varieties of thicknesses and lengths. Stylists choose which lashes to use based on the shape of the eyelid. Some brides have very short eyelashes, and having them curled with an eyelash-pressing device is even more frightening for them than it is for those with longer lashes. The stylist holds the device in an open position as she brings it close to the eye; when she catches the upper eyelashes, she pushes the device closed. The lashes are then curled upward in preparation for the false lashes, which will also curl sharply upward to foster the appearance of big, round eyes like those found on baby dolls (*yang wawa*, literally "Western babies"; see figure 11).

Figure 11. "Western baby dolls" decorate wedding cars; bridal stylists recreate the look of their wide, round eyes on brides. (Photograph by the author.)

Some false lashes are applied in ready-made rows of black lashes to which a fine line of glue is applied, the whole thing carefully pasted onto the line where the bride's own lashes emerge from her eyelid. During the time of my fieldwork, the most fashionable eyelash look required remarkable precision on the part of the stylist. Taking a row of very coarse false lashes in hand, the stylist cuts out tiny pieces of just one "hair" each. On the tiny tip of the "hair" (perhaps two millimeters in size) she applies a minute drop of eyelash glue and attaches the single lash to the tip of the bride's eyelid, perfecting the angle of the lash by holding it with tweezers while the glue dries. Each eye, top and bottom eyelids separately, gets at least ten of these singular, coarse lashes. Next, the stylist applies mascara to the new lashes—bringing the mascara wand as close to the underside root of the lashes as possible, just millimeters away from the eye. Some of the brides I knew prepared themselves for this experience by talking about it with their friends and coworkers who had undergone the procedure for their own photographs. The lashes and glue feel strange to most brides and are sometimes extremely uncomfortable.

Although I found the intimacy and invasiveness of the styling encounter striking, none of my informants mentioned this aspect of styling except when I raised the topic. Most had anticipated the uncomfortable and even frightening parts. None found the invasiveness particularly problematic. Differing cultural understandings of the body account for this (see Brownell 1995; Zito and Barlow 1994). Taiwan's aesthetic salons offer many services that involve intimate physical touching by an aesthetician or masseuse. Often beauty services are advertised in a way that highlights the homoerotic quality of the treatment: for example, one Taiwanese advertisement for women's massage features a nude body draped in towels beneath the hands of a large-breasted masseuse wearing a very low-cut neckline. As in the West, beauty rituals sometimes legitimize "the purchase of human touch" (Freedman 1986: 48). This sort of commercial intimacy in the name of beauty and health, though not uncommon, is expensive. Accordingly, there are class dimensions to its purchase—wealthy women consume the human touch of beauty services, working-class women sell them. Bridal makeovers are expensive, too, but they occur almost universally among Taiwanese brides as a "once in a lifetime" event. The bridal styling experience of physical intimacy with the stylist, then, may be seen as yet another kind of pampering associated with celebrity.

PAINTED LIPS

Next the stylist turns her focus to the lips. She has earlier coated the bride's lips in thick foundation makeup to erase their natural color and shape. Now, using a combination of lipstick colors on a thin lip brush, she paints new lips. Sometimes the bride's lip shape is acceptable to the stylist, and she uses the natural borders of the lips and paints within them. But frequently she paints on lips that are fuller, thinner, longer, or shorter than those the bride provides. As with eye makeup, the style of the lips can vary according to the feeling the stylist wants to give the bride's face. In a beauty school class on makeup composition, the teacher showed slides of different types of lips, teaching the students which ones were sexier, livelier, softer. She said that if she wants to make a face look sexy, she uses softer colors on the eyes and makes the lips full, dark, and shiny. If she wants to a make a face look cute, she uses lighter pink lips that are less full and emphasizes big, round eyes, using the eyelash technique just described.

All of the brides I met were already accustomed to wearing lipstick before their professional makeovers. Lipstick and making up are synonymous in Taipei, and in certain contexts, such as the offices of multinational corporations, it is inappropriate for an adult woman to leave her lips bare. At a makeup class for lay people offered by a European cosmetic company's "education department," the teacher began the class by asking us to raise a hand if we usually wore makeup. Next she asked if by "makeup" we meant lipstick only. Most of us raised our hands. The teacher gently laughed, saying that today she would teach us how to *really* use makeup, not just apply lipstick. Despite her chiding, I found a great deal of seriousness among acquaintances about lipstick wearing. Numerous times during my field research close friends and informants asked, "Don't you want to put on some lipstick?"—politely telling me to apply lipstick before a lunch appointment, after a lunch appointment, or before a snapshot was taken of coworkers enjoying a birthday cake. One friend, a multinational bank employee, complained of her female coworkers who failed to color their lips. Without lip color, she argued, the face looks tired and causes one's colleagues to feel tired, too. Her moralizing on the subject of lipstick and the media attention devoted to mandatory makeup policies at some Japanese corporations suggest that even lipstick use is less widespread than some members of society would like it to be.

By the time the bridal makeup is complete, one to two hours have passed. Having stolen glimpses of herself in the mirror from time to time, finally the bride gets to take a good long look. She first sees herself with newly painted-on eyes and lips, highlighted and contoured makeup, and hair still in curlers among the reflected photographs hanging on the wall behind her. Her new skin, new eyebrows, new eyes, and new lips are remarkably similar to those in the photographs. Stylists do not have time to pause at this point because the bride's nails must be polished, and her hair must be supplemented with hair extensions, curled, sculpted, sprayed, and pinned into shape—another time-consuming, meticulous process—before the shoot can begin.[25] As the last step in the styling process the bride goes off to a bathroom or closet, where she takes off her shirt and the stylist dabs foundation makeup to match the color of her face onto her neck, chest, shoulders, arms, and hands. By the time she is ready for the shoot, three hours have passed.

At the end of the day, when the eight-hour photo shoot is over, the bride redresses in her own clothes and goes home to remove the makeup. If she's lucky, bridal shop saleswomen or experienced friends have warned her to have chemical eye makeup remover on hand. Despite my familiarity with the proceedings, I had failed to plan ahead. First I washed my face with soap, water, and washcloth several times. These washings removed some, not all, of the foundation makeup, but my eyes were still heavily coated in stubbornly undisrupted eyeliner and mascara. I resorted to rubbing off the waterproof eye makeup with petroleum jelly and wiping down my face and eyes repeatedly with a wet cloth until most of the makeup was gone. The final traces of eyeliner wore off over the next two days. I believe I spent about the same amount of time scrubbing off the makeup—half an hour—that most stylists devote to styling the hair *and* face of grooms.

STYLING THE GROOM

Men's styling is comparatively quick. The groom's hair is styled with a brush, blow dryer, and heavy hair-sculpting sprays until each and every hair lines up perfectly, though following the groom's everyday hairstyle. Stylists apply a thin coat of facial foundation to match the groom's skin in a shade darker than the bride's foundation makeup. Occasionally a thin line of dark eyeliner is applied along the lower lashes, and sometimes a bit of rouge is applied to the groom's cheeks.

When photo assistants arrive, the groom hands them his eyeglasses to have the lenses removed, thereby preventing glare in the photos but preserving his everyday look of wearing glasses. Grooms are warned in advance to bring along an extra pair to wear between sittings. Brides, by contrast, must navigate through the day without the benefit of either eyeglasses (which would smudge her makeup) or contact lenses (which would be too uncomfortable in combination with the heavy eye makeup). Although the expectation is that brides should look much more beautiful and quite unlike their everyday appearances, salon staff assume grooms will want to wear glasses if they wear them in daily life so they will look like themselves. Of the thousands of bridal photographs I saw in Taiwan, I found only one photograph in which a bride wore glasses—in a city photo archive among other wedding photos of elite families in the 1940s.

INTERPRETATIONS

An observer can infer much about the bridal portraiture enterprise through the simple fact that stylists work on brides for at least five times the amount of time they work on grooms. Listening to my informants' voices alone, I would have to deduce that the lavish attention focused on women's beauty stems from the essential fact that "girls love beauty" and bridal photography is an inherently feminine enterprise. Unsatisfied with this explanation, I suspect much more is going on.

This chapter focuses upon the bridal face, barely touching upon the other beauty manipulations performed on brides such as hair sculpting and body padding. In almost every instance, the beauty preferences at work idealize Caucasian features over facial features and body shapes common in Taiwan.

The intense, even obsessive, attention given to the eyes suggests that cultural anxieties have projected themselves onto these and other targeted body parts. In most cases, made-up eyes suggest that a woman is overtly trying to attract male sexual attention and mark her as "open" or loose. Often they imply commodified sexuality, as with strip dancers, men's club hostesses, and models (cf. Peiss 1998). In the fantasy world of the bridal photograph, however, everyday cultural logic is suspended; made-up eyes connote the bride's near-celebrity status and worldliness, not promiscuity per se. The bride's beauty is depicted as attracting her groom's romantic affection and devotion, not his lust.

One bride told me, in the company of two stylists, that it is a Chinese custom for brides to be styled by someone else because a bride should not lift a finger (*dongshou*, literally "move a hand") on her wedding day, to insure that she has a comfortable, easy fate in marriage. When I tried to confirm this "custom," others had never heard of it. Old women laughed, saying that young people had surely invented it. My persistent questions left Xiao-lan curious. A bridal magazine editor, she conducted an informal survey of bridal stylists, asking whether they would do their own makeup as a bride. She found that even stylists are styled by someone else for bridal photo shoots and weddings. My friend found this curious, as she felt sure that the reason brides go to stylists is because they lack the knowledge and skill to make up themselves. I would argue that even marrying stylists get styled by another in large part because this beauty ritual is not merely practical; it is a meaningful experience in and of itself (cf. Furman 1997; Rooks 1996). Beauty ritual and marriage are intertwined. The change from young woman to bride on the cusp of full adulthood is not something the woman can do to herself. The transformation is too great, both literally and figuratively.

In times past, weddings centered on the bride because wedding rites served to mark her leaving one family and joining another. Wedding rituals continue to serve this function. Yet vast changes in the practice of marriage and family life have also de-centered the significance of the transfer of a woman from her parents to her in-laws, such that for young people getting married today, the wedding more strongly represents the transition to full adulthood—the shouldering of familial responsibilities and the rearing of the next generation. Why, then, should brides remain the focus?

As we have seen, decreasing female beauty is considered a hallmark of marriage, and the photographs often are talked about as the bride's last chance to revel in youthful beauty. Many brides told me that their extravagantly expensive bridal photographs served to commemorate (jinian) their beauty, captured just before the start of youth's demise. The central emphasis is for the photographs to portray the woman's beauty; depicting the couple's relationship comes in a distant second. Many talked about showing the photographs to future children to prove that their mother was once a beautiful young woman of high status, despite appearances to the contrary by the time the children are old enough to care. Others emphasized that the photographs would remind the husband that he had married a beautiful woman. Later, they could be used to show him how much he (and his family) had taken away from her. The loss of beauty, in this line of reasoning, is a result of all that a woman sacrifices of herself in marriage, not for her own benefit but for the benefit of her husband's family line. The bridal styling and photographs anticipate the restrictions on women's freedom of movement due to familial responsibilities, the loss in status married women experience vis-à-vis male peers who no longer court or "seek" *(qiu)* their attentions, and the degrading of women's appearances in marriage when women are thought to lack the incentive, time, and money to devote to beauty. While men's lives change after marriage, too, these changes are not viewed as a loss to the degree that changes to women's lives are. Only women, after all, become "inside people." This cultural logic makes sense of the focus on brides in styling and in photo albums. The drama of the wedding, from the point of view of young people, is all about the bride.

Traditional parent-dominated wedding rites take marriage as a family affair, but the bridal salon ritual of styling casts the wedding as a rite of passage for the bride as an individual. Although the groom usually accompanies her to the salon, the bride goes through her styling alone. The woman enters the salon a common woman and, after a few hours of sitting quietly, sees herself transformed into a bride.

Victor Turner's (1967) famous essay "Betwixt and Between" explores the liminal period through which young people pass during rites of passage into adulthood. During this period, initiates are no longer children but not yet adults; they are in between culturally recognized states of being. Turner argues that the liminal stage during rites of passage is not merely a waiting period; liminality is a profound, cosmologically significant experience. In the Ndembu initiation rituals studied by Turner, initiates in this stage are said to be as if dead but also as if not yet born—in a superhuman or divine space of nonbeing. Could something so profound take place in Taiwanese bridal salons—temples to consumer one-upmanship? We might expect such depth of experience and intensity of meaning to occur in traditional wedding practices but not in the crass commercial endeavors of the bridal stylists and photographers. Because of the tendency to assume that real human meaning exists only outside the commercial sphere (see Miller 1995b; see Lury 1996), one imagines that Taiwan's bridal industry should be the last place on earth where one might expect to brush up against divinity. Most Taiwanese would agree; bridal salons are never talked about as places of spiritual significance.

And yet, consider that in the transformation from woman to bride, the individual woman is lost. Immobilized by her heavy false hair, false lashes, tight-bodiced gown, and wide skirts with crinoline or hooped slips, the woman loses not only her own defining features but also the ability to move her body as usual. Women who normally need corrective eyeglasses or contact lenses are expected to get through the photo shoot (and, later, the wedding day) without the eyesight to which they are accustomed. Looking and feeling unlike themselves, brides may indeed experience a sense of their own dissolution, perhaps even a sense of entering a temporary state of nonbeing. Similarly, if one takes the concept of "superhuman" broadly, the constant invoking of the bride as celebrity comes to mind. Stuart Ewen (1988: 93) writes of celebrities: "In their ability to magnify, and to create near universal recognition, the mass media are able to invest the everyday lives of formerly everyday people [celebrities] with a magical sense of value, a secularized imprint of the sacred." In a world preoccupied with status competition and upward mobility, celebrities—with their riches, lofty status, and cosmopolitan lifestyles—are rather godlike.

The bride-as-celebrity metaphor also helps to make interpretative sense of bridal stylings. Professional stylists hold sway over celebrities when it comes to their appearance on stage because during a performance the celebrity's body is not her or his own. It does not matter how a star prefers to wear her hair and makeup because when she's on stage her body is not a means of *self*-expression; she is not herself but her character. Film production companies employ armies of professionals to control every minute aspect of a star's appearance. The same, on a much smaller scale, is true of the bridal photography production process. The final product is too important to leave up to the untrained whims of individual brides and their grooms.[26]

Because the context is so divergent from everyday life, bridal styling need not impose its practices and beauty standards on everyday women. Unlike other practitioners of beauty services, stylists have no need to convince their clients of how unattractive or defective their bodies are to sell services or wares that can correct the body's "defects." Admittedly, stylists receive training that constructs their work in terms of correcting the natural defects of Taiwanese skin, eyes, noses, lips, breasts, and hips. The important point is that stylists do not explain their work to their clients; they do not train brides to investigate their bodies for defects that can be corrected for the price of false eyelashes and razor blades. Aestheticians performing facials, by contrast, tend to mention every imperfection as they work ("Your skin is so dry" or "I managed to remove all but one of your blackhead pimples"). Their words have implications for consumption: "Buy this terrific moisturizer" or "Come back soon for another facial before your blackheads become numerous again." Though stylists' work is geared toward bringing normal faces in line with the outlandish, race-crossing beauty norms of the bridal industry, they need not *promulgate* the ideologies of defect that guide their work. Stylists need only create bridal beauty so the final photographs will sell.

The cultural understanding that bridal stylists possess specialized skills and technical training creates social distance between brides and stylists. This has the practical effect of preventing brides from trying to control their looks for their photographs, which helps to keep the bridal business running smoothly and to sell greater numbers of photographs. But the social distance between brides and their stylists has an unintended consequence, too. Because the work of bridal stylists is seen as technical and extremely time-consuming, the beautiful images they create have no bearing on how women ought to look in everyday life. Though big, baby-doll eyes are considered beautiful, people do not expect to see them on a daily basis.

By exposing the realities of the production of high beauty, the bridal industry inadvertently teaches consumers that its beauty standards are not only impractical for everyday life but are also, quite literally, impossible to achieve outside the photo studio. Many brides, and many more grooms, concede that women look terrible in bridal makeup—ugly and even frightening *(kongbu)*. Bridal makeovers are designed for brides' onstage performances, especially for their starring roles under photographers' bright lights. Though in professional photographs they may look beautiful (even if unrecognizably so), in person they look quite bizarre. The work of stylists teaches brides, and grooms, about the constructed nature of commercial beauty images, quietly advising brides not to bother trying to emulate constructed beauty in real life. The experience of being made over, or of watching one's fiancée go through that process, imparts the very lesson that Naomi Wolf argues American women desperately need: that commercially produced images of women are no measure by which to judge human bodies.

Through their bridal salon experiences, Taiwanese women penetrate the distant realm reserved for celebrities and models. Erving Goffman argues that the distance maintained between audiences and performers helps to create the illusion of the performer's "celestial qualities and powers" (1973: 69). By making the bride a "celebrity" for the day, bridal styling and photography break down that distance, exposing brides and grooms to a lesson in the pleasures and problems of stardom.[27] I suspect that former brides can look at women's magazine covers and see fair, flawless skin and big, baby-doll eyes without comparing their own looks too unfavorably. They need only look at their own glamorized, high-tech photographs to see their own faces, rendered almost unrecognizable, with the same fair, flawless skin and big, baby-doll eyes.

CHAPTER 6

Romance in the Photo Studio

For women, the early start time and long duration of their makeovers mark the photo-shoot day as special, but for men, taking the day off from work, rising before dawn, and spending a long day in the highly feminized[1] space of the bridal salon are chores. Grooms and grooms-to-be often brushed off my questions about their bridal salon experiences and photographs, saying that bridal photography is for women. When I chatted with grooms during their shoots, they often showed me that they had brought along newspapers to read in anticipation of boredom. One of the largest Taipei bridal shops goes so far as to provide a men's waiting room stocked with reading material, vending machines, and a television.

While grooms are expected to approach the feminine world of the bridal photography salon with indifference and even disdain, those who take their lack of interest too far cause their brides to lose face. In the bridal industry, where the bride is the star, grooms who fail to cater to their brides according to cultural norms throw the system into laughable relief.[2] Photographers and their assistants enjoyed telling me funny stories about uncooperative grooms. For example, one young man fell asleep during the shoot and refused to be awakened. Another attended the shoot only long enough to pose for a few photos and then went back to work.

Most grooms, however unenthusiastically, cooperate with the demands of the photo session, even though the process—being made up, being dressed and undressed in various costumes, being coddled by the photographer, seeing the photographer idealize the bride—is emasculating. As one young groom-to-be put it, "No girl would marry me if I refused to give her bridal photographs." Female informants agreed wholeheartedly. Occasionally, though, a groom either refuses to pay for the expensive photographs or agrees to pay but refuses to pose. Brides find this extremely embarrassing. The implication is that only a low-status woman would give herself in marriage to a man without receiving compensation in the form of romantic bridal photos.

Photographers treat grooms much as they do studio props—to enhance the beauty of the bride. It is the groom's duty to put up with his objectification gracefully, and this gesture of temporarily accepting a lower status vis-à-vis his bride contributes to the romantic quality of the photographs. However, a groom who is *too* enthusiastic about bridal photographs risks losing face himself. If he fails to exhibit masculine disdain, he may appear too dependent on his bride, too willing to be bossed around by her. Grooms' stance of "aggressive nonchalance," to borrow this phrase from Abu-Lughod (1990), adds to the romantic allure of bridal photography precisely because romance entails the subversion of everyday social norms, where husbands enjoy higher status than their wives. The ritual subversion of gender hierarchies is romantic, an expression of devotion by the groom for his bride.

In the world of transnationally circulating visual imagery, sexuality and romance are central preoccupations. Just as Taipei's bridal salons help brides appropriate mass media influenced standards of beauty, so too do they help couples appropriate images of romance. Even a Taiwanese feminist activist told me that she would want bridal salon photographs to show to her friends, though she views the beauty rituals of the Taipei bridal industry as objectifying. She feared that without a bridal album, her peers might think her marriage lacked romance.

Romantic relations, by definition, must occur through time, even if that time is brief. How peculiar, then, that still photographs can portray romance even in the absence of time. Sociologist Eva Illouz (1997) discusses the "visualization of romantic love" in mass media. Movies and other visual media have trained audiences to recognize certain "visual clichés" that signify romance. For example, a shot of a hand-holding couple walking along a deserted beach at sunset instantaneously speaks of romance without requiring the depiction of romance narratively, through time. Filmmakers rely on such visual clichés to quickly convey the quality of characters' relationships. Advertisers capitalize on the same images in print media, attaching their products to pleasant romantic associations.[3] The bridal photographer's job is to place clients within visual clichés that say "romance" even in the absence of narrative text. They do so by emulating the settings, poses, and facial expressions of romantic images found in movies and advertising photography.

Bride and groom are actress and actor. The photographer directs their performance, helping them strike romantic poses and produce romantic facial expressions. The photographs do not portray the couple's romantic life per se; they are visual constructs bearing the photographer's stamp much more than the stamp of the actual relationship between bride and groom. Photographers do not merely evoke romance; they produce it.

The social significance of emotion lies in its deployment or performance.[4] The ethnographic record is full of instances where emotional performances are socially mandatory. In Chinese weddings, the moment when the bride bids farewell to her family is one such instance. The bride is expected to cry; if she fails to do so, she risks hurting her parents by publicly suggesting that she is happy to be rid of them. This is not to say that brides like Florence, whose wedding-day tears disturbed her carefully placed false eyelashes, do not experience heartfelt sadness; the point, rather, is that we cannot fully understand such sadness in its cultural context without considering its performative aspects alongside its experiential ones. In photo shoots, the couple is expected to demonstrate romantic feelings—real, spurious, or somewhere in between.

What exactly is being performed? The Mandarin term for romance is *langman*—approximating the sound of the English "romance."[5] The concept, like the word that names it, is widely considered foreign. People I interviewed repeatedly stressed that "we Chinese" (in contrast to "you Americans") do not directly express love. The married owners of one bridal salon explained to me that the company's name, Cang Ai, points to a specifically "Chinese" perception of love. *Cang* means hidden or concealed. *Ai* means love. Chinese people, they explained, feel uncomfortable expressing love directly, so their feelings of love for one another are hidden. This bridal salon, like all others, avoids questions of a couple's feelings for each other and of their personal romantic (or unromantic) histories. Bridal salons operate on the presumption that marrying couples ought to feel love for each other but, not being of an American constitution, are unable to express themselves. Thus it is not possible to evoke the *actual* romantic feelings hidden in the couple's hearts. Rather, the bridal salon places couples in the romantic visual clichés of transnational mass media.[6]

Many informants talked about *langman* as a foreign import, but, like many things foreign in Taiwan today, romance has been domesticated.[7] Motorbikes, for example, are not indigenous to Taiwan. Motorbike riding in Taipei carries few of the connotations that it does in the United States. In Taipei, the motorcycle is the most efficient form of short-distance transportation because it allows the driver to weave in and around cars stalled in Taipei's ubiquitous traffic jams. Although some motorcyclists also own automobiles for use on longer or non-rush-hour trips, many own motorbikes because they are cheap, and use them for all kinds of transportation needs. I often saw entire families of four atop a single motorbike. Other examples of domesticated imports abound. BMW automobiles carry connotations of organized crime in Taiwan, for example. In his 1998 mayoral campaign, Taipei mayor Chen Shui-bian sought youth support by associating himself with stocking caps of the sort worn by African American men (as seen in movies and on MTV). The foreignness of items such as BMW cars and stocking caps is not necessarily erased in the process of domestication. To the contrary, their foreign status adds to their allure, contributing to the richness of their local meanings. Recognizing the powerful symbolism that foreign items carry in the Taiwan market, local companies frequently portray local products as imports by giving them English brand names and using Caucasians in their advertising. American, European, and Japanese imported goods connote upward mobility in Taiwan, where consumer consumption is the primary mode of constructing oneself as part of an imagined global elite that includes the well-off nationals of richer nations.

Images of romance are central in the construction of eliteness in globalizing Taiwan. Romance, an individualistic pursuit, takes place in the "outside" world of youth, unconstrained by the "inside" logic of familial duty and the interdependency of kin. People see romance as modern in its individualism, in contrast to marriage and family, which are tradition-bound. Illouz argues that even romance in its American manifestations is "a utopian model of the sovereignty of the individual above and often against the claims of the group" (1997: 9). In Taiwan people say that Westerners are hardened individualists who eschew even basic obligations to kin (such as housing and caring for elderly parents) while pursuing selfish desires for personal wealth and pleasure. That romance is constructed as a Western import in defiance of Chinese family values adds to its "transgressive" character, to borrow Illouz's phrasing.

Romantic photographs, therefore, connote much more than constructed feelings between bride and groom. Romance also marks them as upwardly mobile cosmopolitans who, at least prior to marriage, flout the "inside" values of selfless performance of familial duty. Images of romance serve as symbolic capital wherein couples lay claim to a host of prestige-enhancing meanings that put "the West" to local purposes.

Romance in Taipei, with its cosmopolitan cultural connotations, is prestige-enhancing for women much more so than for men, however. Zhu described her boyfriend's indifference to romance and inability to understand her desire for it as "traditional." He asserts the importance of taking good care *(hao zhaogu)* of his girlfriend and future family but is discomforted by direct expressions of loving feelings.[8] Zhu and her boyfriend's formulation of the problem between them is common. Romance and, with it, "Western" forms of relating expressively are feminized. "Chinese" or "traditional" styles of spousal relations that are more instrumental and less expressive are masculinized. The implied international hierarchy wherein the West is more modern and prestigious than Taiwan is *gendered.* The feminine in this cultural construction becomes the agent of Taiwan's globalization by insisting upon romance. The masculine, associated with parochial traditions, becomes an obstacle to progress.[9] Note, too, that photographic images of romance speak of a time-bound process atemporally through visual clichés but that these same visualizations of romance also speak of time in another sense: feminized romance is progressive and masculinized tradition is stuck in the past.

It is neither a natural outgrowth of capitalism nor a mere coincidence that romance, femininity, and "the West" come together in this cultural logic. Taiwan's transformation from an agrarian to an industrialized capitalist economy happened in the context of direct American political and economic patronage. Republic of China policy makers and educated citizens specifically looked to American models to guide Taiwan's modernization. Information about American society was brought back by scholars who traveled abroad for their studies and was inferred from books, movies, and television broadcasts. American companies sold beauty and hygiene products through ad campaigns that promised modernity together with consumer items such as soap. Women's magazines, for example, held up idealized representations of American marriages and families to serve as models for the Chinese middle class in Taiwan. One such article glorifies the American custom of putting children to sleep early in the evening. This, the author points out, allows married couples time alone to develop their personal relationship, whereas in Taiwan children stay up late and go to sleep with their parents, leaving little time for couples to focus on their marital relationship ("'Tai Kong' Jiating Wenti Duo" 1984). The article denigrates the

"Chinese" practice of keeping children up until adults are ready for bed as putting family over and above the personal relations of marriage. Magazine authors and editors sought to focus greater attention on interpersonal relationships by means of contrasting Taiwan to its wealthier political patron, the United States.[10] These women argued that the people of Taiwan ought to emulate not only American economic structures but American styles of spousal relations as well. They implied that traditional modes of spousal relations were backward while the emulation of perceived American modes was forward-thinking.

There is one more way in which the atemporal visual images of romance produced in bridal salons are relocated in time. The production of those images requires that brides and grooms perform romance in the photo studio in real time. Indeed, the groom's gift to the bride—paying for the photographs and making himself available for the photographer's manipulations—is cast as a real live romantic gesture, not just a constructed image. The groom's gesture of acquiescence to the feminine/romantic/modern for the benefit of his bride is, in and of itself, romantic.

GENDER HIERARCHY AND ROMANCE

The groom's performance in the photo studio is romantic precisely because it topples the expected gender hierarchy of marriage, in which it is the wife who is supposed to acquiesce to the husband. In American media depictions of romance, the romantic moment often hinges on issues of inequality. Janice Radway's (1984) study of mass-marketed romance fiction makes the connection between romance and inequality clear: A beautiful heroine brings forth the feminine, nurturing side of a hyper-masculine hero, who is moved to a dramatic profession of his adoration for her. The climax of these novels shows the once-womanizing hero publicly renouncing his old ways. Whereas he previously treated the heroine as yet another sexual object, now he renounces his masculine prerogative in the name of love. Radway's research among housewives who compulsively consumed romance fiction revealed that such novels were popular because they reversed the everyday experiences of gender relations lived out by the readers. Popular, transnationally circulating Hollywood films very frequently exhibit the same logic, in which the hero, in the end, gives up his old masculine identity (if not his very life) for the heroine.

In real life, romance can work in similar ways. Holland and Eisenhart (1990) found that romance was a game of status differentials played by the white middle-class American college students they studied in the early 1980s. High status for women was marked by their ability to command men's attention in the form of gifts, invitations for dates, and other gestures of esteem without allowing commensurate physical intimacy. High status for men, however, was marked by their ability to demand physical intimacies from women without having to provide romantic gestures of esteem. Dating was a zero-sum game of jockeying for status. Whoever came out on top (by giving less and receiving more) earned a higher ranking on what the authors call "the sexual auction block." When the woman won, receiving male attention without allowing proportionate sexual intimacy, it was romantic. His actions attested to her high status. When the man won, receiving sexual intimacy without proportionate gestures of esteem, it was female promiscuity. Her actions attested to her low status.

If romance is a period of female dominance and male subjugation, the marriage that results generally reverses these relations. Even in the present era of improved educational and career opportunities for women, women in dual-wage-earning families perform most of the household and child care labor (Hochschild 1989).[11] The politics of romance is problematic because romance is short and fleeting—a phone call, a special date, a marriage proposal, a wedding. Romance comes in interspersed moments; marriage comes in blocks of continuous years. Hence, American feminists have often derided romance as mystifying gender relations. Kate Millett, for example, writes that some mistakenly see romantic love as softening the blows of Western patriarchy, but romance, she claims, does not alleviate women's situation economically, socially, or politically: "While a palliative to the injustice of woman's social position, chivalry is also a technique for disguising it" (1970: 37; see also Coward 1983; Firestone 1970). This helps to explain the immense popularity of romance fiction. As Snitow (1983: 252) puts it, women's "one socially acceptable moment of transcendence is romance," making it a point of constant return in fantasy.

I would add to these arguments that romance simultaneously engages both gender and class politics. In romance, women not only attempt to get "the upper hand" (as the women in Holland and Eisenhart's study phrased it) in the relationship with their lovers, but they also negotiate status differences *between* women. Because gender and class are always intimately intertwined, romantic fantasies can also be read as female fantasies about upward mobility.

THE ROMANCE OF BRIDAL PHOTOGRAPHS

I have already argued that the groom makes two sacrifices, two romantic gestures, toward his bride at the bridal photography salon. The first is shelling out the money for a costly package of gowns, makeover, and photographs. The second is posing in the photographs that focus squarely on her, serving as yet another prop at the photographer's command to enhance her beautiful image. Beyond these gestures, though, there is even more romance afoot in bridal photo studios. One photographer, urging me to experience being photographed myself in order to understand it better, told me, *bei pai jiu shi bei ai*—"to be photographed is to be loved"; the verbs here, "to photograph" and "to love," rhyme. Photographers are romantic heroes.

In Taipei, photography is an extremely popular hobby among men.[12] Every woman I met owned an automatic camera, but ownership of specialized photographic equipment and participation in camera clubs were more common among men. I was surprised, frequently, by the extensive and expensive camera equipment that even the least wealthy grooms I interviewed possessed. I sometimes enlisted their help and equipment in making slides of their photo albums, in fact. Women are one of men's favored photographic subjects. A popular dating activity is for a couple to go to a scenic park where the man takes photographs of the woman, who usually poses alone against the scenery.[13] The act of taking a photograph is, in this context, considered romantic. The man, looking at the woman through his viewfinder, demonstrates his appreciation for her beauty by showering her with his photographic attentions. But the cultural logic of the romance of photography is asymmetrical. Men, it is said, like to be behind the camera, not in front of it.[14]

A Taiwanese television commercial captures the association of romance with photography well. A man takes photographs of his girlfriend on generic film and the resulting photographs are poor. The woman, angered by the photographs, throws them at him and turns away from him. When he takes a new set of photos of her on name-brand film, the results are beautiful and the woman embraces him lovingly in response. Similarly, single women sometimes show off photographs taken of them by boyfriends as evidence not only of their own beauty but also of the man's affections. In cultural constructions of photography as a social act, gender often takes center stage.

Bridal photography sessions are loaded with romantic undertones.

Everyone involved professes that the photographs are primarily for the bride's benefit and that providing her with the opportunity to have such photographs is a gesture a man must make for his future wife. The bride is the star. The groom, by contrast, must patiently put up with the emasculating experience of the photo shoot. No longer looking but looked at, he joins his bride in the feminized position of visual object. The groom may pose in only one-quarter to one-half of the shots, in many of which he will be positioned as an accessory to the bride, only occasionally as subject in his own right. And the now-feminized groom must pay for the photographs to boot.

In the photo shoot it is the photographer, not the groom, who lavishes the bride with the special treatment and attention characteristic of romantic rituals. He compliments her beauty repeatedly and treats her as if he holds her in highest esteem. He devotes the day to studying her face and personality to yield portraits that will earn her higher prestige among her peers. If the commercial context were absent, the photographer's actions would certainly be understood as romantic.[15] Photographers I observed at work always downplayed the commercial aspects of their relationship to the bride, seeking to make her feel understood and appreciated as a unique individual. The photographer's incentive, of course, is to produce photographs that will sell, resulting in commissions. If he successfully woos the bride into gorgeous poses, the photographs sell themselves. If he can create the impression that he has served the bride better because of the special, intimate quality of their relationship, the bride may demand that her groom purchase even more photographs to express her appreciation of the photographer and her enthusiasm for his work. The groom buys this experience of idealization for his bride as part of his obligation to her, and he gets at least partial credit for what seem to be the photographer's labors of love.

THE PHOTOGRAPHER AS ROMANTIC HERO

Bridal salon employees construct photographers as artists and invest them with authority. While saleswomen are introduced by name or nickname, photographers are introduced as *sheyingshi* (photography master, photographer). When photographers step onto the shop floor, saleswomen perform gestures of deference by pointing them out and talking up their talents or soliciting their opinions on matters such as the selection of a frame. When saleswomen show their customers sample albums, they emphasize the importance of the photography in ways that suggest reverence for the photographer's artistic capabilities, even though other aspects of the album may actually contribute more to its airs of sophistication. No matter how talented the photographer may be, sloppy graphics, poor-quality mounting work, and a cheap album cover make for a low-prestige album. Once a couple has put down a deposit on a bridal package, saleswomen further talk up the skill of the photographer assigned to their clients by complimenting his work and showing off sample albums that he (is said to have) produced.[16] Stylists, too, defer to photographers' specific requests for makeup and styling changes. In addition to constructing photographers as heroes in the industry through their gestures of deference, the efforts of bridal salon staff to bolster the figure of the photographer serve to reduce production costs. Customers convinced of their photographer's professionalism and high status are more likely to defer to his choices during the shoot and less likely to make time-consuming special requests.[17]

The Photographer holds a certain cultural mystique. Many people believe that Taipei's most famous photographers are outstanding womanizers, sleeping with the many beautiful models and celebrities they photograph in suggestive poses and scanty dress. As in the United States, it is rumored that the best photographers have a seductive effect on women who pose for them, causing otherwise restrained women to want to undress in front of the camera. Although bridal photographers are not specifically coded this way, many actively seek to present themselves within the trope of the famous photographer—fashionable, outgoing, cosmopolitan, and capable of extracting the feelings they want to photograph. Photographers told me that a photographer, even if constitutionally shy, must be outgoing and expressive with clients. Outgoingness is often coded in Taiwanese society as a foreign trait, and the bridal photographer's role is likened to work in show business, where those who work with stars must be worldly and confident as they emulate New York and Hollywood media norms and have frequent contact with sexy foreign models.

These constructions of the photographer as creative, seductive, and skilled at manipulating subjects from behind his camera were probably introduced to Taiwan from abroad, both through the formal training Taiwanese photographers received in Japan, the United States, and Europe and through translated photography writings and advertisements. The earliest Chinese book on photography I found was published in Shanghai in 1930 and makes frequent reference to English photographic terminology, providing translations. More broadly influential in

Taiwan, one imagines, were the photography hobbyist magazines that arose in the mid-1980s, when Taiwan's economic boom and political liberalization fueled the consumption of photographic equipment by laymen. Photography magazines were supported by the advertising dollars of multinational photography supply corporations such as Fuji, Kodak, and Konica. As these magazines helped to popularize photography and spread knowledge of the array of products available to amateur and professional photographers, they also brought masculine constructions of photographers and photography from abroad.

In these magazines, film advertisements frequently presented images of seminude women, and advertisements for cameras likened the lens to a phallus. The photographic gaze, in turn, carries associations of sexual penetration.[18] In the context of bridal portraiture, this penetration is reconstituted as a penetration of the personality *(gexing)*, which photographers seek to "bring out" in the form of natural-looking facial expressions that suggest spontaneity.

Taipei has a growing number of female bridal photographers, whose very presence, one might assume, should undermine the masculinization of their art. In 1997, I estimated that less than one-quarter of Taipei bridal photographers were women. Yet public perception was that photographers should be male. Male photographers and salon owners I interviewed told me that photography is physically demanding work, requiring stamina for moving back and forth from set to camera and strength for carrying the heavy commercial-quality gear on location shoots. In other words, the work is ideally suited for strong men. Female photographers, though they might complain of tiredness after a shoot, told me that the real problem with being a female photographer is that some clients do not trust their abilities.[19] Working in a cultural context where the act of photographing a subject is sexualized, female photographers present themselves in masculinized styles to counterbalance the illogic of a female photographer. They wear youthful clothing, like denim jeans, that is also rugged-looking and comfortable. Their comparatively masculine styles of clothing allow freer range of motion, unlike the fashionable outfits, including high heels and tight skirts, that stylists wear. Female photographers also deploy masculine styles of speech and comportment to appear more like "real photographers" who successfully command and direct action.

Note that photography is a masculine-gendered social act regardless of the sex of the photographer. The photographer occupies a masculine position, seducing the feminized photographic subject into expressiveness. Even if the photographer is female and the subject male, the relation between them is one of masculinized position to feminized. The photographer is in charge; the subject's duty is to obey his commands and respond positively to his talk aimed at making the subject comfortable, relaxed, and responsive.[20]

THE BRIDE AS ROMANTIC HEROINE

Whenever I saw a bride emerge from the dressing room for the first time, I was struck by the recognition that she was no longer an ordinary woman but was now a *bride*. I expected grooms to gush, but they usually did not. One groom smiled broadly and told me, yes, his bride looked beautiful, though he did not say so to her. Another groom laughed and said his bride looked so unlike herself that day that it frightened him; he was repelled. My husband, after our photo shoot, admitted that he had been afraid to get near me after the makeover. I wore so much makeup, and my hair was so sculpted that I seemed like a wet painting, best left alone to dry. Photographers, however, step up and lavish their brides with compliments: "You are *so* beautiful!" Though they act as if their reaction is genuine (and at times it may be), getting the bride emotionally warmed up for the shoot is what is actually at stake.

Many brides, myself included, do not feel quite like themselves in the costume. The foundation makes skin feel thick and artificial. False lashes and eyelid tape, together with many layers of eyeliner and eye shadow, make even the most habitual action—blinking—feel awkward. Afraid they will mess up the fastidious work of hairstylists, brides hold their heads steady and move slowly. The weight of the artificial hair added for extra height shifts the head from its accustomed center of gravity, adding to the feeling of clumsiness that comes from not wearing contacts or glasses to correct eyesight as usual. The dresses seem fragile, as though with one wrong move the clips that hold gown to body might pop open. (Photo-shoot gowns are not altered for use by specific body shapes. They run large in size and are clipped on.) The thick crinoline slips and puffy skirts spanning a diameter of three to four feet add to the sense of ineptness. A bridal costume is quite immobilizing.[21] Immobility, however, suits the bride's role well. She is the object of the shoot, not its agent. Stylists and photography assistants anticipate the bride's awkwardness and guide her through the motions, teaching her how to sit, assuring her that the dress will not suddenly split open or slide off. They take responsibility for every detail of her appearance. She need not powder her own nose, or adjust her own necklace; everything is taken care of by the professionals.

The awkwardness of the bride's costume and the importance of the day's work of producing photographs for public display make many brides nervous at the start of shoots. Furthermore, the photo shoot is itself a marriage ritual not unlike the formal wedding rites that come after the shoot. Although couples do not begin calling themselves married as soon as the shoot is over, couples are very reluctant to turn back and call off the marriage after they have taken this step. It is not only embarrassing but considered a grave waste (and, to bridal salon staff and other outsiders, a humorous event) when the rare couple breaks up after their photos have been produced. Though not the wedding day, the day of the shoot is a big day nevertheless.

The bride's nervousness is a big problem for the photographer. Photos of brides who look terrified do not sell. Photographers, therefore, see themselves as managing not only the lights and equipment but also the emotions in the room. The photographer tells her what sort of feeling *(ganjue)* and facial expression *(biaoqing)* to convey—happy, demure, romantic, cool—and helps her to contain undesired feelings such as boredom, fatigue, embarrassment, clumsiness, or giddy excitement. Rarely, a bride or a groom evidences model-like talent for posing. More often, the photographer must guide each individual in every minute aspect of nearly one hundred poses in a day's session.

While the bride undergoes the final stages of costuming, the photographer and assistants prepare the equipment, loading rolls of the expensive 120-millimeter film onto multiple camera backs to speed up the process. They prepare different types of film—color, black and white, tungsten, and slide films for "cross processing"—for different effects. They also measure light quality across the set and ready backdrops and other props for the first few scenes.

Photographers and their assistants normally have clearly defined roles. Photographers were once themselves assistants. Assistants earn the lowest pay of all the workers in bridal shops. Most are young—recent graduates of vocational high schools or colleges, where they receive excellent training on equipment and technology and little schooling in the essential skills of making photographed subjects feel comfortable and helping them pose. When possible, a photographer always works with the same assistant or two. They form teams and learn to coordinate their efforts easily without requiring many words for effective communication. If the photographer calls out that this shot will use the blue backdrop, the assistant automatically knows what type of lighting is called for and what props to set up. The photographer might then tell the assistant that the first shots will be half-body shots, and the assistant knows how to seat the couple and adjust their costumes accordingly. They must work together efficiently to meet salon owners' expectations of nearly one hundred sellable shots taken in an eight-hour period that includes lengthy breaks for the bride's costume and styling changes.

The assistant in charge of posing (sometimes there is one for lighting and one for posing; sometimes one assistant handles both) goes to work on the subject. Noting that the bride's hair and makeup are still in place, the assistant checks her clothes—folding each crease in the dress just so, checking to be sure the bride's neckline has not dipped so low that her breast padding shows, adjusting necklaces so the pendant hangs right in the center. Next he or she helps the couple pose. Some assistants put their hands on the subjects and move their limbs and bodies into place. Others demonstrate the desired pose, piece by piece. A good pose is complex. Many shots are taken with a shallow depth of field, meaning that the area of the set that will be in focus in the final product is a narrow plane. The effect is to make the backdrop slightly out of focus so that its imperfections are not seen on the printed photograph. The assistant arranges bride and groom within that narrow plane of space, posed so their bodies seem to gesture toward each other even though they are side by side. This requires poses that do not come naturally to the uninitiated—a shoulder pushed back, neck jutted out, head tilted a certain way. The assistant must show the bride exactly how to position her feet, even though they are well hidden under puffy skirts. If she crosses her legs just so, it will improve her posture and help her lean in the right way. Hands, too, contribute to the pose. Assistants instruct subjects on the importance of holding the bouquet extremely lightly so as not to show the slightest tenseness in the hands, arms, and upper body. It is this extraordinary attention to minute details that creates the near-commercial quality of the final photographs.

Shoots I observed involved as many as five set changes and a dozen poses within thirty minutes, before the bride returned to the stylist for a costume, hair, and makeup change. Though assistants know which props to use with which backdrops and do the work of getting them in place, only the photographer looks through the viewfinder and sees which props need to be adjusted, which limbs need to turn a little.[22] Typically, assistants get the major pieces of a shot in order and the photographer makes final adjustments for perfection, such as changing the angle of a basket of flowers or moving the veil so it brushes against the groom's shoulder.

THE PHOTOGRAPHER'S FEMINIZATION

In the 1980s, multiple photographers were stationed in various studios and outdoor locations while couples, dressed in costume, shuffled between photographers to have their photos taken in different settings. Today, photographers take on what they call "cases" and cater to individual brides, rather than specializing in one scene and one pose. The photographer/bride relationship has become personalized, assuming associations of personal intimacy that were absent from photographic relations in the industry in its recent past. The personalization of photographic services is, of course, a sales technique. And it seems to be working. Whereas in the early 1990s a standard album contained perhaps twenty photos, by the late 1990s it was increasingly common for couples to purchase fifty or sixty photos and display two albums and two framed enlargements instead of just one.

A photographer must carefully finesse the relationship with the couple. On one hand, a photographer needs to convey professionalism to elicit the couple's compliance on the set. On the other hand, the photographer needs to come across as warm and friendly to avoid alienating the bride and groom with too much authority-invoking professionalism. If the bride is not comfortable with the photographer, she might produce facial expressions that are stiff or dull. In the context of their brief relationship, a good deal of this trust comes from the photographer's self-presentation—through clothing, gesture, and speech.

Many male photographers in Taipei portray themselves as creative types and rule-breakers who challenge conventional male roles and celebrate the trends of youthful fashion. Ironically, given cultural constructions of the act of photographing as masculine, male photographers often depart from conventional styles of masculine self-presentation (dress, grooming, comportment, and speech). Many male photographers I met wore their hair long, with bleached highlights, and/or wore unusually fashionable clothing by men's standards. For example, Xiao-fang, a photographer in his late thirties, wore his bleached hair cut short and spiked up with stiff hair gel. He wore designer clothing purchased from boutiques for stylish young men. He spoke in a feminized style of expressive speech and used feminized physical gestures as well.[23] Like many photographers (and in contrast to stylists, who are usually quiet), he spoke about his family life in order to warm up brides, even showing them photographs of his baby daughter.

Once a scene and pose are set up just right, the photographer talks to the bride and groom from behind his camera, cooing in gentle tones, "*Lovely*, you're beautiful, just beautiful. Groom, *smile* a little bit. Bride, look at the camera, look up a little bit, not too much! Relax a little. Perfect. Now don't you move! Perfect. Beautiful. One-two-three!" Photographers' talk is peppered with elements of baby talk—the tones more sing-songy, the pitch higher, the mood overly enthusiastic, commands softened with diminutives like "a little bit" *(yi-dian)*, words repeated twice *(hao de, hao de)*, and sentences finished in "ah" sounds *(bu yao dong a!* instead of *bu yao dong!)*.[24] This type of speech and accompanying behavior is called "sweet talk" (described as *hong hong*), used especially for talking to small children or beloved pets. When spoken to an adult, sweet talk conveys a sense of both intimacy and hierarchical relations, for it evokes the image of a parent speaking to a child. Lovers sometimes speak to each other this way in private, conveying intimacy and nurturance. Photographers thus talk to brides from behind the camera as if they were intimate. If in any other context a man were to speak to her in this tone and lavish her with so many compliments, any woman would assume he was expressing a sexual interest in her. Female photographers I observed at work also spoke sweet talk to clients when behind the camera and took this a step further than most male photographers dared by calling the groom "handsome boy" or "stud" *(shuai-ge)*, whereas male photographers tended to use the less-diminutive names "husband" and "groom." Photographers of either sex, however, call the bride "wife," "bride," "beautiful bride," "princess," or "beautiful lady."[25]

When I interviewed photographers about their peculiar manner of speech, they expressed instrumental motives. Most explicitly, the purpose is to direct the subject's pose from afar. The assistant has set up most of the pose; now assistant and photographer must be out of the way of the lens. Only the bride and groom are left on stage, bright lights in their eyes, trying to hold their bodies in awkward poses without looking too stiff while trying to produce natural-looking facial expressions, anticipating the flash of light to come while repressing the need to blink. The photographer uses his voice to soothe them while directing their posing as if by remote control. The camera, perched on a large rolling stand, sits behind the lights in the darkness of the studio. Since the bride and groom have their eyes fixed on a designated object and cannot clearly see the photographer's face, the photographer's voice carries the weight of the

Figure 12. Photographers work with the emotions of their subjects to elicit pleasing poses and expressions that look natural, not stiff. The expressiveness of these models is difficult to replicate with real brides and grooms. (Image courtesy of Cang-ai Bridal Photography Co., 2003. Photographer: Jenny Chang.)

interaction between them. Photographers explained to me that they must be careful not to sound too direct or harsh, which might make the couple feel inadequate and nervous. Hence, they sweet-talk their subjects into cooperation with their directions.

Coaxing clients to behave rather unlike themselves and still look "natural" requires a complex set of skills. Photographers use the word "communication" *(goutong)* as a gloss for the work they do in controlling and bringing out the subject's feelings and sometimes talk about their work as the management of emotion.[26] Most reported that they focus on the personal details offered by the bride and groom, especially their occupations, to infer personality characteristics and forge bonds with their clients. Referring to the bride and groom's occupations or personal backgrounds makes them feel understood: "You're in public relations; you're not a shy person! Let's see you smile." Photographers work to photograph very different moods (see figure 12). Depending on the desired feeling for a group of photos, the photographer may try to make a woman feel glamorous, sophisticated, cutesy, or demure, using words that connote the desired feeling and describing images for the couple to visualize as they pose. The kind of emotion work that photographers do, moreover, is not typically masculine behavior in Taiwan; rather, the bridal photographer brings himself/herself into a feminized position of service vis-à-vis the subject.

Photographer Xiao-yu described one incident in which her attempt to elicit emotion from a bride went too far. The bride was one of the very small minority who invite parents to be in some of the bridal photos. As the bride and her mother were primped for the shoot, Xiao-yu (herself unmarried) talked about how sad it is to leave one's home at marriage. She had hoped to capture the bride's and mother's culturally honored sadness in some photographs. Perhaps because the daughter, dressed as a bride, was beginning to feel the part, and causing her mother to feel the part too, both mother and daughter became more than a little sad. Not only did their tears create a dilemma for the makeup artist, but the bride remained pensive for the rest of the shoot, even after her mother went home. The photographer had been *too* successful at eliciting the subjects' feelings, and the photographs turned out looking too grim.

Photographers frequently complained to me of the difficulty of bringing introverted *(neixiang)* subjects out of their shells enough to look "natural" in poses and express feeling on their faces. It seems to me that the problem of shy subjects is actually a problem of the genre of photographs and the importance to studios of selling a great many photos. If a couple is reluctant to take up poses that are lively *(huopo)*, sexy *(xinggan)*, or cutesy *(ke ai)*, the photographer's repertoire of varied shots is diminished. Couples are not likely to buy more than their package's base number of photographs if all of their shots are similar in facial expression and pose, and photographers know that a cutesy pose with a serious or lifeless facial expression is unlikely to sell.

Photographers often contrasted their introverted clients with Americans, whose (imagined) styles of interaction they try to get their clients to emulate. One photographer put it: "We Chinese are not as outgoing as Americans. Americans are easy to photograph because they aren't embarrassed to express feelings openly."[27] The "problem" of Chinese people not being enough like "Americans" points to the character of bridal photographs in Taiwan; they are explicitly working to create Westernized representations of the couples in which even the shiest selves come out and express themselves openly for public viewing in photographs. Of course, not all Americans behave like the characters seen on television! Although Taiwanese associates considered me a paragon of American outgoingness, I found posing extremely difficult, and as a result, my photo album does not contain the wide variety of feelings that photographers aim to produce. From my point of view, many brides and grooms I observed at shoots seemed far more comfortable than I was in front of the camera.

Often photographers use the bride's chosen dresses as cues for the mood of the photographs they design for the couple *(bang tamen sheji)*. During Florence's shoot, the young, energetic photographer went to her side as the stylist changed her hairstyles and prepared her for the next round of photos. She had chosen a straight gold lamé gown that exposed much of her back. The stylist paired the gown with matching gloves that reached to her elbows. Having read the gown according to his own associations, the photographer announced that the next set of shots would be very cool, cold *(wo bang ni pai ku-ku, leng-leng)*. As Florence stood ready for the shoot, David teased her about her exposed back and the gown's sexy style. The photographer fussed with a tall sheet of corrugated blue plastic and special lights, repeating that the feel of these shots would be very cool. Florence said she did not know how to pose cool, so the photographer showed her how to hold her arm out straight in front, palm facing the camera, as if to say "stop." He positioned her partially behind the plastic sheet as if she were about to hide behind it. Finally Florence got the idea and provided a facial expression to match—a cool gaze with no smile, chin tilting down a bit. The photographer encouraged her, saying, "Great, excellent, very cool," and released the shutter.

Sometimes the photographer's design intentions are less clear to the couple. Many photographic subjects will stare blank-faced at the camera until told where to look and how to gesture. Others, unsure what feeling the photographer has in mind, ask out loud, "Should I smile?" "Should my expression be happy?" Photographers and assistants frequently find that they must demonstrate the desired pose and facial expression themselves—again, placing the photographer in feminized postures that would be unbefitting of a commercial photographer.

Although photography in many other contexts is sexualized (especially commercial and erotic photography), bridal photographers must explicitly desexualize their work, even though it involves much more intimate physical contact with the photographic subject than is typical in commercial shoots.[28] Both photographers and assistants frequently come into bodily contact with the bride. The photographer might have to touch the bride's neckline to adjust it perfectly or lift the bride's skirt to reposition her legs. An assistant may stand behind a bride seated on a low stool and hold up the back of her gown so its fabric forms the backdrop for a close-up of her face. Bridal salon workers become physically intimate with the bride in ways that are otherwise restricted to sexual partners, masseuses, and physicians. Photography staff, in contrast to most stylists, are predominantly male. The bride-touching they do takes place in front of the groom and is explicitly asexual, but all are aware of the occasional awkwardness it nonetheless provokes. If they must touch her body or lift her skirt, it is understood that they do so for the bride's benefit, not for their own pleasure. The attention to her every detail and focus upon her alone are, rather, for *her* pleasure—the pleasure she will take in the gorgeous photographs.

Sometimes a photo session does not go smoothly. One problem, as photographers reported, is customers who try to design the photographs themselves. This happens remarkably rarely, but all the photographers I interviewed had had at least one experience of this sort, usually of a bride who had a plan of her own for the photographs. Experienced photographers do their job well because their work is highly routinized. They have a repertoire of poses and props that they like to use, that they feel go well with particular backdrops. When clients ask for specific scenes, poses, or locations of their own choosing, photographers can get thrown off. During Florence's shoot, for example, she and her groom asked to pose for photos on a couch. The photographer agreed willingly (as was his duty), but it was clear from his actions that their innovation was difficult for him to photograph. He moved an old sofa (not a prop but used for seating at the back of the studio space) in front of the camera and draped it with satin fabric from another backdrop. He fussed with the couch, turning it first this way, then that way, experimenting with different angles and imagining how the couple would sit on it, how he would pose them. He then experimented with them. The bride lying down with the groom leaning on her back did not seem right, so he tried having the groom stand behind the couch as the bride lounged on it. After shooting just a few frames, he announced it was time to change scenes. The preparation time involved for these few frames of film was much more than the normal yet already high ratio of preparation to shooting time. In the end, although posing on the couch was their idea, Florence and David did not select a couch pose for their album. It had been a waste of time and energy for the photographer, but had he not complied, the couple might have been angered and their dissatisfaction might have harmed the rest of the shoot.[29]

Photographers must finesse their way through the contradiction between the photographer's need for tight control over the shoot and the centrality given to the bride on this day. To accomplish this, photographers told me, strong interpersonal skills are necessary. Photographers are keenly aware that theirs is a service industry and that success depends on happy customers. Whether the bride is difficult because she challenges his design authority or because she is nervous and therefore difficult to pose, the photographer must tailor his work style to accommodate her personality and needs. The bridal photographer, then, exhibits a complex kind of subservience to his or her clients. Broader cultural constructions of photographers as masculine are aided by the salon staff's demonstrations of deference to imbue the photographer with masculinized, professional authority. At the same time, photographers must perform deference to the women in the form of sweet talk and feminized comportment. That bridal photographers work in a retail service industry in itself serves to feminize them—which is not the case for commercial or fine art photographers. Bridal photographers are viewed as occupying a low rung in the ranks of their profession, even though they often earn more money than commercial photographers.

The deference photographers perform for brides is made clearer by comparing bridal photo shoots to model photo shoots. I found striking differences even when bridal photographers shot models for company advertisements. In such cases, photographers often work silently or call out simple directions to the model without any trace of sweet talk or expectation that the photographer must manage the model's emotions. Managing emotional expressions is the model's job, not the photographer's. Shoots move much more quickly as a result. Comparing my observations at bridal shoots and model shoots confirmed that a great deal of a bridal photographer's work is in building personal relationships with brides (and, to a lesser extent, grooms) and has relatively little to do with the formal work of composing photographs.

In bridal shoots even the space of the photo studio is feminized. When photographers engage in masculinized behaviors such as smoking or betel nut chewing, they wait until costume change breaks and leave the studio. The hallways outside photo studios become a masculine refuge, with smoke-filled air and masculine styles of speech and gesture prevailing.

Despite their status as paying customers, grooms know to leave the studio to smoke (and to refrain from chewing betel, which stains the teeth red). I sometimes observed grooms chatting with photographers during smoke breaks, leaving behind the airs of subservience of the photo studio and speaking to the photographer on personal terms (about age, marital status, stories, etc.). One photographer even took out his portfolio of nonbridal work to show a groom during a lengthy costume change for the bride, with photographs of nude women figuring prominently among photos of natural scenery and an old-fashioned fishing village. Bridal costume changes usually take a half hour or more, so grooms spend a good part of the day waiting for the photo shoot to resume. These waiting periods, however boring, provide a respite when the groom is no longer on stage and can engage in his everyday habits, such as smoking and reading newspapers, even while dressed in tuxedo.

CONCLUSIONS

What do photographers think about the other roles in the ménage à trois of photo studio romance—those of the bride and groom? On separate occasions several male photographers told me that they saw bridal photography as pleasurable for their female clients precisely because the photographs (and the photo shoot) reverse the gender relations of marriage by elevating women and subjugating men. They each talked about the photographs as the last time a woman can enjoy herself in this way before she spends the rest of her life as a married woman subject to the drudgeries of family responsibilities. If marriage in Taiwan today constitutes a loss in status for women and takes away women's beauty and charm—turning them into "yellow-faced wives"—then the huge, beautiful, and costly bridal photographs are the least grooms can do to recompense them for submitting to marriage.

Photographers may be more cynical than most because of their role as the constructors of romance,[30] but the view that marriage is drudgery and depletes women's beauty is much more widespread. One young, unmarried man remarked that he sees bridal photos as a "sugar-coated pill" because they make women's subjugation in marriage easier to swallow. It would be an oversimplification to say that the groom's temporary self-subjugation entails a covert agenda of procuring unpaid labor in the form of a wife, however. On some level a bride may have her own instrumental reasons for wanting the glamorizing photographs. The larger-than-life portrait hung above the couple's bed may serve as a perpetual reminder to the husband of his wife's sacrifices to him and his family over the years, evidenced by the decline in her beauty, and may be deployed by the wife to help keep her husband in line. In this sense, photographers may be seen as pawns in the battle of the sexes.

The presence of male workers in the service industry sector of Taipei is low, and male workers in beauty services are even more rare. The bridal

Figure 13. Bridal photographs, such as this streetside display outside a salon, play up the power of the bride; this one is unusual in that it anticipates the reversal of power dynamics after the wedding. (Photograph by the author, Taichung, 1997.)

photographer holds a unique social position, and his unique positioning contributes to the allure of bridal photography. The actions of the photographer—unintentionally, as far as I can tell—do far more than produce photos. The photo shoot, like the makeover, is not merely a means to an end but is a marriage rite in and of itself. In contrast to family betrothal and wedding rites, which de-emphasize the relationship between the bride and groom, the photo shoot ritualizes romantic relations. The bride is idealized and elevated by her groom at his expense, both literally and figuratively. The groom need not romance his bride himself but can still get credit for doing so. He pays the photographer to do the emotion work.

Taiwanese bridal photographs emulate "the West" on two levels at the same time. Superficially, they emulate romantic visual clichés found in movies and advertising photography, but producing such images requires *substantive* behaviors. To attain these images, couples must act out romantic practices that are seen as Western. Grooms perform romance by putting up with the demeaning shoots and by purchasing the photographs and the experience of being a star for the bride. Photographers also practice a kind of romance, seducing the couple into desired poses and expressions even though this requires photographers to feminize their demeanor in ways many men refuse to do. Questions about the off-stage relationship between bride and groom are entirely bracketed. Romance, like beauty, is bridal salon art and artifice. It is purchased. It is temporary, though its traces, recorded photographically, last a lifetime.

CHAPTER 7

Contextualizing Bridal Photos in Taiwan's Visual Culture

Photographs seem to have a unique relationship to reality because they represent a slice of actual time. One can paint, but not photograph, someone who exists only in imagination or memory. Roland Barthes argues that the photograph (the signifier) and the pictured subject (the signified) are always "glued together." When we look at a photograph we tend to see only the pictured subject; the photograph itself is as if invisible (1981: 6). Susan Sontag (1977: 154) points out that a photograph is "a material vestige of its subject," like a footprint. Photography's unique claim on reality allows it to serve as a surveillance tool of the state, in the form of mug shots, passport and driver's license photos, and FBI files.

Taiwanese bridal photographs belie photography's claim on reality. The bride frequently looks so unlike herself that her portraits might as well be paintings. The bridal portrait production process is so time-consuming, in fact, that the bridal industry could surely save time and money if the portraits were produced by painters and computer imaging. Salons could eliminate the labor costs of styling, shooting, and retouching and do away with supplies such as cosmetics, wigs, gowns, lights, cameras, film, backdrops, and props. The production process is already loaded with artifice; why not take the next step and produce beautiful brides directly rather than working on and with real women, since managing their looks and emotions is so troublesome? The reason is obvious: Without photography, bridal portraiture would lose its claim on reality and, as a result, lose its power. Even though couples may hardly recognize the bride in the final photographs, they know that the image is *of* her even if not *like* her. They were there. They endured the styling, felt the gowns, experienced the poses. With the groom made to look very much like himself, friends and family are assured that the bride posing with him must be his wife, especially if the photographer succeeded in getting shots in which she produces a signature gesture or expression that could only be hers. As the years pass, it does not matter that the woman and the bride bore little resemblance to each other at the time of the wedding. The image of the bride displayed above the couple's bed becomes memory (cf. Kuhn 1991).

What makes photography special is not its ability to capture reality but its propensity to mediate and manipulate reality while passing the photograph off as Truth. Countless observers have demonstrated the myriad ways that photographs can lie, cheat, and steal.[1] The camera decontexualizes; it fragments space, freezes time, manipulates light, and pictures subjects that are always already culturally framed both in the settings in which they were photographed and in the ways photographs are displayed, captioned, sequenced, and viewed (Burgin 1982a; see also Benjamin 1985; Eco 1982; Metz 1985). Cultural training teaches us not to see the photograph and its machinations but to look straight through to the subject instead, ignoring the powerful processes through which it is pictured.[2] The photograph's tendency to serve as an invisible medium makes it doubly powerful.

The power of photography is often implicated in lived struggles for social and political power. Photographs have had decisive influence in American military affairs in recent decades. To cite some obvious examples: Emotionally wrenching images of conflicts in Vietnam and Somalia caused American public opinion to sour on American military involvement in those places. Photographs of the aftermath of the attack on New York City's World Trade Center towers led to public demand for the American bombing of Afghanistan.

Feminist critics point to the role of photographic images in magazines and on billboards in colonizing, figuratively speaking, the white, upwardly mobile female body. These images, they say, encourage some young women to become disabled with preoccupation over their bodies' failure to conform—to norms of slenderness, for example. Just as white, middle-class women gained greater access to career mobility, body image disorders stopped some potentially upwardly mobile young women in their tracks (see Faludi 1991).

Photographs have also been used in projects of not just figurative but actual colonization. Most anthropological studies of the power of photography concern the misrepresentation, exploitation, and objectification of marginalized peoples in imperialist contexts, tracing the political manipulations of the photograph by powerful interests (e.g., Lutz and Collins 1993; Pinney 1997; Poole 1997; Vergara 1995). The consensus is that photographs serve imperialist interests by visually colonizing the Other, creating images that confirm imperialist beliefs and stereotypes.

Christopher Pinney's (1997) study provides an important counterexample, however. He found that people in contemporary India put photography to their own culturally specific purposes. They revel in photographers' ability to create highly manipulated images using composite printing and overpainting. In the city of Nagda, portraiture is an avenue for Indian self-expression, not objectification. Indian conceptualizations of personhood (also reflected in films featuring flying objects and magical transformations) make the photographer's manipulations attractive in ways that Europeans—who are culturally accustomed to perspectival representation, Western filmic conventions, and the belief in moral physiognomy and an essential, immutable selfhood—find difficult to comprehend.[3] Depending on one's worldview, photography's powers of manipulation may be used to defy reality or to create images more true to the real than the eye alone can visualize. Pinney's study reveals that photography, in the hands of Nagda photographers, does not colonize Indians even though photography had often been used for this very purpose under British rule. The problem, then, is not photography but *people.*

Does the gaze of the Taiwanese bridal photographer colonize young women in Taiwan? There are potentially two ways one might argue that it does. First, Taiwanese bridal photographs clearly objectify brides and embody potentially harmful beauty standards, whereby the natural forms that faces (and other body parts) take in Taiwan require drastic efforts to "repair." I have argued, however, that the ideas about beauty evident in bridal photographs do not spill over much into everyday life precisely because the process of producing such beautiful photographs reveals how unrealistic those beauty practices are for everyday life. Second, the photographs very clearly propagate a fantasy world in which upward mobility entails increasing acceptance of perceived Western values, especially individualism. Does this constitute another kind of colonization? On the surface it would seem so, but closer inspection reveals that bridal fantasy worlds are exaggerated opposites of the lived experiences of many couples. Young people find themselves drawn into the "inside" world of family life through marriage after years of life "outside" family domination in Taipei's vibrant urban landscape. The photographs celebrate the last hurrahs of youthful freedom before young women and men are engulfed by the demands of family life (or so young women often fear). Because the photographs appropriate the West for local purposes of creating prestige and meaning in globalizing Taiwan, it would probably be more accurate to argue that young women in Taiwan colonize the West through their photographs than vice versa.

The West as referenced by Taiwanese bridal photography is a haphazard conglomeration of projections produced especially in places like New York and Hollywood but also in Rio de Janeiro, Bombay, Tokyo, Hong Kong, and Taipei. Most often, these projections are produced with the goal of selling something: automobiles, movie tickets, deodorant, or credit. The people who absorb these projections are bombarded by so many of them that they cannot afford to seriously contemplate them all if they are to carry on with life. Given the competition for attention, the more outlandish an ad image is, the better.

Photography is a powerful advertising tool because "the power of the disembodied image is that it can free itself from the encumbrances posed by material reality and still lay claim to that reality," making photography "the land of dreams come true" (Ewen 1988: 90). In advertising photography, the substance of life is banished. The spaces pictured are "sanitized," with "no intimation of any significant action outside the frame" because "all elements of lived experience constitute potential flaws" (Ewen 1988: 89–90). The dreamland is created not only through photographic and computer trickery but also by the work of casting directors, who, for example, assemble body parts from different models to make a single perfect image. As one commercial photographer put it: "It's difficult to get the foot, ankle, and calf perfect on the same leg" (quoted in Ewen 1988: 87).[4] The idealized images produced for advertising purposes do not, argues Goffman (1979), represent human beings at all. Rather, they represent "femininity" and "masculinity" in abstract form.

Though the perfect leg that results from the assembling of body parts may be beautiful to behold, many critics have charged that such images create standards of beauty to which even the three models whose legs were used in the preceding example will compare themselves unfavorably. In societies inundated by photographic images, Sontag argues, photographs have a tendency to "usurp reality" and incite people to judge and shape social lives according to photographic standards and pho-tographable events.[5] Photography's claim on reality, after all, is a major source of its appeal and its power. Taiwanese bridal photographs join the game of usurping reality; they usurp the images and practices of com-mercial photography. In the process, the constructed nature of the "real-ity" that ad photos depict becomes clear.

LIGHTING, FOCUS, AND OTHER PHOTOGRAPHIC TECHNIQUES

The quality of light in a photograph is like the soundtrack of a film. Eerie music in the background prompts the viewer that something bad is about to happen to a favored character. Light similarly provides a subtext to the photograph and tells the viewer, indirectly or even subconsciously, how to evaluate the pictured objects or persons. Light, then, speaks about issues of social positioning.[6]

A photograph consists of chemical traces produced by light refracted through a lens onto film. Bridal photographers manipulate light in numerous ways. First, they use artificial lights: soft light boxes and white bounce umbrellas in the studio, portable spotlights on location. Colored lights create background effects. Photographers also use reflectors to fill in where artificial light sources leave off in the studio and to increase con-centrations of natural light on location shoots. Second, photographers regulate the flow of light into the camera both by setting exposure lengths and depth of focus and by exposing different varieties of film to produce desired effects. Third, photographers and assistants retouch the negatives, further manipulating the already controlled image. Fourth, photo processors regulate the outflow of light (exposure times and light diffusion) from the enlarger onto the print paper. Fifth, photographers and assistants retouch the print, hand-painting on its surface to fill in spots, cover imperfections, and add color.

The craft of bridal photography in Taiwan works from the observa-tion that commercial fashion/beauty photography deploys light in highly formulaic ways. Simulating commercial photographic techniques per-forms two different beautifying functions on brides. First, the techniques reduce the appearance of aesthetic problems. The absence of visible pores, wrinkles, and pimples is considered beautiful by many viewers. Manipulations of light that minimize the appearance of such "imperfec-tions" beautify a photograph greatly. Second, the highly formulaic tech-niques of beauty photography mark a recognizable visual genre. Viewers already know various visual genres of photographic imagery, even if they often cannot point to the visual qualities and codes that mark a given genre. Eco (1982) delineates ten different culturally contingent "codes" that mediate the relationship between the viewer and the photograph. Hard and soft focus, and large or small grain on the print, carry cultural connotations (especially gendered ones) to which viewers react, though often unconsciously (Burgin 1982b: 65).

The simulation of commercial beauty photography techniques codes the bridal portrait as belonging within that genre and, therefore, deserving the fame and idealization otherwise reserved for models and stars.[7] The presentation of bridal portraits in luxurious albums and frames further indexes fame and wealth. This move is not unlike staging a publicity event in which crowds of people are paid to act as though a person standing on a stage before them is a famous rock star. The viewer of such a scene is likely to infer that the unknown person on the stage is famous. Bridal photographers create the visual equivalent of a mob of fans for the bride by usurping the visual conventions of advertising photography. Just about everyone in Taiwan knows about bridal photography, and only the rare viewer would mistake a bridal photograph for a real magazine photo. Similarly, only a rare onlooker in Taiwan would be likely to mistake even the best karaoke singer for a real pop star.[8]

Taipei bridal photographers and photography instructors taught me the tricks of the trade. Liao Hong-peng, a bridal-photographer-turned-teacher, explained that the difference between a good-looking and a bad looking face in a photograph hinges largely on the appearance of lines running from the sides of the bottom of the nose to the sides of the mouth. The lighting determines how these lines will appear in the photograph. If the lights cast a shadow in them, the face will not look good. If light fills up the lines of the face, the lines become invisible in the photo. Other lines, such as wrinkles on the forehead and eyes, are similarly affected by light.[9] Bridal photographers use large light boxes (two or three of them, sometimes in combination with reflectors) to flood the bride's face in light from all angles. Using lots of light enables photographers to create high-key images in which relatively low variances in light (lines on the face, wrinkles and other details on the gown) are washed out while higher contrasts are emphasized. As a result, darkened brows, eyes, and lips stand out in the image against an otherwise washed-out face. The technique (and the result) is precisely the opposite of how Ansel Adams created a highly detailed nature photograph or how Stieglitz depicted O'Keeffe's face in similarly high detail.[10] Bridal photographers typically set the negative exposure time to create a standard exposure (that is, according to the specifications made by photographic equipment manufacturers), but in film processing they shorten the exposure of the print to wash out the appearance of fine lines, bumps, and pores. Underexposure also whitens a photograph, making the bride's face appear very fair. The combination of manipulating lighting in the studio and exposure in printing is a powerful tool for vanishing detail in bridal photography—and in commercial beauty photography generally— where homogeneity is valued and detail is considered ugly (see figures 14 and 15).

During the period of my fieldwork, most bridal photographs were shot without a light-diffusing filter on the lens. A more subtle diffusion is possible by using a diffusion filter on the enlarger during printing. Without creating an overly soft or blurred look, the enlarger's diffusion lens softens the photograph just enough to hide the remaining imperfections on the skin; it is a "realistic" level of blur. Because the final portraits are hand-printed, the printer can also cast a slight diffusion over selected areas of the print—the face—while leaving the rest in clear focus to show, say, the finer details in the gown.

Cross-processing was another technique I commonly saw used in Taiwan's bridal salons for creating glamorous images. Shot on slide film but developed through a special process that produces a negative, cross-processed photographs flatten out subtle light distinctions such that in many photographs the bride's nose disappears; only the dark shadows of her nostrils remain. The variations in light that would otherwise make apparent not only the sides of her nose but also the lines and bumps on her face are washed away. In the past, similar imperfection-erasing operations were accomplished through heavy diffusion, which produces a soft focus. Today, many couples see heavy diffusion as "unnatural"; they prefer photographs that have a sharper focus. Cross-processing, like the low-level diffusion filtering done at the time of printing, vanishes detail well without the telltale blurring associated with heavy diffusion.[11]

The popularity of photographic techniques that vanish detail calls into question the value of facial "three-dimensionality" often cited to me by stylists, who work to make the eyes appear deeper set, the nose more prominent.[12] There are, in fact, photographic techniques that can make a face look less flat (not just for race-crossing purposes but for countering the tendency of certain lighting conditions to create flat, two-dimensional-looking images in print). By setting up the lights so the nose casts a shadow to one side of the face while the bridge of the nose catches a highlight, the nose appears more prominent and the face more three-dimensional. Professional portraits in the United States and Europe often make use of light variations upon the face. In Taiwanese bridal portraits, however, light/dark contrasts on the face are rare.

Zheng Wei-wei, a bridal photographer, showed me a sample album of his work using shadows for dramatic effect. Wei-wei had earned a master of fine arts degree in photography at an American university and worked in New York City shooting model portfolios before returning to Taipei to work in an upscale bridal salon. Although he seemed to prefer working in and looking at what he called "cubic lighting," he explained that few clients would accept this style of portraiture. Wei-wei's cubic photographs were very much like high-key photos. Although they contained shadows, the light areas showed very little detail. Still, consumers rejected this look.

Several bridal photographers recommended that I read one or two volumes of an influential series of photography skill books produced by the Eastman Kodak Company out of New York. The entire series is available in Mandarin translation at many Taipei bookstores and libraries. Some photographers I met had taught themselves by reading these and other books. I obtained the English version of a Kodak volume on portraiture and found the following descriptions of high- and low-key lighting. The high-key technique "is excellent for glamorous, female portraits or for soft portraits of babies and children" with its brilliant whites and "contemporary, clean, well-polished look." Low-key lighting, on the other hand, "with its dark shadows and low-contrast level, . . . is dramatic and good for strong, male portraits. Low-key lighting defines strong personalities and determined people like actors and executives. Enhancing textures, emphasizing shadows, and adding a dramatic atmosphere to the photograph are the main ingredients" (Marvullo 1993: 50, 52). Another essay in the same volume devotes a few paragraphs to men's fashion photography and proclaims: "In direct contrast to fashion photography of women, we seldom, if ever, use flat lighting with men. To create the bold, masculine look desired, side lighting with hard shadows works excellently" (Perrin and Perrin 1993: 111).[13] This gendered cosmology of light is being exported to Taiwan both in the form of media images and through photography education.

Although images of the bride alone or the couple together are far more common, many albums contain one or two portraits of the groom

Figure 14. Snapshot of the author in full bridal makeup, in natural lighting outside the bridal salon. (Photograph by Michael Koch, 1997.)

Figure 15. Taiwanese bridal portrait of the author. Notice that the facial lines evident in figure 14 are washed out as a result of high-key lighting in the studio and reduced exposure time on the print. (Image courtesy of Cang-ai Bridal Photography Co., 1997. Photograph by Su Geng-shao.)

alone. In some of these, the formulaic high-key lighting is relaxed and photographers seek to portray the groom in more masculinizing light. I found one set of photographs in a sample album displayed outside a Tainan bridal salon where this was strikingly evident. A two-page sepia spread featured one image of the couple together and one of the groom alone. High-key lighting and careful positioning of lights in the first image flattened and lightened the couple's faces, leaving no shadowing and the appearance of fair skin. The lights in the second image cast a shadow beside the groom's nose, giving him a more dramatic and more three-dimensional appearance.

Extensive retouching contributes significantly to the images seen in advertising and glossy magazines. Images of aging celebrities in the United States, for example, are routinely retouched to remove wrinkles and sagging jowls. Because it is labor intensive and requires skill, retouching is prohibitively costly for most noncommercial photographic purposes (family portraits, for example). The manipulations of light and focus (in combination with the three-hour makeovers) used in Taiwanese bridal photography are comparatively cheap ways to achieve similar ends. Major transformations, however, such as straightening a crooked nose or erasing a double chin, can be achieved only by severely reducing the image's detail in Taiwanese bridal photos. When high-tech computer equipment and skilled technicians are available, however, there is no limit to the transformations one can effect on a photograph without compromising its realism through heavy diffusion.

Although some Taipei bridal studios used computer imaging to insert photographic images of the couple into computer-stored images of exotic destinations (Paris, Rome, and New York were popular), and many salons provided couples with images stored on CD-ROM in addition to photo albums and wall hangings, computer-based retouching work was not standard practice in 1997. Retouching was done by hand, so photographers used expensive 120-millimeter film even for shots they did not intend to enlarge for wall hangings. Using hand instruments, photographers scratch out undesirable spots (wrinkles, bra straps, stray hairs) on the negative. Negative quality suffers, however. Photographers and their assistants must paint over parts of the final prints to hide problems associated with negative retouching, in addition to painting other beautifying add-ons (darker eyeliner added to a close-up of the bride or color highlights painted atop a black-and-white or sepia print, for example). The plastic coating applied over the photograph not only protects the image from dirt and light but also helps to hide telltale signs of retouching. Overlays of graphic designs are sometimes used in lieu of negative retouching. When a bride's undergarment protrudes at the neckline of her gown, for example, photo assistants can cover it with graphics or text, which not only fixes the problem but also makes the album page look like a page in a fashion magazine.[14]

VISUAL CONTEXTS

In addition to indexing glamorizing images found in women's magazines and advertising photography, bridal albums are closely related to another form of photographic practice in Taiwan known as *xiezhenji,* a label that derives from the Japanese term for photography. *Xiezhenji* means generally a collection of portraits of an individual placed in a book or album, but in practice the term has specific connotations. The older and more common understanding of *xiezhenji* is a book of erotic photographs, including seminude and nude poses, of a celebrity or model, usually female. *Xiezhenji* are consumed primarily by men and are just one type of pornography *(seqing)* popular in Taiwan.[15] The newer type of *xiezhenji* is a more recent phenomenon in Taiwan: albums of photos of young single women shot by bridal photographers or other professional photographers specializing in glamour photography. This kind of *xiezhenji* is commonly called *yishuzhao* (literally, "art photography"). In most noncelebrity glamour albums the young, single woman is fully clothed. Although glamour photography albums are a more recent phenomenon than bridal photography *(hunsha sheying),* the terms *yishuzhao* and *xiezhenji* are broader, such that bridal photography is understood as a subset of *yishuzhao/xiezhenji.* This will become clearer as I describe the genre.

Wu Jia-bao—a Japan-trained photographer and owner of the Fototek school of photography in Taipei, which offers classes on *xiezhenji* and bridal photography—explained the history of *xiezhenji* to me. From the 1940s on, it was (and perhaps still is) the custom for a photographer to shoot hundreds of still photographs during the making of a Hollywood film. A dozen or so of these shots were then hung in the hallways of movie theaters. In Japan in the late 1970s, a film production company made a book of leftover images from a Japanese film and marketed it to the public—the first *xiezhenji.* In Japan, *xiezhenji* were not associated with eroticism.

Wu showed me an early-1980s Japanese *xiezhenji* of a star named Hiroko and described it as an important influence on *xiezhenji* photography in Taiwan. The book collects no less than one hundred photographs of Hiroko in various outfits, in various scenes, and with various other people. I noted several ways it differed from Taiwanese *xiezhenji.* Hiroko's skin tones are quite dark, much darker than would be permissible in today's glamour and bridal photography. The images are not underexposed or treated to light diffusion. Hiroko wears little or no makeup. Her hair and dress look casual in every photograph, and many seem to be candid shots rather than posed portraits. In sum, the photographs of Hiroko do not seem to partake of the advertising photography genre that is an important visual context for present-day bridal and glamour photos. The obvious similarity, of course, is the portrayal of a single woman in different settings and different costumes over the course of dozens of images.

Today, *xiezhenji* are produced by celebrities in Taiwan to generate additional revenue and heighten publicity. In 1997, bookstores had about a dozen different *xiezhenji* for sale, all costing upward of NT $500 (then $20 U.S.) and shrink-wrapped. The majority were of female stars, but also included among these was one of Taiwan's most popular male singer, Liu De-hua. I did not spend the $30 U.S. to be able to see inside, but I noted that the back cover pictured him semiclothed and holding a garden hose that was spraying upward from his pants. In sharp contrast, the front cover showed him fully clothed in a cutesy pose. The *xiezhenji* were displayed near other erotic materials, such as a series of much cheaper pocket-sized books. One of these, for example, featured photographs looking up women's skirts to reveal their underwear. Its publisher claimed the images were taken in the Ximending shopping district of Taipei without the knowledge of the women pictured. Local editions of *Playboy* and *Penthouse* as well as other local sex magazines are kept in the same sections of stores.

One goal of all *xiezhenji* (including bridal photography) is to create head-to-toe stylings—one cute, one sexy, one cool, one elegant—so different from one another that the viewer would not necessarily recognize the woman from one photograph to the next. In other words, *xiezhenji* try to depict a woman in numerous roles and multiple manifestations. Glamour albums and bridal albums both explicitly emulate celebrity *xiezhenji* in the repetitious portrayal of the same woman[16] in various costumes and settings (see figures 16–17). Glamour albums *(yishuzhao)*, though they usually do not picture naked women, are also called *xiezhenji*. I have heard the two forms distinguished colloquially as *xiezhenji* (any book of photos picturing a woman as if she is a model) and "real" *xiezhenji* (photo albums that include nude shots).

Some glamour albums are exactly like bridal albums, except that no groom is present and, in most cases, the woman does not dress in a white bridal gown. When a woman has her photos taken at a bridal salon, she selects several evening gowns from the salon's assortment. She may also bring in her own clothes or clothes she has bought or borrowed just for

Figures 16 and 17. Ideally, bridal and glamour photo albums picture the woman in stylings and poses so varied that the viewer could easily forget that the personae on view are all played by a single woman, as is the case in these photographs. (Images courtesy of Cang-ai Bridal Photography Co., 2003. Photographer: Lin Jian-bang.)

the photo session, since bridal salons generally do not offer the casual outfits or lingerie or other sexy clothes (tight leather pants, thigh-high vinyl boots) that are popular in glamour albums.

The line between bridal photography and glamour photography can be blurry. I have seen glamour photo albums that included photographs of an unmarried woman dressed in a white bridal gown. I have also seen bridal albums that included only one photograph of the groom because he refused to, or was unable to, stay for the whole shoot. I have seen, as well, glamour albums in which the young woman's boyfriend poses with her.

Typically, the pages of glamour albums are much smaller than those of bridal albums. And the covers, unlike the heavy carved wood exteriors of bridal albums, are thin and look like magazine covers, featuring the young woman's face and sporting English headlines and graphics. The companies that manufacture the graphics as sheets of rub-off transfers seem to make separate bridal and glamour graphics. Glamour photo albums are more likely to have text around the images that says "Fashion" or "Beauty"—not "True Love" or the English lyrics to a love song, which might appear in bridal albums. In 1997, the price for a glamour album started at NT $3,000 ($120 U.S.) and could run as high as a bridal package, depending on the number of photographs selected.[17] Some bridal salons advertise glamour album specials just after the Chinese New Year and during the Ghost Month of late summer, when bridal business is slow.

Glamour albums first became popular in Taipei around 1990. In 1997, some girls told me that "everyone" at their vocational high schools had had them done. Glamour albums were not as popular at the more prestigious academic high schools and universities, though they were popular enough that it was easy to find women attending top-rated National Taiwan University who either had a glamour album or planned to get one made. Among the glamour albums I saw, a high percentage contained at least some overtly sexualizing photographs, such as a young woman wearing an extremely short skirt and posed so that the viewer just misses seeing beneath it, a shadow cast between her legs. Some glamour albums contain images of the woman lying on an unmade bed in silky pajamas.[18] But most glamour images, like bridal photographs, are merely glamorizing without overt sexual connotations. Cutesy styles are extremely popular in glamour albums, for example.[19]

The two "real" xiezhenji I purchased also contain some fully clothed images of the celebrity subject and close-up images that focus on the face. For example, a best-selling xiezhenji in 1997 (featuring Deng Jing-chun, a model famous for her work for a breast-size-enhancement company)[20] included, out of approximately one hundred images, only about one dozen that did not reveal bare breasts or buttocks. A glamour album, by contrast, might picture a woman dressed in five to eight different stylings, of which two or three might include a very short skirt, a nightgown, or a partially unbuttoned blouse. Some young women pose for nude photographs exactly like those found in celebrity *xiezhenji,* though they intend these for themselves, not for publication. Rumor has it that photographers in the glamour album business prey upon such women (and try to talk every female client into posing seminude) by shooting extra frames and selling the photographs.[21]

The parallels among celebrity *xiezhenji,* glamour albums, and bridal photos are many. The same photographic techniques are used—high-key lighting, slight blurring, and heavy retouching. Celebrity *xiezhenji* include graphics and text (English, Chinese, Japanese) much like those found in glamour and bridal albums. All three types of albums, like the early Hiroko book, picture just one woman and show her in various settings, costumes, hairstyles, and attitudes. Deng Jing-chun's *xiezhenji* contains several images of her dressed in a silver evening gown and elaborate jewelry, posing in what looks like an expensive European restaurant (the kind of place bridal photographers may recommend to their clients for location shoots). The gown is identical to the type worn in glamour and bridal albums.

Throughout my fieldwork, I periodically heard stories of couples who had posed nude for their bridal albums. At first I heard this from taxi drivers and other informants not well known to me, and I assumed it was urban folklore. When I mentioned these reports to friends outside the bridal industry, they reacted with great surprise. One married young man replied that he was very surprised to learn that people in Taiwan could be so open *(kaifang).* Later, three people I knew well told me on separate occasions of nude bridal photographs they had seen first hand. I had asked one of them, a photographer, during my interview with him on a bridal salon sales floor, if he had ever heard of couples posing nude in their bridal albums. Lowering his voice, he told me that one time a couple had asked him to take nude photographs. He was shocked and embarrassed but felt he had no choice but to agree to the customers' odd request. It seems that couples who want to pose nude often create two photo albums. One contains standard portraits and is shown to family and friends and displayed at the wedding banquet. The other contains nude photographs and is considered more private, though such couples apparently show their photographs to friends at times. One purpose of nude bridal portraits, like all bridal portraits, is to capture the youthful good looks of the bride and save them to remember her once-beautiful appearance. The nude bridal photographs not only go one step further in emulating celebrity *xiezhenji* but also go one more step toward documenting a young woman's beauty for her own future use and pleasure. Overwhelmingly, people in Taipei did not speak of bridal photographs as erotic, but the genre's growth out of a form of erotic photography and the placement of framed enlargements over couples' beds are suggestive.

PERSONAE, NOT SUBJECTIVITIES

Putting aside the intriguing idea of nude bridal photographs, what is perhaps most important about the *xiezhenji*/bridal photography connection is the common creation of a string of personae set in a series of different places and periods. This has its roots in Hollywood movies and movie advertising. The still photographs taken from movie sets fragment the film's narrative into frozen moments. In bridal albums, the variety of costumes and settings suggests a process in time, just like celebrity *xiezhenji,* which include shots taken in disparate places, including foreign countries. The economics of celebrity *xiezhenji* and bridal or glamour albums are very different, of course. Few couples can afford to fly to Athens for a few shots and to Paris for a few more. A celebrity *xiezhenji* may contain photographs shot over the course of months or years, much like the photo album published by the American celebrity Madonna in the mid-1990s. Bridal and glamour albums are shot in a single day but attempt to give a similar feeling of traversing a variety of roles and places nonetheless—*as if* the woman captured the photographer's attention through time. David Harvey's theory of time-space compression explains that postmodernism refuses the notion of progress and "abandons all sense of historical continuity and memory, while simultaneously developing an incredible ability to plunder history and absorb whatever it finds there as some aspect of the present" (1989: 54). Precisely because viewers know that bridal and glamour albums are shot in a single day, the images and albums are fragmenting, discontinuous, even "schizophrenic" (Jameson 1991). The albums reject narrative and, instead, arrange the photographs to heighten the sense of novelty and the inchoateness of the images.[22]

Given their celebration of artifice and interest in representing bodies in as many different unrecognizable forms as possible, bridal photography seems a quintessentially postmodern endeavor.[23] Over the course of field research, I came to realize that the enormous portraits hanging above couples' beds are not the testaments to individuality and selfhood I once presumed them to be. Then, I was reading them according to my own cultural background, where portrait photographs make assertions of unified selfhood and authenticity. It would be a grave misreading, I think, to assert that the fragmented, discontinuous, artificial personae represented in bridal photography are profound reflections of women and men's experiences of subjectivity in late capitalist Taiwan. The photographs do not represent selves and subjectivities at all; they picture overtly constructed personae. In some respects, then, they are empty signs, or signs of meaninglessness.

Although bridal photos are sometimes said to contain a woman's fantasy world, in fact too many aspects of bridal photography are obligatory and regimented to be able to capture adequately any individual woman's fantasies. Although photographers and bridal salons talk up their "personalized service," in fact the bridal photography production process leaves little space for individual agency on the part of brides and grooms. Their ability to express themselves in their photographs is limited, in most cases, to a checklist of preferences for blue, red, yellow, or green backdrops and romantic, cute, cool, stylish, or sexy attitudes. Of course, a shopping list of choices is precisely how agency is conceptualized in consumer cultures. The choices are many, but they are all different versions of the same thing (Ewen 1988; see also Bordo 1997).

If bridal photographs are representations of fantasy, then clearly young women are expected to dream the same dream with only microvariations in style, despite individual women's different ethnic and class positionings—not to mention their personal histories of family conflict and cohesion, loves lost and found. Bridal photographs represent not individual women's fantasies but a collective fantasy about what young women at marriage *ought* to be fantasizing about: glamour, beauty, and romance. Beneath the photograph's representation are just more representations. It is signs all the way down.[24]

Hence, bridal photographs neatly fit Baudrillard's theory of the simulacrum. Simulacra, by replicating or simulating the real, are "the death sentence" of the signified (1994: 6). He writes: "To dissimulate is to pretend not to have what one has. To simulate is to feign to have what one doesn't have. One implies a presence, the other an absence" (1994: 3).

The simulacrum points to the absence underneath the image's surface and, potentially, mocks or parodies the very idea of the real. Creating simulacra and hanging them over one's bed seem to me to be a perfectly reasonable response to consumer capitalism in Taiwan.[25]

Stuart Ewen (1988: 85), like many feminist cultural critics writing on beauty, argues that the "studied perfection" of commercially produced images leaves real people feeling inadequate about the lack of perfection in lived lives: "Passing by shop window displays, broad expanses of gleaming plate glass, people confront a reflection of themselves, superimposed against the dream world of the commodity. An invidious comparison is instantaneously provoked between the 'off guard' imperfection of ourselves—suddenly on view—and the studied perfection of the display" (1988: 85). Taiwanese bridal photography responds to just this scenario by allocating to married women their own sets of perfect images.

Jhally writes: "The function of advertising is to refill the emptied commodity with meaning. Indeed the meaning of advertising would make no sense if objects already had established meaning. The power of advertising *depends* upon the initial emptying out" (1989: 221, quoted in Lury 1996: 62). The bride too is "emptied out," both in the styling process, where makeup and hair styling radically transfigure her, and again in the photographic process, where the photographer "designs" the bride's style and uses lighting, focusing, and retouching to remove from the bride all of her surface individuality. As in advertising photography, the bride is refilled with meanings the photographer gives her (following the checklist of colors and attitudes she indicates as preferences). Just as advertising makes beer stand for manliness and denim stand for rebellion, bridal portraiture makes the bride stand for celebrity beauty and marriage stand for romance.[26] Just as there is no promise that the consumer will get manliness, rebelliousness, beauty, or romance from the object, brides and grooms certainly do not expect their photographs to transform their lives.

By making these photographs, brides, grooms, and the bridal industry at large symbolically reject the notion that beauty, originality, and authenticity exist in the mass media forms that they imitate. Although the fetishization of bridal photographs in Taiwan initially struck me as a sign of mass media mystification, in time I came to realize that the bridal photography form openly celebrates artifice and rejects claims to authenticity; I was the one mystified. My informants felt free to play with signs and appropriate them without losing sight of their meaninglessness (see Lury 1996: ch. 3). Perhaps this freedom is created precisely by the exclusion of Taiwanese faces and values in a large portion of the mass media images that saturate Taipei's landscape. New meanings accrue to this form of play along the way—the act of *making* the photographs takes on ritualized forms and meanings, even as the imagery's essential emptiness is retained.

CHAPTER 8

The Context of Looking

What Taipei Viewers See

When I first became acquainted with Taiwanese bridal photography, my attention focused on elements that are so common, so taken for granted, in this genre that spectators in Taiwan seldom comment upon them. A foreign observer's eyes, much like a child's, are useful for raising questions that people accustomed to a practice are less likely to consider. Many practitioners of Buddhism highly value the cultivation of "beginner's mind," which does not take for granted that which is taken for granted. Anthropologists appreciate the usefulness of beginner's mind in studying sociocultural phenomena even while valuing "native" understandings. What do those who are already initiated into the world of Taiwanese bridal photography talk about when viewing photo albums? What, for them, *is* remarkable about this cultural practice that they find to be rather unremarkable?

HOW MUCH MONEY AT WHAT SALON?

Weddings in Taiwan (and elsewhere) serve, to some degree, as "rites of distinction" wherein couples and their families display their economic clout, social standings, and cultural competencies through consumption (Argyrou 1996). When friends visit the bride in the "new room" to peruse her new album, their talk usually includes discussion of how much money the couple spent for how many photographs at what salon. Women often seemed more interested in the cost of the photos than in the photos themselves. In part, these women are engaging in comparative shopping. They talk about which salons are expensive, which are cheaper, which are overpriced, which provide good value, which have the best dresses, which have the best stylists and photographers. In a similar fashion, they also discuss how many photographs the couple purchased and compare (for example, "I have a coworker who bought sixty photos. Sixty is too many. She paid almost NT $80,000! I like your album of forty photos. Forty is a good number"). Although I often heard women criticize the albums of friends, relatives, and coworkers not present for the conversation, I seldom heard the same type of criticism spoken directly to the bride or groom whose photographs were at hand. However, friends may tease brides and grooms for loving their photographs so much that they bought so many.

Even after time has passed, the cost of the photographs remains a central issue for bridal album spectators. My friend Xiao-lan told me that at the time she thought the photographs were important, but now, years later, she feels that buying so many was a waste of money. "Would you do it again?" I asked. "Yes, but I would buy fewer photographs," she told me. At first she looked at her photo album frequently and took it out to show to friends and coworkers, too. After awhile she put it away, and now she seldom looks at it. When she does take out her huge album, however, the photos serve as a reminder of how her priorities have changed.

THE BRIDE DOESN'T LOOK LIKE HERSELF

Both in their conversations with me about bridal photography as a cultural phenomenon and in their conversations with others about specific photos, people often raised the subject of a bride not looking like herself in her photographs. This subject was raised more often by friends and family of brides than by brides themselves. However, one young woman who felt that her photographs looked nothing like her reported that she looked at the photos multiple times every day to get used to them. Some brides acknowledge that their photographs do not resemble them, and others do not. For example, Bao-hui arranged for me to interview her two sisters about their photographs. She told me beforehand that the photos of her older sister, Bao-yu, were really ugly (chou) because they looked nothing like her sister. "Does she say this, too?" I asked. "Wait and we'll see," she said. Unsure of how to broach this topic during the interview, I had the good luck of having it done for me. We had all gathered at the home of Bao-hui's youngest sister, Bao-mei, who lived with her in-laws. Bao-mei's mother-in-law came into the living room as I looked at Bao-yu's photographs with her and her husband of almost ten years. Bao-mei's mother-in-law said sweetly, "You haven't changed at all!" Bao-yu smiled and thanked her. Bao-mei (the youngest) teased her sister that the photographs did not look like her *(bu tai xiang)*. Bao-yu disagreed, and her younger sister quickly added, "Just kidding!"

Other women point out their own unrecognizability and laugh about it. Married ten years prior, Yong-xiu told me that her young son had asked her, "Who is that auntie with Daddy?" Similarly, Florence, anticipating her transformation, warned me that I would probably not recognize her when I met her at the photo studio for her shoot, after the makeover.

When my own mother saw my album her first response was: "This doesn't look like you!" When I brought my album to my dissertation writing group, a male classmate who arrived late looked at the photo inset on the wooden cover and asked, "Who is this?" When I see the photographs, I see myself in that not-too-recognizable face. I know the photographs are of me partly because I know that I was there, that the woman in the photographs could not be anyone but me. Furthermore, each time I flip through the pages of the album I further my own conviction that the image is of me.[1]

Talk about the bride not looking like herself in her photographs points to another way that acts of looking at bridal photos are culturally structured. Viewers are *required* to compliment the bride's beauty when they view her photographs. This cultural requirement, however, breeds its opposite: Under the right circumstances, viewers (including the bride herself) enjoy talking about how unlike her everyday image the photographs are. In the interaction between Bao-yu and Bao-mei, Bao-mei incorrectly thought that by now it was safe to tease her sister about her photographs. When she found out Bao-yu did not want to hear it, she backed off. Standard practice is to behave as Bao-mei's mother-in-law did—praise the bride's beauty and keep quiet about the fact that her beauty in the photographs is very obviously constructed.

The silence on this issue is particularly striking, given the wider cultural contexts in which conversations at the office, on buses, over tea often involve women telling each other, "You look fatter today; you shouldn't eat sweets!" or "My, you have a lot of pimples lately!" (North American women I met in Taiwan often complained of feeling offended by such comments, but I was always happy to hear about my imperfections because, to me, it meant I was being treated as a friend.)

UGLY GROOMS

Discussion of the groom's less-than-perfect looks, however, is fair game. In the "new room," a bride's friend leafed through the bride's album, pointed out one shot, and said, "This one would be better if you had cut the groom out," while covering his image with her hands. In the backroom of French Riviera salon, where workers retouched printed photographs with colored paints, mounted photos to album pages, and affixed graphics, two employees talked about how ugly the groom was in the photos they worked on. Again, the sense was that he was ruining the good looks of the bride's pictures. Another time, I watched as a saleswoman placed proofs into proof-viewing albums while holding the manager's two-year-old son on her lap. She pointed to the groom's image and taught the little boy to say, "Ugly! Ugly!"

One explanation for these comments is that stylists do very little work on grooms in comparison to the long stretches of time and baskets full of supplies they expend on perfecting the bride's looks. The expectation is that grooms should retain their everyday looks in the photographs, wearing their glasses and usual hairstyles. In fact, if stylists transformed grooms to the same extent that they do brides, banquet guests might not believe the photograph was really of the couple. Yet the styling of the bride, the lighting, the retouching, and the graphics all work to make the photographs look like magazine layouts. The groom, retaining his ordinary looks, appears out of place. People who look real—with unadulterated eyebrows, common-looking eyes, or out-of-style eyeglasses— seldom appear in fashion magazines. The problem, of course, is not that men are uglier than the women they marry as a rule but that cultural practices conspire to marginalize men in the bridal photography production process. For their part, most men seem to prefer it that way.

There may already be a trend toward bringing grooms more thoroughly into the bridal photography fold. Although brides have been wearing special, rented gowns in various styles and colors in their professional portraits since the birth of the bridal industry, only in recent years have bridal salons expanded their offerings to include multiple changes of costume for grooms. The groom usually wears his best suit and tie for some of the photos but later changes into salon-provided tuxedoes in assorted styles and colors, selected by stylists and photographers to coordinate with the gowns the bride has selected for herself. Nonetheless, throughout my field research period most grooms did not want to undergo the vast transformative works done on brides. One photographer, Wei-guo, for example, showed me photos in which the groom had terribly pockmarked cheeks. Wei-guo said he had asked the groom if he wanted his scarred skin to be "corrected." The groom declined, saying that he preferred a natural look. Wei-guo complied, even adjusting the light in a few portraits of the groom to accentuate the lines and contours of his face. Despite all the industry and consumer rhetoric about preferring the "natural," no stylist or photographer would think to ask a bride whether or not she wanted her pockmarks to show in her bridal portraits. They would automatically use makeup, lighting, and negative retouching to correct her skin. It is not simply that the cultural preference is for men to look themselves; rather, men are not responsible for looking good. Beauty is a woman's responsibility.

A male graduate student in gender and literature (who participated in a group interview I organized) offered another explanation for the groom's ambiguous status in the photographs: "In bridal pictures, the man is constantly absent. The focus is on the bride. So when the man appears in a picture it doesn't matter what he's wearing because most people looking at the photo will only notice the bride. Actually, I think the bride is the active partner of the couple in these kinds of pictures." Perhaps, then, the numerous comments I heard about the groom looking ugly or detracting from the photograph should be taken to mean simply that the groom is extraneous because the focus is, of course, on the bride.

LOOKING AT BACKGROUNDS AND CONTEXTS

Many conversations around photo albums concerned not the people in the images or their elaborate costumes but the background in the image. The most cherished type of background was "natural" (meaning real, not virtual) scenery found in parks, gardens, and beaches. Certain locations—for example, the Chinese-style gardens beside the Chiang Kai-Shek National Monument and the National Palace Museum—appeared so often in bridal albums that they no longer elicited much discussion. Couples and photographers sought out more and new location spots to spice up the photos. One bridal salon owner in Taipei contracted for exclusive photographic use of a restaurant with unusual interiors so couples could go there on location shoots and be assured of an uncommon background. The owner of Sesame Bridal Photography built a "wedding castle" outside Taipei with elaborate gardens and rooms decorated according to various themes (one a cave, another a jungle, another referred to as "European"). Beach and seashore shots were popular, even though the long drive from Taipei to the beach made photo shoot days longer than the typical eight hours, resulting in additional fees. Also popular were location shots in upscale retail shopping districts, including the sales areas of bridal salons. One couple decided to have their location photos taken at the station for Taipei's new light-rail train line.

The couple's choice of location spots, especially, is taken as suggestive of their tastes. If they choose a common spot like Chinese gardens, they seem conservative. If they choose a highly unusual spot, they seem daring and fashionable. If they choose a very beautiful but not-too-common spot, they seem refined. Though there is little room for individual agency in the making of bridal photographs, the choice of a location spot is one instance in the process where couples both exert and express themselves, and this is precisely the point that viewers are most apt to discuss. For most viewers, looking at the beautiful brides and romantic poses in bridal albums is boring. Talking about the backgrounds can sometimes spice up the experience of looking.

"NATURAL" PHOTOGRAPHS

When I inquired as to the basis of couples' selection of one salon over another, very frequently they reported choosing a salon that offered more natural *(ziran)* photos. When I asked couples about specific instructions they had given their photographer, many said they had requested naturalness. When I observed viewers looking at and talking about specific photographs, often they would point to certain pictures and praise them, saying, "Very natural." Interestingly, when viewers talked about the feeling of particular photographs as cool, sexy, soft, elegant, romantic, cute, or high fashion, I almost always understood and agreed with their readings. I had expected to (and indeed tried quite desperately to) uncover a uniquely local Taiwanese or at least Chinese perspective on what is cool, cute, or romantic, but by the end of my research I had learned to accept that their readings of these photographs were rather close to my own, even though our critical evaluations of the beautiful and the tawdry were often not in line. When it came to informants' use of the word "natural," however, I found myself bewildered and amazed.

Qiu-mei, for example, reported that she had selected a salon called Taipei Spain because when she and her husband visited a bridal fair held at the convention center at the Taipei Municipal Airport, they found this salon's style to be most natural. Looking at her photographs, however, it was obvious that Qiu-mei wore wigs, false eyelashes, heavy foundation makeup, and breast padding in every image. "What," I asked her, "do you mean by 'natural'?" Qiu-mei complained that some salons have backgrounds that are too colorful and busy; the stylists apply makeup too heavily; the photographers set up poses that do not look natural. Another time a saleswoman proclaimed, "Our photos are natural," as she and I viewed a sample photo album picturing a bride decorated with glittery purple hair gel. Couples pay exorbitant additional fees to go out on location shoots because outdoor shots are more "natural" than studio ones. While it is true that outdoor shots picture backgrounds that are real (not painted or computer-generated), photographers seldom rely on natural light for outdoor portraits. The lighting of bridal portraits is extremely important and highly formulaic, hence seldom left up to the sun alone.

On my first location shoot, the couple, photographer, assistant, and I were out at a private park with beautiful gardens for a couple of hours in the late afternoon. The photographer instructed the bride and groom to climb down near a babbling brook and sit on some rocks. The bride sat down first. The early evening sun happened to touch her face at a low angle, creating what I considered very beautiful lighting conditions. The photographer then instructed the groom to sit down next to the bride where his position blocked out the sun, so that both their faces were now entirely missed by direct light. I watched silently, sure that the photographer would move the groom to the bride's other side or otherwise adjust his angle to retrieve the low-angled sunlight in the frame. Instead, she instructed her assistant to beam the portable spotlight straight onto their faces. Though we had traveled to the park at great expense to the groom to make more "natural" portraits, the use of artificial lighting was, for the couple and the photographer, perfectly acceptable, even natural.

Naturalness was often attributed to the work of Taipei stylists and photographers in explicit contrast to that of southern or rural salons. A related term, *suqi,* meaning "simple and elegant," was also used to praise elite Taipei photographs and styling in contrast to the exaggerated *(kuazhang)* and tawdry *(su)* styles preferred by Taiwan's less cosmopolitan people. The Taipei discourse on taste has it that the bridal styles preferred by those who are southern, rural, low-class, or old (parents, grandparents) are overly complicated and vulgar, whereas the elite, young, fashion-knowing Taipei set has more refined, less ostentatious tastes. Tawdriness is also associated with modern bridal styles in Mainland China, while elegant simplicity is associated with the contemporary bridal styles of "Europe."

Taipei brides sometimes pursue extreme measures to avoid the exaggerated styles of country stylists for their rural weddings. When a young woman who has lived in Taipei for all or much of her adult life marries a groom whose parents live in the countryside, she may fret over the unnatural, tawdry look that country stylists are notorious for. For additional fees, many Taipei stylists will open their salons in the middle of the night to complete a three-hour makeover in the city and still allow time for several hours of driving to the countryside before 9 A.M., when wedding ceremonies usually commence. Although the bride pays as much as triple the price for her makeover, goes without sleep the night before her wedding, and endures a very long day of wearing the thick, theatrical-like makeup and elaborate bridal hairdo, some brides believe this is a reasonable price to pay to avoid an unrefined look produced by a country stylist. For an even greater fee, some Taipei stylists will travel to rural areas to perform on-site stylings.

Taipei consumer demand for the natural, however, has definite limits. One of Taipei's many failed bridal salons of the late 1980s was called "Naturalism" (Ziran Zhuyi). Naturalism's owner/photographer disliked the use of filtering and high-key lighting and promoted a different photographic style that he considered more natural. His shop quickly went out of business. The owner reopened the salon under a new name and separated his aesthetic preferences from his everyday bridal photography work.[2]

Similarly, though consumers often proclaimed to loathe the exaggerated styles of rural bridal photography in preference for more simple looks, two celebrities who opened a bridal salon promoting a "simple and elegant" style of bridal photography also met with failure. Television personality Cao Qi-tai and film star Xia Ling-ling opened a bridal salon and jewelry shop by the name of "Mr. Ms." in an upscale Taipei neighborhood away from the two main bridal districts. At first, Mr. Ms. seemed a sure success because it received tremendous publicity. In addition to their bridal salon, Cao and Xia launched a new bridal magazine, *Mr. Ms.*, to coordinate with Cao's new television show, *Red Bomb*. On *Red Bomb*, couples dressed in bridal wear discussed their relationships with a panel of middle-aged marriage experts in a game show format. Some of the shows featured a segment where a male gynecologist met with the contestants, in sex-segregated groupings, to address intimate topics such as changes in vaginal shape as a result of childbirth. In 1997, Cao and Xia staged an elaborate marriage ceremony and wedding banquet to celebrate their wedding anniversary. The event was a media splash; all the major media outlets reported on the wedding banquet and made mention of the bridal salon, the magazine, and the television show. Shortly after, in the winter of 1997, I paid a visit to the Mr. Ms. bridal salon with Xiao-lan, who was an editor for a competing bridal magazine. Xiao-lan pretended to be a bride-to-be. The saleswoman we met showed us a sample album and explained the salon's philosophy to us. The sample album was extremely unusual in the world of Taiwanese bridal photography: the bride wore the same white dress in every photograph. Moreover, the background of every shot was all white, and there were no graphics overlaid on the photographs to make them look like magazine layouts. The saleswoman explained that the salon's idea was for brides to wear only one dress and have the photos very simple and clean. Xiao-lan, perplexed, asked if they provided evening gowns (gowns in colors, not white). Yes, said the saleswoman. Wearing only one dress was just an idea, but a bride could have the photographs any way she wants. Because the shop had just opened, she explained, they did not yet have other sample albums. (Other newly opened salons get around this problem by purchasing sample albums from other salons and showing them as their own.)

As we left the expensively decorated glass, wood, and marble shop, Xiao-lan shook her head in disbelief. To her, the idea of wearing only one gown was preposterous. Sure enough, the bridal salon and magazine were out of business within six months. Although the natural was extremely popular and sought after, Mr. Ms. apparently did not adequately capture the essence of it according to Taipei consumers' understanding.

When lay people talk about photographs in everyday conversations, the word "natural" especially comes up about photographs that appear to be candid shots. Mei-hua, showing me her younger brother's photo album, pointed out a "natural" photo in which the bride was tugging at the groom's ear while he laughed. Mei-hua felt that the photograph captured a spontaneous facial expression. In photo shoots I observed, photographers tried to get a few shots of this sort (perhaps three frames out of one hundred). Some of these shots caught the couple off guard. In one instance, for example, the bride stuck out her tongue in embarrassment after blinking during a shutter release; the photographer quickly shot another frame to capture her reaction.

Other times I saw photographers set up poses that involved movement. For example, a photographer handed large stuffed animals to the bride and groom and then asked them to stand back to back. She demonstrated how she wanted them to move: On the count of three, they were both to jut their arms out straight while holding the toy, bend over at the hips, and turn their faces toward the camera. It took the couple numerous tries before the photographer was satisfied that she had captured the image she wanted. In such shots, that the photographer must press the release at just the right moment, whereas in the majority of shots, the photographer sets up the pose and adjusts every microdetail to perfection before shooting. Photos of this kind of constructed naturalism were a new product in the late 1990s and were selling fairly well. Though consumers were not interested in buying many photos of this sort and seldom selected them to serve as wall hangings or thank-you cards, they were delighted to include one or even a few in their albums. These photographs often received the most attention from friends.

The formulaic, highly prepared and posed nature of the vast majority of bridal photographs apparently created a certain enthusiasm for its opposite: the natural. The unusual wedding video of one couple brought forth this theme beautifully and evoked tremendous laughter and joy every time it was shown. Produced by a professional television cameraman who was a friend of the groom, the video took a light-hearted, joking approach to the representation of the wedding. The video begins with a comical two-minute version of the whole day in super high speed, focusing on key moments such as the bride entering the black Cadillac that transported her to her new home. Although the video contains more serious moments too (such as a close-up of the bride crying), the couple and their relatives were clearly charmed by the video's comic moments. Much of its humor hinges on precisely the kind of thing that bridal salons attempt to prevent—images of the bride taken when her perfect appearance comes undone momentarily. For example, the bride is shown entering the new room. The groom removes the white veil from her face and kisses her on the cheek. She has been crying. It is a tender moment. The camera zooms in on the bride's left eye, where her false eyelashes are coming undone and hanging down. The bride, eyes closed, tries to put it back in place. Subtitles appear at the bottom of the screen, saying, "Her eyelash is falling off!" At other, more serious moments, the same type of characters appear to say standard well wishes like "Next year have a son!" Another comical moment occurs when the wedding banquet guests shoot off firecrackers from tiny plastic "champagne" bottles. One guest shoots a firecracker too close to the bride. Its contents of curly paper hit her on the forehead and the loud noise startles her, causing her to cover her ear. For dramatic effect, the camera freezes on this very moment when the bride, walking down the aisle in formulaic form, is momentarily knocked out of her highly scripted role into a spontaneous, natural response. A few moments later the action proceeds (the couple walking down a red-carpeted aisle) as if nothing had happened.

What made this video so enjoyable to the couple and their relatives, I believe, was that it pitted natural moments against the standard, highly perfect public representations of weddings so common in bridal photography. By focusing on moments when the bride's perfect image came apart, the videographer highlighted her constructedness without resorting to a documentary style that revealed too much of the real. Instead, pointing out the constructedness of the bride in this fashion served to make her seem even more like a star. Media representations of celebrities often depict "backstage" behavior in an attempt to give the appearance of authenticity and humanness to stars.[3] Taiwan, like the United States, has a vast entertainment media that purports to offer the real, behind-the-scenes scoop on celebrities. By digging out moments that seemed more natural or authentic, this wedding video treated the bride just like a real star, further edifying and glamorizing her by suggesting that these off-stage moments were remarkable. At rural weddings, the ribald jokes offered by emcees and the teasing by drunken male banquet guests similarly bring the bride back down to earth from the elevated, idealized status her elaborate costuming creates (see Bahktin 1968). Whether borrowing from the logic of celebrity or of rural wedding banquets (or both), this wedding video got at the heart of why the natural is prized in bridal photography.

COMMEMORATING WEDDINGS AND PRESERVING YOUTH

When I asked brides and grooms why they wanted so many and such large photographs, the word *jinian* inevitably was part of their answer. *Jinian* translates as "to commemorate, mark, or record," and its first character means "to record" or "to remember." Part of what I found curious about Taiwan-style bridal photographs is that the photographs do *not* record the events of a wedding; they make no pretensions of documenting the coming together of two families in reportage form.[4] Although some families, especially wealthy ones, hire professional videographers to record engagement and wedding ceremonies and shoot footage at the wedding banquet, professional videography and reportage photography of wedding events are relatively uncommon. On the other hand, professional bridal portraiture is nearly universal. More commonly, family members peripheral to the ceremonies (siblings, aunts and uncles) take snapshots as the events unfold. Some families hire photographers to make day-of portraits of the entire family or to shoot pictures of guests posed with bride and groom on their way out of the banquet. Day-of-wedding photographs are typically stored in photo albums provided free of charge by photo finishers in three-by-five-inch and four-by-six-inch formats. Most households I visited have dozens of such photo albums, holding thirty-six images each and containing snapshots of tourist spots, family events, and the like. These small photo albums are taken out for viewing and shared with relatives, coworkers, and friends as much as the huge, formal bridal albums are, if not more, due to their small size and light weight. They are treated, however, just like snapshot albums of vacations. Wedding-day snapshots are also described as "commemorating" events, but their small scale demonstrates that they are simply not as important as the pre-wedding bridal portraits that receive prominent display. After the wedding, wedding-day snapshots are far more likely to be displayed in relatives' homes than are copies of the bridal portraits, however.

I debated, in English, the meaning of *jinian* in the context of bridal photography with a neighbor by the name of Mei. Mei was in her late thirties, the mother of two boys. She held a graduate degree from a prestigious university, and she had recently moved back to Taipei from England, where she and her husband and sons had lived for several years. I told Mei my perspective on American wedding photographs—that the photographs often serve to document the wedding as an event. In Taiwanese bridal photography, in contrast, not only are the photographs taken on a day far in advance of the wedding but the gowns the bride wears in the portraits are not even the same ones she wears on the wedding day. From my point of view, I told Mei, the photographs do not "record" the wedding, do not document it. Mei agreed, saying that her bridal portraits are not "evidence" of her wedding. For evidence of the marriage, her in-laws had hired a photographer to shoot a large group portrait on the wedding day. This photograph hangs in the living room of her in-laws' home, while the much larger, framed bridal portrait hangs in Mei's bedroom. The bridal portrait wall hanging and album are the couple's own, "a personal thing," totally different from photographs of the wedding day itself.

Bridal photographs do not document weddings; they construct brides. One photographer described his work as dream building. People in Taipei find the lack of truth in the photographs an obvious and unremarkable fact. Of course, they said, the bride wants to preserve images of herself that are more beautiful than she really is. Aside from the untruths of the images of her face are many other elements of artifice, such as wigs, padded breasts and hips, gowns worn nowhere but the photo studio.

Like the temporary nature of the bride's relationship to the gown, the bride and groom's relationship to the backdrops, location sites, and props is fleeting. In the favored scenes in bridal portraits, not only are the close ties and interdependencies of couples with their kin excluded; so are the daily physical and spatial experiences of life in Taipei. The spaces pictured in photographs are pristine scenic spots—litter removed from the ground and passersby cut out of the frame—or studio setups simulating foreign spaces, such as dimly lit studies equipped with antique-looking European furniture and shelves full of leather-bound books, or abstract, brightly colored backdrops reminiscent of MTV-produced spaces. Spaces and items evocative of everyday hassles and discomforts in Taipei life, like overcrowding, traffic jams, gigantic cockroaches, and sickly stray dogs, are virtually never pictured in photographs. The dust and grime of the city, produced by its severe air pollution levels and ubiquitous construction sites, are strikingly absent too. Salons often display gowns in glass-enclosed closets to protect them from the Taipei dust. One of the products of consumer culture in Taiwan is brightly lit, open retail spaces decorated in whites and light colors—contrasting starkly with most homes, which are crowded with family members, whose belongings are crammed into every corner, and which are decorated in dark colors, with walls dingy from constant exposure to air pollution and high humidity.

Bridal salon interiors often recreate the well-lit, spacious interiors of designer boutiques to construct themselves as fantasy spaces. Those who enter may feel as though privileged to be in the confines of a pristine, glossy advertising photograph or in the type of modern space seen in movies. Moving in and out of bridal salons' public and backroom spaces dramatizes the contrast. The public spaces (especially the sales area) are immaculately clean, air conditioned, bright, and open, while backroom spaces (hallways leading to photo studios, photography retouching and graphics areas) are grimy, hot, dark, and crammed with objects. I noted the irony of a discussion I had with a bridal salon saleswoman who complained of the "poor quality of life" in Taiwan (referring to air pollution, crowding, and traffic) as we stood in the pristine second-floor space of the salon, expensive and elaborate gowns in a multitude of colors lining the room, track lighting supplementing the natural light provided by ceiling-to-floor plate glass windows on two sides. Inside, we were protected from the noise, heat, and fumes of Taipei's oppressive traffic, unlike the newsstand keepers, betel nut sellers, and motorcycle repairmen working streetside in the open air.

Bridal salons construct fantasy worlds. They do not pretend to record or document the real. When people told me their bridal portraits serve to *jinian,* they used the term in the sense of commemorating or memorializing. The portraits commemorate the bride's youthful good looks, which, she fears, will be lost soon after the wedding. Like a picture postcard that serves to commemorate a tour of New York, the image is *of* the place one visited but often does not look like what one saw there in person. The litter, rain, and beggars that structured the experience of the place are sanitized from the image that commemorates it. Taiwanese bridal photographs seem to approach life in a similarly touristic fashion. And yet, I think consumers of Taiwan's bridal photographs are wise in their recognition that beauty in late capitalist Taipei is, in fact, very much like a tour of New York. It is short-lived, a professionally orchestrated production, and detached from the realities of everyday life. While internationally known Hollywood starlets like Meg Ryan miraculously retain the looks of twenty-something young women well into the fifth decade of life, acknowledgment that the looks of youth are fleeting is a worthwhile, even important cultural project. In this sense, Taiwanese bridal photographs tell the truth about the constructedness of images even as they revel in artifice.

Reframings

Lisette, a Taipei fashion industry executive, lived in Europe for several years after growing up in Taipei and completing college there. In Europe, she fell in love with a Swiss man. I met her about one year after they had moved to Taipei, married, and been honored at a wedding banquet. Lisette loathed the typical bridal gowns and photographs well known to any resident of Taiwan, and she refused to conform to convention. She commissioned a custom gown made from imported designer fabric in red. The style, as she described it to me, differed from styles common in Taipei in that it had a dropped waist and A-line cut rather than a fitted bodice with full skirting. She chose red fabric rather than white because of the traditional association of red with Chinese weddings. Nonetheless, her mother disliked the gown, favoring the white wedding gowns with full skirting that are now customary. Lisette and her groom hired a fashion magazine photographer to make portraits, but rather than choosing an album of photos and a huge, framed enlargement, they ordered just a few prints. Lisette flatly refused to display photographs at the wedding banquet her family hosted at one of Taipei's most expensive hotels. Her mother protested, arguing that a bride must "give guests a look" *(gei keren kan)*. Lisette argued that she was there in person for guests to see; why did they need to look at her in a photograph? She was baffled by her sister's decision to spend a huge sum of money on bridal portraits. Lisette asked me, "Why do people here love these pictures?" Her mother agonized over how terribly embarrassed she and her father would feel by their daughter who refused to wear a regular gown and refused to display bridal photographs. Other young women who told me of similar conflicts with parents gave in, but Lisette was stubborn. Her mother ultimately signaled defeat when she said, in disgust, "You've already become a foreigner!"

Lisette refused to wear a bridal gown inspired by those of Victorian England and to pose for and display photographs that devote considerable resources to portraying couples as Westernized. Instead, she wore a comparatively simple red gown that, she argued, drew her closer to Chinese tradition on her wedding day. For this, her mother accused her of failing to be Chinese, of becoming a foreigner. What in the world is going on?

On the surface, everything about Taiwanese bridal photography seems Western. The enormous framed portraits look like testaments to individuality, in stark contrast to the focus on family one might expect of photographs in Taiwan. On further inspection, though, the photographs leave little room for individual expression. They are highly formulaic, created under the tight control of professional stylists and photographers. A key goal of the photo albums, moreover, is to picture the bride in multiple personae, presenting her not as an individual character but as plastic, capable of assuming any number of varying roles. Artifice, not individual substance, is the name of the game. Lisette's mother, I suspect, accused her of becoming a foreigner out of frustration with Lisette's presumption of a right to individual self-expression at her wedding. Lisette is certainly not the only young woman who dislikes bridal industry conventions. Not all young women love them as much as her sister did. But she is one of the very few whose worldview led them to demand the right to have their weddings their own way. Though at first glance the photographs on display seem to parade individualism, weddings and even bridal portraits are not places for individual self-expression.

Contradictions abound. The photographs mimic globe-trotting mass media images that treat Woman as a commodity; they transform real women, unique in their personal experiences, beliefs, and tastes, into the generic Beautiful Bride. But these photographs are produced through a laborious, time-consuming process that presents brides and grooms with lived experiences that some young people may find more meaningful than the traditional family wedding rites put on by their parents. The photographs reproduce the visual codes of advertising photography, where Woman is a commodity, and take up many of the same beautifying techniques that U.S. critics argue alienate women from their bodies. Yet the photographs and their production process are perhaps *so* very alien-ating for women that they cease to alienate. Instead, they have the poten-tial to teach young women, fearful that their good looks can only go downhill after marriage, that beauty as defined in the mass media is an artificial construct. With enough time and money, virtually anybody can attain it. Failure to look like a fashion magazine model in everyday life is no failure. Making up is like putting on a costume, not to be confused with correcting one's "defects" so as to be minimally presentable in the social world.

At first blush, Taiwanese bridal photographs seem to be horrifyingly empty images, a blind pursuit of Westernness likely to land people in a state of cultural anomie and social illness. Given the serious attention they deserve, however, Taiwanese bridal photographs overflow with meaning.

In *Mimesis and Alterity,* Michael Taussig argues that cultural copies are never exactly like what they mime. This is certainly true of Taiwanese bridal photographs. They may be decent copies of gown advertisements in U.S. bridal fashion magazines, but they are terrible copies of American wedding photographs. Taussig contends that the slippage between the original and the knockoff provides a rich space for momentary flashes of self-awareness.

If I look at Taiwanese bridal photography as holding up a mirror to the West, I have two choices. The easiest choice is to reject Taiwanese bridal photography as a ridiculously poor, inauthentic copy of the origi-nal. When brides in Taiwan don white bridal gowns, several different ones for each bride, they are getting it all wrong. They miss the central point that the bridal gown is, for many Americans, a one-of-a-kind object invested with meaning and value. For a mother to see her daugh-ter wear her gown is often a mother's dream come true. The photographs ought to picture and preserve the very gown that the bride wore on her wedding day. Renting gowns, wearing different gowns in the photo-graphs from the ones worn on the wedding day, changing into three dif-ferent gowns on the wedding day—these practices show that people in Taiwan just don't get it.

There is, however, another way of looking in the mirror of Taiwanese bridal photography. How many American weddings are staged for the momentary, experiential pleasures of weddings as events in and of them-selves? Much about my wedding, I know, was staged primarily for the photographer's camera, not for the joy and transformative properties of the ritual in the moment. American weddings are certainly not immune from the kind of jockeying for status and construction of memory that goes on in Taipei weddings. To the extent that many American weddings may be what Daniel Boorstin (1972) calls pseudoevents—happenings that are staged for the express purpose of being made into events by garnering media attention—perhaps, then, Taiwanese bridal salons have it right. The compulsion to photograph life events throws into question the very meaning of "event" outside its photographic representation (Sontag 1977). Many parents today (in the United States *and* in Taiwan) experience their children's birthday parties and dance recitals primarily through the viewfinder of a camcorder. When unexpectedly presented with a stunningly colorful sunset, my cultural training leads me to reach for a camera, not to pause and enjoy such momentary pleasures in and of themselves. The image, and the compulsion to make images, often takes precedent over experience and substance. Rather than staging an event just to create photographic memories of it, why not skip the event altogether and focus one's resources on producing the most beautiful images? Perhaps the lack of authenticity that Taiwanese bridal photographs seem to show is not for being botched copies of the original but for being *too* good at mimesis? If so, the very emptiness of Taiwanese bridal photographs is a source of insight, of meaning. Taiwanese bridal photographs do not *create* the image/substance split; they merely dramatize it. Through their dramatization and mimetic excess, they unintentionally throw that which they mime—the West—into clearer relief.

Mimesis is potentially revolutionary, according to feminist theorists such as Luce Irigaray and Judith Butler. Noting that sexism is deeply and irrevocably entrenched in the very structures of Western thought, Irigaray (1985a) questions the very possibility of thinking outside sexism. While it is not possible to think or speak outside one's cultural structures, according to Irigaray, it is possible to undermine those structures by mimicking them. Building on this insight, Butler (1990) calls attention to the power of parody to transform consciousness. Drag performances, she argues, can powerfully disturb deeply held cultural views about sex and gender. The copy calls the presumption of an "original" into question; the parody creates space for critical reflection not otherwise accessible.

This ethnography of the Taiwanese bridal photo suggests that in media-saturated Taipei, where Western visual images and their local copies abound, the enormous gulf between local social realities and mass media images may be of both social and intellectual value. Where the distance between surface and substance becomes so evident, media images may lose their hold on everyday life. When the highly constructed nature of media images becomes widely known, media-based standards for appearance and conduct cannot serve as standards for lived realities. The distance created between image and reality, sign and referent, becomes a space for play and appropriation in social life.

Another reflection Taiwanese bridal photography mirrors back to the West is the emptiness of consumerism, a way of life that Herbert Marcuse describes as "euphoria in unhappiness" (Marcuse in Tomlinson 1991: 126–27). Consumer pleasures serve as compensation for capitalism's pitfalls, though momentary experiences of consumer euphoria never really erase the underlying unhappiness. In fact, as Colin Campbell (1989) points out, daydreaming about consumer ecstasy is often more pleasurable than attaining the goods. Consumers in Taiwan seem to know this when they buy highly romantic and beautiful photographs without *buying into* them. Though real life is not as grand as it appears in the photographs, having fabulous images of oneself provides a bit of compensation. If women at the time of marriage are sacrificing part of their happiness, at least dreaming about and experiencing momentary stardom soften the blow. Because of the environmental consequences of consumerism, the global familiarity of this logic ought to be of more concern than the visual emulation of the West seen in Taiwanese bridal photography. The "euphoria in unhappiness" approach to life, which depends on high levels of consumption, has worked so far only because such a tiny fraction of the world's population has lived this way. The same logic that makes luxurious bridal photos important in Taiwan exists in countless other acts of consumption. Taiwan, of course, is but one small island nation. The environmental implications of the spread of consumerist lifestyles become more worrisome in view of the fact that Taiwan's successes are emulated in China. The specter of more than one billion individuals in China in their own fossil-fuel-driven automobiles demands that those of us living in capitalist, consumerist societies— whether in Topeka or Taipei—make a choice that has profound implications. We in consumerist societies can try to prevent the vast populations of the world's poor countries from attaining *our* version of "the good life" or, better yet, we can look for new means of pursuing happiness, beyond the temporary euphoric highs consumerism has to offer.

When anthropologists writing on globalization insist upon asserting the endurance of the "local" in the face of globalization, they risk missing the nature of globalizing processes altogether. I might have constructed this study around Chinese or Taiwanese traditions of visual representation and assimilated the bridal photographs into a local framework. In fact, I tried hard to make sense of the photographs in resolutely local terms—with reference to *local* cosmologies, *local* perspectives on the body, and *local* definitions of personhood. But the people among whom I worked in Taipei could not fulfill my desire to find local resistance to the global in the bridal salon. Their sources of creative inspiration are not temple paintings of the gods but foreign magazines, MTV, and Hollywood movie advertisements. This is not to say that there is nothing local about Taiwanese bridal photographs. To the contrary, I have argued that everything from mass-media beauty norms to mass-mediated representations of romance takes on local meanings, gets assimilated to locally salient contests over status. Were I to insist on their Taiwaneseness to the exclusion of considering the mimetic, imitative nature of Taiwanese bridal photographs, however, I would miss the lessons about globalization that they teach. Among those lessons is the point that Taiwanese bridal photography is not merely a response to Taiwan's rapid globalization but is itself part of the globalization process. The photographs, and the people who make them, define and refine what people, places, gestures, things, and ideas count as cosmopolitan and, by their exclusion, what people, places, gestures, things, and ideas count as backwardly local. Taipei's bridal photography thus provides a window into how people living in a global city negotiate which aspects of their lives come to be considered elements of local culture and which come to be considered cosmopolitan global culture.

The executives of multinational beauty corporations need not advance one particular beauty ideal for women around the globe. To the contrary, they have learned that there is no need to replace local beauty standards with foreign standards to generate profits. Rather, they promulgate the subtler, underlying idea that physical beauty (however that is construed in particular locales) is vitally important, that women can and *should* improve their appearances through consumer consumption. In the beauty business, the specifics of beauty norms are not nearly as important as the fact that unrealistic norms exist such that most bodies will not live up to them. Even more important is spreading the notion that displaying beauty is "Woman's" duty, for "she" is "to-be-looked-at" (see Mulvey 1989). In this respect, the long-standing idealization of fair skin in Chinese societies, which finds new expression in modern photography, seems less notable than the newer obligation for women of all social groupings in Taiwan to achieve fair skin through the use of commodities lest they be deemed not just low-class but ugly and lazy, too. It is not enough to understand globalization through the lens of particular cultural practices like the preference for fair skin. One must also look at the social contexts of such practices, considering who is practicing them and why.

The globalization of beauty, in essence, is not about the specific content of beauty but about beauty's increasing social importance and its feminization. Mary Wollstonecraft, writing in 1796, argued that physical weakness resulting from particular beauty practices in her day was but one of the problems with social demands on women to beautify. The focus on physical beauty in one sex—too often to the exclusion of what she called "intellectual beauty and grace"—is harmful not only to women but to all members of society. Today, critics still argue that our focus on the visual distracts from matters of moral and political substance. Attention to the gender dimension of this problem is important. It is not that the pressures for women to beautify leave women more distracted by visual surfaces than men but that Woman is often the very means of distraction. The struggles for gender and global justice are profoundly interwoven.

Transnational cultural flows very often occur on the level of the image because surfaces divorced from substance travel freely. Many critics fear globalization will lead to cultural homogenization. Instead, globalization produces diversity precisely because people in places like Taipei can and do play creatively with transnational visual images. This is not to say, however, that globalization is unproblematic. Structuring all that diversity are, on the economic level, powerful multinational corporations that control the conduits of transnational flows and, on the cultural level, the compulsive focus on visual images to the neglect of substantive issues. If the importance of the visual influences American presidential elections and determines the flow of capital in Hollywood, what difference may focusing on the visual make for Taiwanese gender relations and Taiwanese families? With multinational beauty corporations defining Woman as a transnational symbol par excellence and casting the female body as a key site for the work of commodities—purifying, primping, correcting, and glamorizing—there's cause for concern about subtler, structural kinds of global homogenization even while surface cultural differences seem to flourish. In Taiwanese bridal photography, young people talk back to the globalizing processes that form the context of their lives. What do the photographs say? That Woman is a construction, that the Bride is framed. The problem is in holding onto that insight and the critical consciousness contained therein.

Lisette was one of the few brides who refused to be framed. On the surface, she appears to be a rebel resisting Taiwan's globalization. She wanted to wear a single red gown made just for her wedding, much like brides wore in the old days. Her refusal to adopt the bridal image demanded by her society and her parents, however, struck deep. She tipped the delicate balance of power between the generations that is a strong undercurrent in Taiwan's bridal industry. The now-customary Western bridal images were not compelling for Lisette because she was already—substantively—living the values they embrace. Lisette had no need to play with those superficial images, and that was the core of her conflict with her mother. If a Taiwanese bride in red is more Western than a bride in Victorian white, understanding culture and globalization clearly requires digging beneath the surface.

Notes

INTRODUCTION. FRAMINGS

1. The distinction between bridal photographs and wedding photographs is important. In Taiwan, *hunsha sheying* is occasionally reduced to its most literal meaning: a photograph of a person dressed in *hunsha*, a white Western-style gown that, the term implies, is accompanied by a veil or hair accessory of white, gauzy fabric. In practice, not all *hunsha* include a veil or gauzy hair accessory. Readers outside Taiwan might assume that "bridal photographs" necessarily include a woman who is on the verge of or in the midst of getting married—a bride. In fact, *hunsha sheying* is also used to describe photographs of a woman dressed in a white bridal gown who is not a bride. In other words, the appearance of being a bride is more important than the fact of being one. When speaking of *hunsha sheying* in English, people familiar with Taiwan usually call them "wedding photos." For reasons that will become increasingly clear to the reader, I reserve the use of "wedding photos" for photographs taken at wedding ceremonies or banquets and use "bridal photography" to refer only to professional posed portraits made by photographers employed by bridal salons *(hunsha sheyingshi),* whom I refer to as bridal photographers. Bridal industry photographers do not typically work as wedding photographers, and professional wedding photography, in contrast to bridal photography, is not universally practiced because reportage-style photographs are not as prized as carefully crafted, highly posed portraits.

I use the pinyin system of romanization for all Mandarin words except place names, for which I use the standard romanizations used in Taiwan. Pinyin for "Taipei" is "Taibei." "Taichung" is "Taizhong." This disparity is caused by the now nearly universal use of pinyin in North American sinological scholarship despite Taiwan's continued use of an older system of romanization.

2. When I met up with Hui-zhu again two years later, she had a one-year-old son, and her fear of losing her career had not been realized. Her brother-in-law was still unmarried.

3. Prior to conducting dissertation research fieldwork in 1996–1997, I lived in Taipei for two months of Mandarin language study in 1994, and for three months of Mandarin and Taiwanese language study and exploratory research in 1995. As already mentioned, I had also spent a year there for Mandarin language training and English teaching in 1992–1993.

4. I later learned that she sent out the Chinese headlines to a translation company that, however, provided absurdly poor translations, often nonsensical and containing grammar and spelling errors. When I asked why she did not fire the translation company and print the magazines with no English headings, she claimed that the bridal magazine in particular had an international audience of Singaporeans, Chinese Malaysians, and Chinese Americans, so English was necessary. I find this explanation highly questionable. All three magazines, like most glossy magazines on the Taiwan market, contain English headings. The headings seem to serve more as decoration or graphic art than as informational headings. To that end, the errors are irrelevant. What is important is the cosmopolitan *look* that the English text provides.

English words decorate many items in Taiwan, from T-shirts to umbrellas. I once rode in a Taipei taxi whose seat covers had English text printed on them. The text seemed to have been copied from something like a high school science textbook. The recent popularity of Chinese characters on all manner of fashionable objects in the United States is a similar phenomenon. If the characters are misprinted, few who enjoy them would mind because they cannot read them anyway. For example, I once visited an upscale futon store in New York where a futon cover decorated with four large Chinese characters was displayed upside down.

5. During my first visit to Taiwan, taxi drivers often told me that I spoke with a more standard Mandarin accent than they did. Trained in this accent, however, I was unable to understand what they were saying in my first few months and would respond with a polite and naive "I'm sorry. I can't understand." In addition to differences of pronunciation, there are also differences in preferred word usage and grammar.

6. In Taipei, young people tend to speak Taiwanese-influenced Mandarin in their interactions with one another. In recent years, it has become fashionable in elite, academic crowds to pepper conversations with bits of Taiwanese, yet most young and middle-aged people I observed spoke to each other in Mandarin even when both were native Taiwanese. When I spoke to elderly neighbors, often they understood my Mandarin but I could not understand everything they said, so I relied on interpreters (middle-aged neighbors or exceptionally well-educated old Taiwanese) to carry out such conversations.

7. Glamour photos *(yishuzhao)* are discussed in chapter 7. Professional photographs of couples who were not engaged to be married were uncommon in 1996–1997, though gay and lesbian couples may have been more likely to commission professional glamour shots of themselves as couples than heterosexual

couples were. My research focused on bridal photography, thereby excluding sustained attention to either individual or couple glamour photo albums. My study, as a result, has a heterosexist slant. I have some misgivings about this even while I believe that a rigorous, contextualizing study of Taiwanese bridal photography must hinge on the study of heterosexual institutions: weddings and family. Glamour photography became popular in Taiwan only after the contemporary bridal industry and its style of glamorizing bridal portraits rose to prominence. In later chapters I argue that bridal photography has deep roots in lived experiences of heterosexual courtship and weddings as they relate to families. When homosexual couples commission photographs that emulate those of their married, heterosexual peers, how do the photographic results differ and why? This question is ripe for further research. See the conclusion, however, for discussion of how mimesis reveals as much or more about "the original" than it does about "the copy."

8. These include the National Central Library, the Taipei Central Library, the Taipei Wen Xian Hui collections, the Institute of Ethnology and Institute of Taiwan History at Academia Sinica, the Women's and Gender Studies library of the Population Studies Center at National Taiwan University, and the photography archive at the Council for Cultural Affairs.

9. See Tomlinson's (1991) eloquent demonstration of inadequacies of the notion of cultural imperialism.

10. Daniel Miller (1995a, 1995b) goes so far as to argue that anthropologists cling fast to "the local" to legitimize anthropology's role as the periphery's representative to the center in these times of rapid, intense globalization, when the distance between center and periphery seems to be closing. Miller claims that when an anthropological study like Moeran's (1993) of a Japanese advertising firm reveals not local specificities but global homogeneity, the work is subject "to the rather cheap criticism from the traditional anthropologists that the differences were there if only he had looked 'deep' enough" (Miller 1997: 14).

11. Here I paraphrase Chakrabarty's (2000: introduction) analysis regarding a related but different problem.

12. Japanese magazines and television shows are another source of inspiration, especially for the "fun" photos interspersed among the more serious Western-inspired bridal photos.

13. "The West" is built through the same process revealed by Anderson (1983) in his work on nationalism as "imagined community," a concept I borrow later in the paragraph as well.

14. The body, particularly the female body, has become a site of cultural anxiety and corrective commodity action in recent decades (e.g., see Bordo 1993, 1997; Featherstone 1991; Radner 1995; Wolf 1991).

15. I do not mean to suggest that no one in Taiwan is critical of bridal photography. The perspectives of the rare critics I found willing to talk are highlighted throughout this book, in fact. Feminist activism and scholarship in Taiwan are, to my knowledge, not quite as focused upon beauty and body issues as is presently the case in the United States, where alarming rates of body dissatisfaction among girls and women have recently captured feminist attention (see,

however, Lan 1995 on the "politics of cosmetic sales"; Lin 1996, 1998 on weight-loss advertising; and Zhuang 1998 on *Beauty* magazine). More pressing feminist concerns in Taiwan have been divorce law reform, workplace discrimination, wife battering, rape, child prostitution, prostitutes' rights, and gay rights.

As John (1996) argues, U.S. feminists ought to acknowledge and historicize their research questions and political battles as particular to key times and places and as shaped by culturally, historically specific discourses. My own research interest in beauty and representations of "Woman" developed, in part, out of my experience with Yale students in an introductory women's studies course. My students wrote and spoke powerfully on their personal battles with body dissatisfaction and the contradictions they experienced between their self-images as elite college women focused on school and career who nonetheless had profound desires to alter their bodies through diet and cosmetic surgery. I was struck by their stories of competition among young women over how little they could eat in the dining halls and by their feelings of shame about their vain body obsessions. Students believed that their intense concerns about physical appearance suggested disgraceful flaws in character—that "feminine" narcissism and vanity stand at odds with academic seriousness in career-minded, independent women.

16. Lest I overstate this point, let me note that many bridal salons seek to expand business by promoting anniversary photographs and other portraiture. Many bridal packages in Taipei during the period of my fieldwork included the "lifetime membership" benefit of a free small-sized portrait every year for the couple's anniversary. The free portrait session, however, did not include the costs of the necessary makeover. The hope, moreover, was that couples would eventually purchase new albums of photographs and new wall hangings. It is difficult to estimate the present popularity of return visits for portraits. Many informants expressed interest in having anniversary or family portraits taken at a bridal salon where the quality is generally high, but it seems that fairly few people devote the time (and the money) to making portraits again. Bridal salons promote the idea, however. Romantic Bliss salon, for example, sent out flyers to all its previous customers on the occasion of Mother's Day, suggesting that a family portrait would make the perfect Mother's Day gift.

CHAPTER 1. HOW CAN THIS BE?

1. I thank Chen Ming-chi (n.d.) for sharing his unpublished literature review on class stratification in Taiwan.

2. On the complexities of class mobility and the life cycle in Taiwan, see Gates 1987. On Taiwan's new middle class, see Hsiao 1993.

3. Taiwan's bridal industry differs from other arenas in Taiwan, where parochialisms are downright celebrated, including wedding ceremonies, which are discussed in a later chapter. Old-fashioned Taiwanese-style restaurant/bars offering foods and decor of the Japanese colonial era have recently become popular. Like other instances of "self-Orientalization" (Said 1978), the commodification of Taiwaneseness is easily incorporated into broader streams of consumption. A fashionable young couple may eat out at a "Taiwanese" restau-

rant one night and the next day eat lunch at a restaurant specializing in the foods of China's former emperors. Also, see Hsieh (1994) on the marketing of Aborigine "culture" to Taiwanese tourists.

4. Zhang Yuan-ling (1997) kindly gave me a copy of her master's thesis on bridal photography in Taipei. She finished the paper around the time that I was concluding field research. In her thesis, Zhang constructs a history of the bridal photography industry based on her interviews with Taipei photographers, some of whom I had also interviewed. It was a bridal photographer/salon owner who put me in touch with Zhang, in fact. Though I tell the history differently than Zhang does, there is no conflict between our different tellings. She gives greater weight to particular individuals. My telling focuses more on underlying social factors and the broader context from which modern bridal practices emerged.

The only published work on bridal photography in Taiwan is a highly theoretical essay written by Zheng Wei-wei (1995). Zheng completed a master of fine arts degree in photography at Ohio University. After working for a short time as a modeling portfolio photographer in New York City, he returned to Taiwan and began working as bridal photographer, photography teacher, and magazine photography consultant. The volume in which this essay appears is extremely difficult to find and is not held by any of Taipei's major libraries. I received my copy from the author.

Unpublished works related to the bridal industry include two business administration master's theses, one on bridal exports (Su 1988) and the other on consumer behavior in the bridal market in Kaohsiung (Huang 1994).

5. May Fourth Movement (1919) writers and activists targeted marriage practices and the oppression of Woman (itself a newly constructed category at that time; see Barlow 1994) as a source of China's national weakness in the face of Western imperialism (Gilmartin 1993). The Republican and Communist governments each made consent by the bride and groom a legal prerequisite for marriage (Wolf 1984). Footbinding, concubinage, the seclusion of women, and exclusion of women from the examination system were also banned. In China in the 1950s (and until the 1980s), the state frowned upon traditional or feudal wedding customs and promoted modernized, nationalistic weddings that displaced ancestors and vertical (grandparent-parent-child) family relations from center stage. As with other matters of religious practice, the state in Taiwan was far less interventionist.

6. For more on the American wedding market and the internationalization of gown production, see Ingraham (1999).

7. The Suzukas advertise in Japanese tourist magazines and have arrangements with certain tour operators. In an interesting gender twist, some of these Japanese tourists are men who want to be made up as beautiful women and be photographed.

CHAPTER 2. FANTASY FOR SALE

1. Hochschild (1983) writes of the "commercialization of human feeling" in the American airline industry, where stewardesses similarly form pseudopersonal relationships with customers to serve airline interests.

CHAPTER 3. INNER AND OUTER WORLDS IN CHANGING TAIPEI

1. This trend marks a distinct break from the past, when men traveled alone to the Americas to work as "coolies" and sent money back to their wives and children in China. In many cases, a mother and child travel to the United States to live with relatives who are green-card holders, entitling the children access to public education. There are at least three important perceived benefits to a foreign education. First, the children will learn to speak English or another foreign language fluently, a highly valuable skill in Taiwan's job market. Second, the children will have better access to prestigious foreign universities. American, European, and Australian university degrees are extremely valuable in Taiwan. Third, boys who leave Taiwan to live overseas may be able to avoid compulsory military service if they spend no more than a few months in Taiwan each year until the age of thirty.

2. Similarly, the many Taiwanese businessmen who work in mainland China are known to have mistresses there.

3. The term "bride-price" is commonly used in the literature on China, and therefore I use "bride-price" rather than "bridewealth," which is common in anthropological literature more generally. There is a great deal of debate over the terms (see Goody and Tambiah 1973). The subjects of dowry and bride-price in Chinese weddings have attracted much more Western scholarly attention than have wedding rites themselves (see Ebrey's 1991 review of the literature on marriage and Mann's 1991 essay in the same volume on the mid-Qing). The relative importance of bride-price and dowry differs according to social class, region, and historical period (see Siu 1993; Yan 1996).

4. For literature on this topic outside Taiwan and China, see Burbank (1995) on Australian Aborigines, Collier (1997) on Spain, Hendry (1981) on Japan, Hoodfar (1997) on Egypt, and Rebhun (1999) on northeast Brazil. Friedrich Engels, in *Origin of the Family, Private Property, and the State,* first predicted that wage labor would have this impact on precapitalist marriage systems.

5. Self-selection of spouses—and with it greater independence of marrying couples from their parents—was practiced by the urban elite in Taiwan long before it became a widespread phenomenon (Thornton and Lin 1994). The history on the mainland is slightly different. There, free marriage and nationalism have close ties. May Fourth writers attacked the traditional Chinese family system as a cause of China's degeneration and its failure to prevent European and Japanese conquest. Two categories, "woman" and "free marriage," became repositories for beliefs about nationhood and modernity, though concern for the welfare of real women—such as the wives abandoned by male activists who took new wives in the cities—was overlooked (Gilmartin 1993; Gilmartin et al. 1994; see also Lin 1992). The People's Republic of China later sustained this commitment to liberating marriage from the traditional patriarchal family system (see Wolf 1984 and the other articles collected in a special edition of *Pacific Affairs* devoted to discussion of the 1980 marriage legislation in China).

Susan Brownell (1995) adds that discourses on the oppression of women in China were elite perspectives not shared by the masses. She argues that support for women athletes is high in China because of the belief that women, more than men, are able to withstand the "bitterness" of physical training and competition, since rural Chinese women are raised to perform the most strenuous tasks and survive with fewer resources (food, education) allocated to them.

At the time of the May Fourth movement in China, Taiwan was under Japanese colonial rule and was relatively unaffected. The Republican Chinese government that took over from the Japanese, however, brought its marriage laws to Taiwan and began teaching May Fourth writings in public schools. Although the bridal industry's romantic images certainly represent modernity, the association between romance and nationalism was absent in 1990s Taiwan.

6. In fact, wage labor did become a way of life for women *after* marriage (though not *in place of* marriage) in the 1970s and 1980s. Young married women left their childcare and household duties to their mothers-in-law and performed many kinds of small-scale rural factory work. See Gallin 1984, 1986; and Sando 1986.

7. Many Western romantic love stories also locate romance outside the social order, depicting the bliss of romantic love as conducive of social chaos, destruction, and death. The cultural logic of romantic love, argues sociologist Eva Illouz (1997), is utopian; romantic love requires stepping outside the mundane world of semiscripted social roles so that lovers can experience themselves as unscripted and authentic. For the same reasons that romance is utopian, however, romantic love is also antisocial; its preoccupation with individualistic pleasure and freedom often does not coexist comfortably with social order. Hence, explains Illouz, "Nature" and vacationing are closely associated with romance in mass media imagery because romance requires spaces outside everyday social experience where lovers may shed their social roles. By this same logic, the exclusion of romance from proper spousal relations and its seclusion in extramarital relationships make sense. The Romeo-and-Juliet conception of romantic love, whereby the individualistic bliss of romance produces social chaos and terrible (yet romantic) suffering, seems incompatible with marriage and family. Some contemporary American commentators (advice writers and radio show hosts, for example) would agree with the Taiwanese villagers interviewed by Margery Wolf: marriage is too important to leave to individualistic whims of romantic passion. They call, instead, for Americans to reduce the divorce rate by regarding marriage as an obligation, not a source of self-fulfillment and pleasure.

8. Abu-Lughod eloquently describes the culturally appropriate attitude of Bedouin spouses toward each other as "aggressive nonchalance" (1990: 31). She argues that sexual bonds and feelings of attachment in marriage are, in many patricentered societies, considered threatening to the solidarity of paternal kin. Abu-Lughod thus argues that the "veiled sentiments" contained in love poetry seem to suggest that beneath the veil of modest nonchalance, men and women often have strong feelings for each other. The disinterested attitudes expressed in nonpoetic forms of communication enact deference, especially for male elders who are most indebted to the patrilineal social structure. Abu-Lughod resists the temptation to view the feelings expressed in poetry as somehow more real than those expressed in other forms of communication where professions of romantic love are disallowed. Instead, she argues that in the same way that expressions of disinterest in the opposite sex mark modesty and honor, professions of the sub-

versive sentiment of love are valued because they suggest other cultural values—autonomy and freedom.

9. See Jankowiak (1993) and Whyte (1992) for Mainland China. See Schak (1975) for Taiwan.

10. The pattern is different in other parts of Taiwan because young adults often leave their homes to move to large cities, especially Taipei. People who grew up in Taipei frequently told me they preferred Taipei to other parts of Taiwan, which are considered backward in contrast to the capital city, so moving away from Taipei to live independently of one's parents was not an attractive option.

11. I thank Lisa Rofel for offering this wording. Beth Bailey (1988) makes the same point for the shift from calling to dating in the United States. See also Simon (2003) on the importance of public spaces for conducting gay social life in Taiwan.

12. In a similar vein, D. Wu (1997) describes how McDonald's serves as a comfortable hang-out spot both for high school students in search of study space and for a young mother who, after picking up her child from school, delays going home until her husband also returns home from work, to avoid spending time alone with her mother-in-law.

13. One report declares that the percentage of teenagers reporting premarital sexual experience (31.4 percent today) has nearly tripled in the past twenty years and that the percentage of teenage girls engaging in sex has risen more quickly than that of boys (Wang 1999). Here, however, I am writing about women and men past their teen years.

14. Notably, however, sexual morality probably plays a smaller part in the silence about dating than Americans might assume. In Taiwan, the critical code of ethics pertains to familial relations, not sex per se. Western observers of gay rights issues in Taiwan, too, have pointed out that anti-gay sentiment in Taiwan is primarily focused on the lack of filiality gay people exhibit toward their families by refusing to marry and produce sons, rather than on sexual morality as distinct from filiality. See also Brownell 1995 on athletes' transgressions of family ethics.

15. Taiwanese and Hakka both fall into the category *benshengren,* in opposition to Mainlanders, who are *waishengren* and more recent immigrants to Taiwan. Hakka or Kejiaren speak their own language, different from Taiwanese or Minnanhua because their ancestors hail from different parts of China. The Hakka are a very small ethnic group and are well integrated with other Taiwanese, though they may speak Hakka at home.

16. Early in my field research I made a point of following the television serial dramas aired nightly because they are full of romances found and broken. When I tried discussing the plot lines with informants, I found that fairly few young people ever watch the shows because they are too busy avoiding their homes, where the older generation sits watching television.

17. They say women who are "already married," but what I think they really mean is mothers. Newly married couples without children whom I met—particularly those who lived with the husband's parents—usually followed the pattern of unmarried people, spending a lot of time away from home.

18. In the late 1990s, the problem of discrimination against married women

in the workplace held the national media spotlight. Japanese firms, in particular, were known to fire women shortly after they married in anticipation that married women could not devote themselves to the office, work overtime as needed, and be available for company excursions and activities. These discriminatory practices were determined unconstitutional and crackdowns ensued.

19. Martin (1988) and Stockard (1989) each report that, in various times and places, Chinese people talked about marriage (specifically sexual relations and childbirth) as ritually polluting. The dread of marriage and the drop in women's status after marriage I describe in this chapter may be seen as continuous with these attitudes of times past.

20. Polygamy was outlawed in Taiwan in 1945 by ROC law, but nonetheless many people use the term "wife" or "little wife" *(xiaotaitai* or *xiaolaopo)* when referring to a mistress. Other terms used include "girlfriend" *(nüpengyou)* and "the third party" *(disanzhe)*. Some women I know refuse marriage outright on the basis that husbands, even those who are tender and caring before marriage, will ultimately take mistresses and neglect their wives sexually, emotionally, and financially in middle age and beyond. See Chang 1999.

21. James Watson's (1988: 9–11) description of the emphasis on performance over belief in Chinese ancestor rituals resonates strongly with Foucault's work on "discipline" and is considerably more concrete.

22. Judges required either a photograph of the husband engaging in sex with another woman or a police report indicating the same. Married women seeking divorce and child custody, accordingly, developed the practice of hiring private detectives to follow the husband into a hotel. Detectives called for a police escort at just the right moment and paid hotel staff to provide a key to the room. A successful "bust," as one can imagine, could be very difficult to accomplish. Most divorced women, therefore, lost custody of their children.

23. The topic of substituting insurance policies for the social insurance provided through marriage merits further research. Based on some of the stories I heard, I feared that insurance salespeople might have played on these young women's anxieties. I did not investigate the policies to learn if they were sound investments.

24. Due to a sex ratio imbalance and to multiple marriage among wealthy men, the percentage of men who never married is higher. In 1905, it was 3.2 percent, and in 1990, 9.2 percent (Lin, Lee, and Thornton 1994: 204).

25. Students who attended college in the early 1990s, for example, were likely to look askance at couples spending the night together in the rooms of student apartments. By the late 1990s there was greater acceptance of sexual relationships between students.

CHAPTER 4. FAMILY WEDDING RITES AND BANQUETS

1. Goldstein-Gidoni (1997) and Edwards (1989) argue that the Japanese customs Mr. Xu idealizes are, in fact, recently invented traditions.

2. This approach to culture is precisely what David Harvey (1989) places under the rubric of "postmodernity." He contends that the experience of time-

space compression in post-Fordist or late capitalism produces, among other things, cultural forms where appropriations across time (history) and space (cultures) are common.

3. Meskill's (1979) study of the Lins of Wu-feng provides a history of one such wealthy family, though the author does not specifically discuss weddings and wedding costume. See Garrett (1994: ch. 12) for discussion and illustration of imperial wedding attire.

4. The old-time photos these couples ridicule practice some of the conventions described by Stuart and Rawski (2001) for imperial-era ancestral portraits.

5. Some fortune-tellers have graduated from training institutes, complete with formal classes and textbooks. These institutes may exert standardizing forces on weddings as families consult their graduates on wedding ceremony specifics.

6. In the 1950s and 1960s, when childbirth occurred at home, parents sought to register their daughters' birth at a favorable time and date to improve their marriage chances (Wolf 1972: 118). With childbirth moving into hospitals and the advent of modern obstetrics in Taiwan, wealthy parents who want to improve their children's fates do so by planned Cesarean section and a hefty *hongbao* (red envelope of cash) for the obstetrician.

7. Pregnancy is not necessarily considered unbecoming for a bride. One aspect of this story that may not be clear to non-Taiwanese readers is that Xin-de and Yu-ling's presumption was that families would want to *protect* the health of the pregnancy by refraining from the use of a Taoist symbol over the bride's head. There is nothing scandalous about a child being born only eight months after his or her parents' wedding, though often people politely pretend that the bride's first sexual experience will occur the night of her wedding. About the same time as this event, a friend called Mei-hua to invite her to his wedding banquet and proudly boasted that his "wife" was already expecting. Occasionally couples use premarital pregnancy as an excuse to force their parents to agree to their marriage—a less reputable situation than a bride who becomes pregnant after her engagement but before the wedding. See also Hu 1984.

8. See Chan (2000) for a critique of U.S. anthropologists' interpretation of bridal laments.

9. Watson (1997: 19) argues that the celebration of individual birthdays was unknown in much of East Asia until McDonald's introduced children's birthday parties.

10. Red, both historically and in the present period, is the color associated with weddings, though pink, or "light red" *(fen hongse)*, is a widely accepted substitute. On other occasions as well, red suggests happiness, vitality, and fertility (Wolf 1970).

11. The Japanese colonial administration in Taiwan took interest in family matters such as marriage and child rearing only insofar as to keep careful household registration records but did not attempt to change or actively control marriage practices. Toward the end of the colonial period, during years of intense fighting on the Chinese mainland (1937–1945), the colonial administration launched the Kominka movement to "Japanify" Taiwan's Chinese population, encouraging the adoption of Japanese styles of clothing and spoken Japanese

even among Taiwanese (Chou 1991). During this brief time period, some Taipei families may have adopted Japanese wedding practices, and many urban couples probably wore Japanese-style bridal attire. See also Ching 2001.

12. Compare with Wolf (1972), where the go-between's neutrality is important.

13. Margery Wolf (1972: 117–18) claims that parents who disapproved of a match experienced misfortune, such as broken rice bowls around the house, during the period they took possession of the potential spouse's eight characters *(bazi)* as a way out of the negotiations without causing a loss of face to either side. As my primary research was not on wedding negotiations but on bridal salons, I am curious whether I coincidentally missed talk about *bazi* undermining love matches in favor of talk about bride-price or whether the older generation today is less likely to find fault with the *bazi* in favor of causing difficulties over monetary aspects of the exchange. Cases where parents begin marriage discussions and then end them for any reason may be uncommon. The balance of power between parents and their grown children has changed, and parents do not have complete control over their children's marriage choices.

14. Hu's (1984) ethnography of rural change in 1970s Taiwan documents that in Liu T'so village the value of women's earnings was carefully calculated into bride-price negotiations. The parents of sons used premarital pregnancy to hurry up marriage negotiations and begin receiving a daughter-in-law's earnings, while the daughters' parents sought to delay marrying out daughters to continue benefiting from their earnings a bit longer (1984: ch. 6). Hu argues that wage labor among young women drove up the rate of premarital pregnancy, increasing women's age at marriage, elevating bride-price, and lowering dowries. In Taipei today, where the degree of couples' independence from their families is greater, the significance of women's wages is slightly different. Although married couples commonly provide partial or complete financial support to elderly and disabled members of the husband's family (primarily his aged parents but also siblings), in the early years of marriage, when the groom's parents may not yet have retired, the importance of the wife's wages to his parents is less direct, as the parents are probably self-supporting. Couples commonly contribute money (and sometimes labor) toward the support of the *wife's* elderly parents too (see Lee, Parish, and Willis 1994). In very wealthy families, moreover, the husband's parents may demand that his wife refrain from paid employment altogether, even if she has university degrees. In sum, the significance of women's wages depends greatly on the social class and life circumstances of the husband's family, which makes it difficult to generalize about the meaning of bride-price given my limited data.

Siu (1993: 170) makes the point that in post-Mao Nanxi Zhen, Guangdong, dowry and bride-price represent "intense and rapid devolution of property" from the older generation to the younger at the time of marriage, rather than transfers between groom's and bride's families per se. Siu argues that what may appear to be the revival of traditional bride-price and dowry practices in China in the 1980s and 1990s is, in fact, a new type of cultural practice to China. In Taiwan, where bride-price and dowry practices were never subject to a state ban, marital transfers have certainly changed but are by no means new inventions or reinventions, as in China. Nevertheless, Siu's insight about the changed significance of bride-price applies to Taipei.

15. These cakes often look like large, thick cookies and have the consistency of a rich, very moist cake. Many are imprinted with a design on the top, such as the double happiness character.

16. Not all brides dress in evening gowns for engagement ceremonies, but this bride's family was throwing an engagement banquet for their family and friends that day. In some parts of Taiwan, the bride's family sponsors a banquet the day after the wedding. Occasionally the bride's family co-sponsors the wedding-day banquet and invites its friends and family then. This family's custom was to entertain on the engagement day, however, and the bride dressed up accordingly.

17. Round foodstuffs—oranges, eggs, and balls made of glutinous rice—appear frequently at engagements and weddings. I have heard of the groom taking a hard-boiled egg whole in his mouth during the ceremonies, and I myself, along with all other guests, have been asked to eat many bowls of sweet *tangyuan* soup containing glutinous rice balls, and round fruits and nuts, at weddings.

18. During my field stay, two men were arrested for mail fraud when they sent fake wedding invitations to hundreds of strangers. The thieves used common surnames on the invitations. They were found out on the banquet day, when guests showed up to find no banquet. As the men had anticipated, quite a few invited guests sent their *hongbao* in advance. Interviews with victims of the fraud revealed that although they did not recognize the couple's names, they feared these were children of important family friends or were former friends they had forgotten, so they sent cash gifts for fear of violating reciprocal obligations.

19. At least one Taipei entrepreneur recognized a market for entertainment services at city weddings and created an "elegant" show of classical music and dancers available for wedding banquet performances. In 1997, however, such a thing was extremely rare.

20. Charsley makes a similar point about the role of the bride in contemporary Scottish weddings, where the bride

> is unquestionably the focus of attention. . . . She is the star of her day, the day on which, in an ancient structuring of priorities, it is for an instant bride and groom—the bride and her bridegroom—before the twist of marriage makes it husband and wife. But it is what the bride represents for others that gives the role its widest significance. It submerges a woman's individual personality and makes her an instantly recognizable object, a source of interest, attraction and often emotion even to people who know her not at all. . . . [The bride] can stand for youth and beginnings and hope, for freshness and innocence, for successful growing up, for the passage of generations, for love and romance. (1991: 182)

21. Mass weddings such as this one have historical roots in state ideological campaigns promoting frugality among the Chinese people in order to save the nation. The Chinese Communist Party promoted mass weddings in mainland China and, during the Cultural Revolution, banned large, private wedding celebrations.

CHAPTER 5. MAKING UP THE BRIDE

1. For an interesting but possibly unreliable source on the use of makeup in Chinese history, see *Zhongguo Huazhuangshi Gaishuo,* published in association

with Shiseido's institute for research on beauty (Li 1996). The author discusses makeup use from the Qin dynasty (221 B.C.E.) to the present.

2. I found soap and skin bleach advertisements in early- and mid-twentieth-century Taiwan newspapers that are similar to those McClintock (1995) describes for nineteenth-century British colonies.

3. My younger informants, stylists among them, told me that it is mandatory (in the eyes of the older generation in particular) for brides to wear their long hair in pinned-up styles, as this is Chinese tradition—even though older informants' wedding photographs make it clear that this "tradition" was not in practice in the immediate past. Today, all but a few women require artificial hair extensions to create the mandatory long curls pinned in piles on top of the head. Freedman (1970) notes, of Chinese weddings of the more distant past, that the pinning up of the bride's hair marked the wedding as an initiation rite for the bride. (Cf. Watson 1998 on another association for long hair in Chinese cultures, mourning.)

4. Taipei has two districts known for face-peeling treatments: one near the Shilin night market and another near the Xingtian Temple in a pedestrian underpass beneath the street. Practitioners also visit neighborhood markets from time to time. Their customers are primarily old women, who have their faces peeled in preparation for special occasions like the lunar New Year and family weddings.

5. Though he does not discuss face peeling, Dikötter (1998) describes historical Chinese cultural beliefs about body hair (mao) and the association of hairless skin with high civilization. The relative hairlessness of female bodies in Taiwan is one physical trait that women there considered more beautiful than Caucasian traits. Many Taiwanese are surprised to learn that Caucasian women have heavier body hair than they upon encountering them in person. Signs of body hair are usually erased from the media representations of women through which many Taiwanese come to "know" foreign female bodies.

6. Though most cultural studies scholars credit Foucault for bringing attention to the body as a site of political and intellectual significance, feminist thinkers prefigured Foucault's notion of "docile bodies" as early as Wollstonecraft (see Bordo 1993: 17–23).

7. For example, see Firestone 1970; Holland and Eisenhart 1990; Wollstonecraft 1796.

8. See Zones 1997 on public health risks and cosmetic products. See Scott 1985 and 1990 for his theory of "weapons of the weak" and argument against the notion of false consciousness.

9. Laura Miller (1999) describes how a Japanese aesthetic salon uses a microcamera to show the subject a view of her wrinkles in extreme close-up and high detail in order to sell her additional expensive skin treatments.

10. Wolf and other writers (such as Faludi 1991 and Chernin 1981) have argued that a new emphasis on women's appearances is a cultural backlash against women's advancements in the public sphere. Such authors imply that the recent intensification of the cultural imperative of female beautification ought to be understood as part of a patriarchal conspiracy against women. I find Bordo's perspective that problems with beauty stem from wider elements in consumer society more compelling. Her work on bulimia (1993), for example, sees the binge-and-purge cycles of the bulimic as the perfect enactment of capitalist cul-

ture. Other critics of consumer capitalism similarly note the high level of anxiety about the body and relate this problem to broader social forces (for example, Baudrillard 1998; Featherstone 1991). Ewen argues that the American cultural belief in the power of consumer objects to transform lives and souls points to a serious underlying problem: "The extent to which objects seem so promising may be but an index of the extent to which the human subject is in jeopardy; destined only to be defined as *consumer*" (1988: 91; italics in original).

11. Haiken (1997: 94–95) argues that in the 1920s and 1930s the psychological notion of the "inferiority complex" came to justify the practice of cosmetic surgery by credentialed medical doctors. Previously, the belief that legitimate medicine was used only for healing (not for beauty) kept cosmetic medical practices outside mainstream, legitimate medical practice and schooling. The association of good looks with social and economic success (and bad looks with mental illness) permitted surgical intervention in cases of physical "deformity." Over time, "deformity" as a category came to include more features, including common ones such as bumps on noses and nonfolded eyelids. As Zones (1997: 265) aptly puts it, plastic surgeons now consider appearance to be "a bona fide medical problem."

12. Mass media products available in Taiwan come from the world over, including Hong Kong, Japan, China, Singapore, India, Europe, Australia, and the United States. (And, of course, Taiwanese media products also travel the world over.) Media from particular places have particular valences in Taiwan. Hong Kong kung-fu *(gongfu)* movies are important in Taiwan but are not particularly relevant to bridal photography. Japanese television shows and magazines have extremely strong influence on hair and clothing fashions. Notably, fair skin and double eyelids are considered desirable in Japan, too. Laura Miller's (personal communication) research shows that these traits were culturally valued long before Western mass media images were everyday objects in Japan, as may also be the case for Taiwan. Nevertheless, images of Caucasian bodies carried particularly high symbolic capital in 1990s Taiwan. Local advertising campaigns frequently employed foreign models because associating a locally made product with (white) Westerners added value to the product by conferring cosmopolitan status upon it.

13. "Western" is not an accurate designation because stylists do *not* emulate the looks of many residents of North America and Europe who are not Caucasian. "Caucasian," however, is not a perfectly suitable term, either. The looks considered superior are certainly not shared by all Caucasians, a social group that has only recently come to include curly-haired Jews such as me.

14. In contrast, Haiken (1997: 203–5) reports that cosmetic surgeries became popular in Vietnam as a direct result of American military presence there. Vietnamese women saw employment and marriage opportunities in molding their bodies to American beauty preferences for larger breasts and rounder eyes and hips.

15. Many thanks to Lisa Rofel, who reminded me to point out how offensive we *yang guizi* (foreign ghosts) are.

16. In Taiwan, beauty schools offer "medical" aesthetic training certificates, and physician supervision is not required for many procedures.

17. In Taiwan, it is not considered rude for a woman to apply makeup in public; however, beauty preparations such as facial treatments and body slimming take place in hidden-away, quiet places, in stark contrast to bridal styling.

18. I met only two male stylists during the course of my research. One was a student stylist who aspired to making up movie stars. The other seemed to serve primarily as the bridal salon's manager. There may be more male presence in film and television styling, but generally beauty schools—which also serve as consulting firms for commercial styling projects—are female-dominated, though some are male-owned, and male ownership in the beauty sector is probably quite high. I would estimate that male stylists in the noncommercial beauty sector account for less than one percent of stylists.

19. I thank Joseph Lipton, who shared this observation with me and introduced me to physiognomy more generally.

20. Stylists often earn less than successful saleswomen because they do not work on commission. Instead, they are often paid on a scale that takes into account how many stylings they perform each month. Their income may, in some salons, include a small commission to reward them for work that produced more sales and to tie their interests with those of the company as a whole. Experienced, successful stylists are not likely to style in bridal salons for many years. Instead, they might become part-owners or go to work as "consultants" (freelance stylists) or beauty school teachers.

21. Taiwan has hostess clubs quite similar to those described by Allison (1994) for Tokyo. The women who work as hostesses at many such clubs are presumed available for the purchase of sexual services. Although much less common, Taipei also has clubs that reverse the gender roles: Men serve as hosts and women as clients. I was told that these clubs are extremely expensive and that the fee for male sexual services is much higher than for female sexual services. Rumor has it that the women who patronize such establishments are not female executives but the wives of executives who, like their husbands, seek extramarital sex.

22. Interestingly, the use of foreign models was infrequent in bridal magazines during my research period. Earlier bridal magazines, unearthed in the National Library and at used bookshops, pictured foreign models extensively, however. Among the important changes I observed in bridal magazines over the years is the growing importance of local bridal salons as advertisers, which may account for the change to local models.

23. Concerns about "cultural imperialism" or the erasure of cultural difference run high, at certain times and in certain contexts, in the United States and other Western countries. Tomlinson (1991) and others have argued that American and European interests in retaining cultural difference often amount to wanting to preserve that difference purely for the sake of Western aesthetic and tourist appreciation. Difference, like any novelty, is valued for its consumptive possibilities; and global capitalism, in important ways, seeks to create and structure such variation in order to sell "difference" to wider markets (Wilk 1995). In 1996–1997, the multinational razor manufacturer Schick promoted the idea that women in Taiwan ought to shave their armpits, not because American

women do so (as a result of ad campaigns in the United States during an earlier period, when beards had become fashionable for men and the market for razors was diminished) but because, according to a Schick survey, a high percentage of men in Taiwan "prefer" shaven armpits on women. One wonders if this ad strategy, too, was designed to cater to an American marketing manager's anxieties about cultural imperialism and the desire to construct uniquely local beauty needs.

24. Colleagues tell me that in Japan and Korea tanned skin, indexing leisure and vacation, has become stylish for women.

25. I could have written this chapter with a focus on hair instead of makeup, as the manipulations performed on hair in many ways parallel those done on faces. The preferred styles are extremely labor intensive, requiring dozens of hairpins. Hairstyling is generally less invasive than makeup styling at the start of the day, but in upper-echelon salons, where hair is restyled to match each costume change, hairstyling changes can be quite painful. The sculpting lotions and hairsprays applied to hold curls in place stiffen the hair and glue it to the head. Stylists take down the piles of pinned and glued curls and brush out the stiffened hair before repinning and gluing new curls into place for each slightly varied hair design.

26. Just as parents regard marriage as too important to be left up to the preferences of individuals.

27. Gamson's work (1994) on the phenomenon of celebrity in the United States points to the activities of celebrity producers, who maintain an air of authenticity for celebrities, and celebrity watchers, who seek to disrupt the protected distance given to celebrities in order to catch glimpses of the real person lurking behind the staged persona.

CHAPTER 6. ROMANCE IN THE PHOTO STUDIO

1. I use the terms "feminized" and "emasculated" interchangeably in this chapter and in those that follow. These are my terms and analysis, not the words of informants, though I believe that this analysis strongly resonates with their experiences. I use these terms because they bridge two levels of gender analysis: gender roles and gender as a metaphor for power relations (see Scott 1988). Grooms are twice feminized by bridal photography. First, they step out of conventional gender roles by sitting for the photo session rather than acting as photographer. Second, for men, stepping out of conventional gender roles is usually a step downward in status. In this second sense, "feminization" stands as a metaphor for movement downward in the status hierarchy.

2. Goffman (1973: 14) refers to such instances as "disruptive events"— something that occurs to disrupt or contradict the actor's performance and thereby reveal its constructed nature.

3. Illouz (1997: 46–7) argues that contemporary U.S. perspectives on romance emphasize intensity, whereas Victorians emphasized romance as a "slow, gradual courtship process" entailing introspection and revelation. The current focus on romantic intensity as opposed to romance as a time-bound process dovetails with the "visualization" of romantic love as an *atemporal* state.

4. See Abu-Lughod and Lutz (1990), who explain why anthropologists ought to take a practice or performance-centered approach to emotion. One of the best-known anthropologists of romantic love, however, writes from a different perspective; William Jankowiak introduced his edited volume of fifteen papers on romance with the following:

> It has long been taken for granted that romantic love is the fruit of cultural refinements and not an experience readily available or accessible to non-Westerners in general. Indeed, it has become axiomatic among Western literati that the experience of romantic passion is a mark of cultural refinement, if not obvious superiority, and that the less cultured "masses" are incapable of such refinement: desire and lust, yes; romance and love, no. The hidden inference of this assumption may be that romantic love is the prize or reward of true culture. (1995a: 1–2)

Jankowiak finds evidence of the presence of romantic passion—defined as "any intense attraction involving the idealization of the other within an erotic context"—in nearly 150 different cultures (1995a: 4–5; Jankowiak and Fischer 1992). I find this type of research dissatisfactory because of its perspective on culture (viewing "cultures" as reified objects) and its ethnocentric understanding of emotion. The conceptualization of emotions as having ontological status and as natural, universal, and internally located within persons partakes of modern Western psychological notions of self, personhood, subjectivity, and embodiment (see Lutz and White 1986). Anthropological scholarship on emotion that takes account of these criticisms investigates ethnopsychologies (e.g., Potter 1988 on China), reveals the culturally constructed character of emotions, calls attention to their being situated in power relations (e.g., Hochschild 1983, Rebhun 1993), and challenges the Western thought/feeling dichotomy (e.g., Lutz 1988, Rebhun 1993).

5. Like most loan words from English, which are reshaped to fit the sounds of Mandarin, the meaning of the word *langman* has no relationship to the characters used to make it. One of Taipei's older bridal shops was known as Luomen, a competing pronunciation of "romance" that fell out of use.

6. Occasionally photographs may replicate couples' own experiences of courtship (shopping together, sipping from a single glass through two straws). When the photographs and actual courtship activities dovetail, however, they do so in large part because courtship activities themselves often imitate mass media images.

7. See the introduction for a discussion of cultural hybridity—the appropriation and domestication of foreign practices, objects, and ideas.

8. Reviewing psychological and sociological research on the United States and other Western societies, Cancian (1986) describes the different approaches that men and women have to love and argues that love in the United States has increasingly come to be defined according to feminine norms following the polarization of home and workplace that took place under industrialization. Cancian criticizes scholars for having contributed to this trend by defining love according to feminine definitions—communication of feelings, expressions of tenderness, and the emotion work of being caring and supportive toward another. Men, the research on the United States indicates, have a "distinctive style of love that focuses on practical help, shared physical activities, spending time together, and

sex" (702). Cancian further argues that culturally defining love in a feminized fashion is politically problematic for a number of reasons: men's style "involves giving women important resources, such as money and protection that men control and women believe they need"; the feminized definition of love "reinforces this power differential by leading to the belief that women need love more than do men," which studies suggest is untrue; sex gets defined as men's terrain; the emotion work that women do "is either ignored or redefined as expressing feelings" when studies suggest that it ought be seen as a type of essential work; the association of love with femininity serves to legitimate "impersonal, exploitative relations in the workplace and community," defined as masculine spaces; and "the feminization of love intensifies the conflicts over intimacy between women and men in close relationships." She continues: "One of the most common conflicts is that the woman wants more closeness and verbal contact while the man withdraws and wants less pressure. . . . Intimacy is her 'turf,' an area where she sets the rules and expectations" (704–8). I would argue that a similar phenomenon is at play in Taiwan, where American representations of romantic love have played an important role in the restructuring of intimate relationships that occurred alongside Taiwan's process of capitalization. "Taking care of" another by providing financial and other types of resources, including familial belonging in a patriline, gets constructed as the "traditional" form of loving, while communicating and expressing tenderness are associated with modernity.

9. Romance, too, sometimes forms the basis for globalization—as when romance ensues between people of different national origins—and this, too, is gendered. It is taken as common knowledge in Taiwan that Western men find Chinese women attractive as marriage partners. Common knowledge also maintains that Western women are less likely to regard Chinese men as attractive marriage partners, a subject on which I was frequently quizzed by Taiwanese taxi drivers. Note that in this sexual political economy, it is women who are the agents of Taiwan's reach to the West, not men. By contrast, people also commonly speak about Taiwanese men's affinity for women of poor neighboring countries, who are widely considered more submissive than Taiwan's women (see chapter 3). Hence, Taiwanese men's romantic pursuits pull Taiwan's reach away from the West even as Taiwanese women's romantic pursuits reach toward it in a game of transnational hypergamy.

10. In that time period, Taiwan was called "China" in magazine articles such as this.

11. The literature also documents that in divorce, women experience downward class mobility while men fare better economically, even though the data suggest that un-remarried men have higher mortality rates, implying that their emotional dependence on women may be underestimated by cultural beliefs (see Cherlin 1992; Newman 1987).

12. Bourdieu (1990) notes the popularity of photography as a hobby among men, not women, in France and observes that those who make photography a hobby construct their work as masculine—in explicit opposition to the everyday use of cameras for family photography, in which women, even if they do not always hold the camera, organize the photographable events.

13. I know also of a photography club in Taipei that pays nude female mod-

els, usually Caucasian, to pose for a group of male photographers on weekends in remote nature reserve areas.

14. Sontag's (1977) analysis of photography as social practice emphasizes the use of words such as "shooting" and "capturing" to describe the act of "taking" a photograph, which, she argues, is always an act of aggression. Sontag and numerous other commentators note that photographs objectify their subjects even as they idealize them. Note the parallel to romance, wherein a woman is simultaneously idealized and, if she accepts her suitor's overtures, captured.

15. My analysis of performative aspects of photo-shoot behavior draws from Goffman's dramaturgical theory of social life. In *The Presentation of Self in Everyday Life* (1973), Goffman takes many of his examples from workers in service industries (for example, waitresses, physicians). See also Hochschild (1983) on flight attendants.

16. I use the pronoun "he" because the majority of bridal photographers I met were men. Later in this chapter I discuss women photographers at length.

17. Photographers enjoy high status even when customers are not present. Contributing to their idealization is the international market for Taiwanese-style bridal photography. Local salon owners who invest in China's bridal market, for example, must convince photographers from Taiwan salons to spend lengthy periods of time in the People's Republic training new photographers. Financial incentives and flattery accomplish this. Additionally, Japanese, Korean, Singaporean, and Malaysian investors send photographers to Taipei to study bridal photography with local photographers. This international attention further serves to bolster the status of photographers.

18. Sontag (1977: 13–14) discusses similar associations made between sexual conquest and photography in Euro-American contexts. My investigations into photography archives in Taiwan suggest that the art of portraiture was not so focused on young, female subjects before the 1960s. All of the photography manuals and magazines published from the mid-1960s onward that I located take up young women as their primary photographic object (with animals and aborigines as secondary objects) and contain very few photographs of Chinese men. The samples of photographers' work from the 1940s and 1950s collected in archives, however, include portraits of both men and women, young and old.

19. Male photographers told me that customers are similarly skeptical of young photographers. The thinking is that photography is a skill that takes many years to develop and therefore young people cannot be high-quality photographers. At the same time, photographers are expected to be in touch with young people's values and youth consumer culture.

20. Sex and gender often operate in distinct ways, not just in Taiwan. See the classic statement for gender as an analytic category distinct from sex in Scott 1988.

21. Gillis (1988) claims that the new bridal wear that emerged in Victorian times sought to cover the body and restrict bodily movement because middle-class ladies designed the new "sentimental rituals" in explicit contrast to earlier wedding rites, which had centered upon the body and bodily movement. The bride's immobility represented the association of marriage with mind over body and sentiment over sex.

22. The photographer's restricted use of the camera is one of the many ways that photographers keep their status distinctly higher than that of an assistant. When photographers deem the timing right (and given other conditions of their relationship to an assistant), they will occasionally invite the assistant to look through the viewfinder and perhaps even release the shutter. Assistants accept their low pay (just over NT $15,000 per month before commissions) in part because they are apprentices.

23. To my knowledge, clients did not read these feminized styles of comportment as "gay," merely as unusually personable for men.

24. I seldom heard Taiwanese spoken during Taipei photo shoots, even though photographers sometimes spoke with their clients in intermittent Taiwanese outside the studio—further evidence of the role-playing that takes place at bridal photo shoots. Switching to Taiwanese during breaks conveys the sense of being off-stage.

25. After observing a close friend's photo shoot, I found that she and I had noted very different things. For example, she did not realize that the photographer had been using this peculiar form of speech until I pointed it out to her. Rather, she came away from the shoot feeling that the photographer genuinely liked her and *particularly* enjoyed taking *her* pictures.

26. Hochschild (1983), in her study of flight attendants, describes something similar as the "commercialization" of feeling.

27. This is not my wording. I take pains in this ethnography not to essentialize my subjects, but my subjects do so themselves.

28. Although I attended comparatively few glamour photography *(yishuzhao)* shoots of young single women, on one that I observed, the photographer explicitly flirted with the young woman. He said, for example, "Oh, you're so beautiful . . . let me look a little longer" (through the viewfinder). See chapter 7 for more on *yishuzhao.*

29. Although bridal photographers are obliged to comply with requests made by clients, I marveled at the high degree of client passivity in shoots. For example, couples very rarely protested the use of color combinations that I found extremely ugly. Eventually I learned that the least attractive backdrop/costume pairings—swirls of rust, brown, green, and ivory with a bride's pink gown, for example—were often used for black-and-white photos. The couples at these shoots were as unaware of the intention to print in black and white as I was. Other photographic techniques of light and focusing can dramatically change the appearance of a backdrop or prop, too. Photographers seldom told the couples what effects they were producing in the photos, yet couples quietly followed the photographer's authoritative lead and the brisk pace he set for the shoot. Only upon viewing the proofs did they understand what the photographer had been trying to do with scenes that during the shoot had appeared so perplexingly unattractive.

30. Goffman (1973) makes this point for all service industry workers: They easily become cynical about their own performances because they are required to delude their audiences for their own gain, the client's own good, or the good of the community. In other contexts, it is much easier for actors to believe in their performances when they don't view their behavior as performative.

CHAPTER 7. CONTEXTUALIZING BRIDAL PHOTOS
IN TAIWAN'S VISUAL CULTURE

1. Burgin and Sontag both concede that lay people are not always mystified by photography's truth claims. From photography's invention in the 1830s, double-exposure prints pointed to photography's ability to create, not just mechanically reproduce. In the 1850s, when photographic retouching was invented, "the news that the camera could lie made getting photographed much more popular" (Sontag 1977: 86).

2. Sekula (1982: 87) puts it this way: "The overall function of photographic discourse is to render itself transparent." He further argues that we ought, instead, to see every photographic image as "a sign, above all, of someone's investment in the sending of a message." Burgin's *Thinking Photography* contains the classic statements on this aspect of photography.

3. See Chalfen (1998) for a review of ethnographic works on what visual anthropologists call "home mode" photography. Newton (1998) provides a useful discussion of anthropologists' tendency to prefer documentary modes of photography, while their informants tend to want control over their appearances before the anthropologist takes their photographs.

4. The same body-part assemblage occurs in Taiwan. I learned, for example, of a Pampers television commercial picturing a mother and baby that required two women and two babies to film these perfected images. A Chinese model was used for the baby's face, but a half-Caucasian, half-Chinese model was used for the baby's buttocks. The darkened skin just above a small child's buttocks (known in English as the "Mongolian spot") is very common among Taiwanese babies but was considered imperfect and therefore unpresentable in the commercial. The model who served as the mother's face apparently did not have sufficiently fair and beautiful arms to be seen lifting the bare-bottomed, fair-skinned baby from a bathtub. An additional model played the part of the mother's arms. I found this example particularly disturbing because it pathologizes the infant's Mongolian spot by banishing its representation without seeming to do so. Editing cuts masked the substitution of babies, of course. I thank the father of the buttocks model for sharing this story.

5. Stuart Ewen (1988) takes up this issue with regard to celebrities who see themselves in highly manipulated images. He notes that one star, Lanie Kazan, reported that she became homebound for seven years because of her inability to accept her own imperfect looks in juxtaposition to her perfected photographs. Another star, Marlene Dietrich, said: "I look at my face on the television screen, and I remember how every tooth was capped, how every inch of skin on that face and neck was dyed and shaped, and in spite of knowing all that, I sit back and say to myself, 'that is *still* the most beautiful thing I've ever seen in my life'" (quoted in Ewen 1988: 89).

6. Goffman's *Gender Advertisements* (1979) decodes the gender problematics of advertising photographs' composition. He notes, for example, that when women are pictured touching something, their touch is always very light, suggestive of caressing, not grasping (as when men are pictured). Virtually all of Goffman's insights apply to Taiwanese bridal photography. The reason for this

Notes to Pages 209–210

confluence, of course, is that the bridal photographs seek to replicate not the gendered constructs as such but rather the norms of advertising photography. For example, a very common pose in bridal photographs shows a bride with one open hand very delicately touching the side of her face. Goffman's analysis would suggest that such photographs construct women as tentative, as mentally absent from the scene, and as delicate creatures. True, perhaps, but viewers in Taiwan also recognize these photographs as referencing Oil of Olay advertisements (the company logo depicts a woman with both hands lightly touching her face in this manner). I do not focus on aspects of pose and photo composition in this chapter because Goffman and others have written extensively on this topic in relation to advertising.

7. The same is true of makeover practices. Some techniques do beautifying work by hiding "imperfections" (foundation makeup), and some techniques do beautifying work by marking cultural associations with prestige and fame (hairstyles taken from celebrities, jewelry that looks expensive), while still other techniques (false eyelashes) do both kinds of work simultaneously.

8. I thank Tao Yi-feng, who served as both native informant and fellow American social scientist, for pointing out parallels between bridal photography and karaoke.

9. Note that the decontextualizing and freezing of the face by the camera are much of what makes the appearance of lines on the face so important. Photogenic faces are merely those that freeze easily and well. Unphotogenic faces are those that tend to pick up shadows in places where shadowing is considered unattractive. A good photographer can easily compensate by filling those areas with light. In lived life, however, the face is never frozen in time and always appears in context, making the same facial shadowing far less problematic for good looks. Ewen (1988: 85) observes, "The ideal photographic model is one who is able to suggest action while standing still, who can imply inner substance or attitude through remote and superficial means. The idealized human becomes the plastic human, able to maintain a perpetual smile, not one whose beauty requires a lingering familiarity, an intimacy."

10. The procedure for making such photographs is to expose for the darkest zones when shooting the film and, later, to print for the lightest zones. This style of portraiture is popular in *National Geographic*, for example.

11. During my fieldwork, there were two bridal photography manuals on the market. Hong (1996) provides sample photographs and details the equipment, film, and settings used to make them. I interviewed a photographer and salon owner by the name of Wang Sir who had published a book on bridal photography emphasizing unusual, or "next generation," shots. Interestingly, Wang Sir told me he produced this book with the intention of earning money on it overseas. In Southeast Asia, Korea, Japan, and Mainland China intense interest in replicating the success of Taiwan's bridal industry has provided Taiwan's photography schools (like Fototek) and photography publications (magazines, books) with a profitable overseas market.

12. In chapter 5 I described stylists' techniques for making the face appear more three-dimensional, including using brown and white highlights on and around the nose. These efforts are designed, in part, to counteract the flattening

effects of the studio lights, though they are also deployed on the wedding day to create the illusion of a more pronounced nose.

13. Laura Mulvey (1989) argues that conventional film practices place male stars in three-dimensional space that seeks to look realistic ("Renaissance space") and female stars in close-ups that fragment the body and appear two-dimensional, as cut-outs or icons. Verisimilitude is required for filmic images of the male star because the narrative requires the viewer to identify with him. The lack of verisimilitude in filmic images of women, she argues, is made possible because the viewer, identifying with the male protagonist, joins the hero in his gaze at the female star. The function of the close-up, according to Mulvey's theory, is not to advance the narrative but to take pleasure in looking. The two-dimensional, unrealistic picturing allows the gaze to fetishize the woman, meaning that the threat of castration she necessarily evokes is deadened by her idealization in an unrealistic image.

14. Photographers' reports of how much retouching they do varied. Some claimed they do a great deal of retouching. Others claimed the opposite. Because retouching entails high labor costs, I suspect the more elite, higher-priced salons can afford to do more of it and therefore produce consistently perfect images of brides without relying as much on underexposure and light diffusion or blur. Hence, their photographs are seen as more "natural" despite the fact that producing them involves *more* intervention.

Taiwanese-style bridal portraiture (and multiple rental gowns) is popular among Chinese populations in Flushing (New York), San Francisco, and Los Angeles, and salons similar to those in Taiwan operate in these cities (though I met several couples who had returned to Taiwan specifically to take their photographs at higher-quality/higher-status Taipei salons). At a bridal fair in Taiwan's World Trade Center, a local bridal salon owner introduced me to a Chinese American bridal salon owner from Los Angeles. The two were negotiating a business deal. The American salon owner explained to me that he needs to send his photo processing work to Taiwan, where the lower costs of portrait making justifies the high cost of shipping the heavy albums and large portraits back to Los Angeles. I suspect two reasons for the big difference in cost. First, although wages in Taiwan are not substantially lower than in the United States for other industries, Taiwan's vocational school system provides children who fail to test into academic high schools and colleges with good technical training, including in photography. Comparable skilled labor in the United States is more expensive. Second, the extensiveness of the bridal photography industry in Taiwan allows for more routinization and mass production than is possible in the United States, where this industry is small. The only comparable U.S. industry I am aware of is the "glamour shots" photo studios that generally operate out of shopping malls.

15. I use the word "pornography" in the less pejorative sense of the word: materials produced for the purpose of sexual stimulation. In the literature on pornography in the United States and Europe, the presumption is that pornographic materials serve primarily as an aid to masturbation. I do not know for certain if this is the precise case for celebrity *xiezhenji* in Taiwan.

16. Men can and do pose for glamour albums, though the overwhelming

majority of glamour albums picture girls or young women. Scott Simon (personal communication) told me that glamour photos are popular in certain circles of gay men. Having visited every major Taipei shopping district where glamour photo studios have streetside marketing booths, I encountered only one that, in 1996–1997, displayed a male glamour album.

17. A low-end glamour photo package in 1997 was NT $3,000. The customer got a makeover with hair styling, several dress changes, and one roll of thirty-six exposures shot by a photographer on 35-millimeter film. The photographer gave the woman small prints of every shot in a free album of clear plastic sleeves along with the negatives, unretouched. Packages that included a professionally assembled photo album of larger prints cost upward of NT $6,000. Many bridal salons that offered glamour photo services shot only on 120-millimeter film and included the high level of styling and photography service provided to brides. In 1997, these packages started at NT $10,000.

18. Sexualizing photographs such as these, by the way, also adorn the walls and storefronts of bridal salons.

19. Japan is reported to be the inspiration for the very popular "cute" bridal styles. For analysis of the popularity of "cute" in Japan, see McVeigh (1996) and Kinsella (1995).

20. I announced my purchase of these *xiezhenji* to a close female friend in her thirties, who said she wanted to see them, as she had never seen a "real" *xiezhenji*. It was she who told me that the model featured was famous for her breast size enhancement ads. My friend commented immediately that these photographs must have been taken before her breasts were nonsurgically enhanced because they appeared relatively small. Another strong possibility, of course, is that the larger breasts pictured beneath clothing in the advertisements were fakes. *Xiezhenji*, unlike other forms of pornography, feature the bodies of people who are famous (models, film stars, singers). Other images of seminude women (found on virtually every cigarette lighter sold at convenience stores and on most boxes of betel nuts sold at roadside stands) typically depict women who are exceptionally large-breasted by local standards.

21. A recent news story entitled "The Mao of Sex: Why Chinese Women Line Up to Take It Off" (Chang 2001), about similar photographs made in the People's Republic of China, appeared in the *Wall Street Journal*. One quote is strikingly similar to what women in Taipei told me about their bridal albums: "I have a pretty good figure and I will be old one day, so if I don't get a record of this I will regret it."

22. When I first became interested in bridal photography, I asked a Taiwanese friend to do some exploratory "shopping" at a bridal salon to help me learn something about the bridal industry. I assumed that Elaine, a lesbian who had been in her current relationship for about one year, had no thoughts about commissioning bridal photographs, at least not anytime soon. I was wrong. It turned out that she had given the possibility a great deal of thought, which became evident shortly after we sat down to look at sample albums with a bridal salon saleswoman. Elaine asked whether the salon had a photographer who could create a *narrative* album that would tell the story of her relationship with her "boyfriend." She envisioned a sequence of photos depicting key moments in

the development of the relationship. The saleswoman said that they had never entertained such a request but promised to consult with a photographer and call Elaine with a reply. As we walked out, Elaine complained about how nonsensical bridal albums are because they never tell a story. In her work as a director of low-budget, heterosexual pornographic films, Elaine had a strong sense of the possibility for telling a story through a sequence of images and hoped, one day, to have such an album made. As this story makes clear, her vision for bridal photography was unique.

23. I'm using the term "postmodern" here following the theory of postmodern culture set out by Jameson (1991) and Harvey (1989). My interest is perhaps more in consumer capitalism than in the theory of the postmodern as such. Ewen (1988), for example, discusses many of the same phenomena under the rubric of modernism. These periodizations are not critical to my argument.

24. My position differs from that of Campbell (1989), who emphasizes the importance of hedonism as a telos of capitalism. Campbell stresses that capitalist hedonism separates pleasure from physical satisfactions. It is a romantic hedonism of longing to experience *imagined* pleasures, while actual fulfillment is impossible. The central importance of imagination, he argues, gives rise to the ceaseless consumption of novelty.

25. In early-twentieth-century America, Ewen and Ewen (1982) argue, advertising and commodity aesthetics spoke to the disorientation and alienation people experienced with modernization, urbanization, and immigration. The emphasis of style over character made sense in a new world where strangers were everywhere and one saw oneself as a stranger in others' eyes.

Harvey (1989: 289) regards the increasing dependence upon images (over substance) as a problem. It "means that the serial and recursive replications of identities (individual, corporate, institutional, and political) become a very real possibility and problem." He cites the forgery of antiques and replications of ancient buildings as throwing authenticity into question altogether and asks, "What happens when the imitations become real?" This type of worry is strikingly absent from bridal salons, which appropriate the distinction between the real and the image as an arena for play, leisure, and even more consumption of images. The few women I searched out who refused to take bridal photographs all cited their dislike for the artifice as their motivation to resist the practice despite pressure from family members and friends.

26. The fact that it is brides, not grooms, who are most central in the commodification process of the photographs is not accidental. As Lury (1996) remarks, many writers have noted that the female body is constructed, in advertising, as the central site for the actions of commodities as well as the central figure of desire. Winship (1987) argues that because women are both the primary sign of advertising *and* the primary market targeted by advertisers, women are construed as consumers of *themselves*.

CHAPTER 8. THE CONTEXT OF LOOKING

1. Compare Barthes (1981: 63) on looking at old photographs of his mother and his dissatisfaction in the struggle to recognize her. He writes: "I never recog-

nized her except in fragments, which is to say that I missed her *being,* and that therefore I missed her altogether. It was not she, and yet it was no one else."

2. I thank Zhang Yuan-ling for relating this story to me (see Zhang 1997).

3. Gamson (1994) takes up the subject of the backstage in the cult of celebrity in Hollywood. He argues that there is seldom a true off-stage moment because backstage footage, too, is performed for the camera. The boundary of the stage, in recent decades, has moved further and further back with efforts to represent celebrities as if in natural or real contexts.

4. Bourdieu (1990) writes that photographs always depict subjects in their social roles and that family photography, more generally, focuses on events that highlight social integration. Wedding photographs, therefore, are particularly important because weddings are high points of social integration. Ironically, Taiwan-style bridal photographs use the cultural emphasis on weddings (as high points of family integration) as an excuse to make highly individualistic photographs. See also Pinney (1997) on wedding photography in Nagda, India.

Bibliography

Abu-Lughod, Lila. 1990. "Shifting Politics in Bedouin Love Poetry." In *Language and the Politics of Emotion*, edited by C. Lutz and L. Abu-Lughod, pp. 24–45. Cambridge: Cambridge University Press.

Abu-Lughod, Lila, and Catherine Lutz. 1990. "Introduction: Emotion, Discourse, and the Politics of Everyday Life." In *Language and the Politics of Emotion*, edited by C. Lutz and L. Abu-Lughod, pp. 1–23. Cambridge: Cambridge University Press.

Ahern, Emily Martin. 1973. *The Cult of the Dead in a Chinese Village*. Stanford: Stanford University Press.

Allison, Anne. 1994. *Nightwork: Sexuality, Pleasure, and Corporate Masculinity in a Tokyo Hostess Club*. Chicago: University of Chicago Press.

Anderson, Benedict R. 1983. *Imagined Communities: Reflections on the Origin and Spread of Nationalism*. London: Verso.

Appadurai, Arjun. 1991. "Global Ethnoscapes: Notes and Queries for a Transnational Anthropology." In *Recapturing Anthropology: Working in the Present*, edited by R. Fox, pp. 191–210. Santa Fe: School of American Research Press.

———. 1996. *Modernity at Large: Cultural Dimensions of Globalization*. Minneapolis: University of Minnesota Press.

Argyrou, Vassos. 1996. *Tradition and Modernity in the Mediterranean*. New York: Cambridge University Press.

Bailey, Beth L. 1988. *From Front Porch to Back Seat*. Baltimore: Johns Hopkins University Press.

Bakhtin, M. M. 1968. *Rabelais and His World*. Translated by H. Iswolsky. Cambridge: Massachusetts Institute of Technology Press.

———. 1981. *The Dialogic Imagination: Four Essays by M. M. Bakhtin*, edited by M. E. Holquist, translated by Caryl Emerson and Michael Holquist. Austin: University of Texas Press.

Barclay, George. 1954. *Colonial Development and Population in Taiwan*. Princeton: Princeton University Press.

Barlow, Tani. 1994. "Theorizing Woman: Funü, Guojia, Jiating." In *Body, Subject, and Power in China*, edited by A. Zito and T. Barlow, pp. 253–89. Chicago: University of Chicago Press.

Barthes, Roland. 1977. *Image-Music-Text*. Translated by S. Heath. New York: Hill and Wang.

———. 1981. *Camera Lucida*. Translated by R. Howard. New York: Hill and Wang.

Baudrillard, Jean. 1994. *Simulacra and Simulation*. Translated by S. Glaser. Ann Arbor: University of Michigan Press.

———. 1998. *The Consumer Society*. London: Sage Publications.

Beausoleil, Natalie. 1994. "Makeup in Everyday Life." In *Many Mirrors: Body Image and Social Relations*, edited by N. Sault, pp. 33–57. New Brunswick: Rutgers University Press.

Benjamin, Walter. [1931] 1972. "A Short History of Photography." *Screen* 13(1): 5–26.

———. 1985. "The Work of Art in the Age of Mechanical Reproduction." In *Film Theory and Criticism*, edited by G. Mast and M. Cohen, pp. 675–94. New York: Oxford University Press.

Berger, John. 1972. *Ways of Seeing*. London: Penguin Books.

Boorstin, Daniel. 1971. *The Image: A Guide to Pseudo-Events in America*. New York: Atheneum.

Bordo, Susan. 1993. *Unbearable Weight: Feminism, Western Culture, and the Body*. Berkeley: University of California Press.

———. 1997. *Twilight Zones: The Hidden Life of Cultural Images from Plato to O. J.* Berkeley: University of California Press.

Bourdieu, Pierre. 1984. *Distinction*. Translated by R. Nice. Cambridge: Harvard University Press.

———. 1990. *Photography: A Middle-Brow Art*. Stanford: Stanford University Press.

Brownell, Susan. 1995. *Training the Body for China: Sports in the Moral Order of the People's Republic*. Chicago: University of Chicago Press.

Brumberg, Joan Jacobs. 1997. *The Body Project: An Intimate History of American Girls*. New York: Random House.

Burbank, Victoria Katherine. 1995. "Passion as Politics: Romantic Love in an Australian Aboriginal Community." In *Romantic Passion*, edited by W. Jankowiak, pp. 187–95. New York: Columbia University Press.

Burgin, Victor. 1982a. "Introduction." In *Thinking Photography*, edited by V. Burgin, pp. 1–14. London: Macmillan.

———. 1982b. "Photographic Practice and Art Theory." In *Thinking Photography*, edited by V. Burgin, pp. 39–83. London: Macmillan.

Butler, Judith. 1990. *Gender Trouble: Feminism and the Subversion of Identity*. New York: Routledge.

Cai, Shang-ji. 1995. *Renxiangxue Mingyun Miji*. Taipei: Yi-qun Shudian.

Campbell, Colin. 1989. *The Romantic Ethic and the Spirit of Capitalism*. London: Blackwell.

Cancian, Francesca. 1986. "The Feminization of Love." *Signs* 11(4): 692–709.

———. 1987. *Love in America*. New York: Cambridge University Press.

Canclini, Nestor Garcia. 1995. *Hybrid Cultures*. Minneapolis: University of Minnesota Press.

Chakrabarty, Dipesh. 2000. *Provincializing Europe*. Princeton: Princeton University Press.

Chalfen, Richard. 1998. "Interpreting Family Photography as Pictorial Communication." In *Image-Based Research*, edited by J. Prosser, pp. 214–34. London: Falmer Press.

Chan, Wing-hoi. 2000. *Writing Women's Words: Bridal Laments and Representations of Kinship and Marriage in South China*. Ph.D. dissertation, Yale University.

Chang, Jui-shan. 1999. "Scripting Extramarital Affairs: Marital Mores, Gender Politics, and Infidelity in Taiwan." *Modern China* 25(1): 69–99.

Chang, Leslie. 2001. "The Mao of Sex." *The Wall Street Journal*, August 10, sec. A, p. 1, col. 4. Accessed via Lexis-Nexis.

Chapkis, Wendy. 1986. *Beauty Secrets: Women and the Politics of Appearance*. Boston: South End Press.

Charsley, Simon. 1991. *Rites of Marrying: The Wedding Industry in Scotland*. New York: Manchester University Press.

Chen, Ming-chi. n.d. "Class Stratification in Taiwan." Unpublished paper.

Cherlin, Andrew. 1992. *Marriage, Divorce, Remarriage*. Cambridge: Harvard University Press.

Chernin, Kim. 1981. *The Obsession: Reflections on the Tyranny of Slenderness*. New York: Perennial Library.

Chiang, Lan-hung. 1989. "New Social and Economic Roles of Chinese Women in Taiwan and Their Implications for Policy and Development." *Journal of Developing Societies* 5(1): 96–106.

Chiang, Lan-hung Nora, and Lin-ku Yen. 1985. *Past and Current Status of Women in Taiwan*. Taipei: Population Studies Center, National Taiwan University.

Ching, Leo. 2001. *Becoming "Japanese": Colonial Taiwan and the Politics of Identity Formation*. Berkeley: University of California Press.

Chou, Wan-yao. 1991. "The Kominka Movement: Taiwan under Wartime Japan, 1937–1945." Ph.D. dissertation, Yale University.

Chow, Rey. 1991. *Woman and Chinese Modernity: The Politics of Reading between West and East*. Minneapolis: University of Minnesota Press.

Chung, Lawrence. 2001. "Growing Number of Single Women in Taiwan." *The Straits Times* (Singapore). November 4, p. 27. Accessed via Lexis-Nexis.

Cohen, M. L. 1976. *House United, House Divided: The Chinese Family in Taiwan*. New York: Columbia University Press.

Collier, Jane Fishburne. 1997. *From Duty to Desire: Remaking the Family in a Spanish Village*. Princeton: Princeton University Press.

Comaroff, Jean, and John Comaroff. 1991. *Of Revelations and Revolutions:*

Christianity, Colonialism, and Consciousness in South Africa. Chicago: University of Chicago Press.

Constable, Nicole. 1997. *Maid to Order in Hong Kong: Stories of Filipina Workers.* Ithaca: Cornell University Press.

Coward, Rosalind. 1983. *Patriarchal Precedents: Sexuality and Social Relations.* Boston: Routledge and Kegan Paul.

Davis, Kathy. 1995. *Reshaping the Female Body: The Dilemma of Cosmetic Surgery.* New York: Routledge.

de Beauvoir, Simone. 1952. *The Second Sex.* New York: Bantam.

de Lauretis, Teresa. 1984. *Alice Doesn't.* Bloomington: Indiana University Press.

Diamond, Norma. 1975. "Women under Kuomintang Rule: Variations of the Feminine Mystique." *Modern China* 1(1): 3–45.

Dikötter, Frank. 1998. "Hairy Barbarians, Furry Primates, and Wild Men: Medical Science and Cultural Representations of Hair in China." In *Hair: Its Power and Meaning in Asian Cultures,* edited by A. Hiltebeitel and B. Miller, pp. 51–74. Albany: State University of New York Press.

Dirks, Nicholas B., Geoff Eley, and Sherry B. Ortner. 1994. "Introduction." In *Culture/Power/History,* edited by N. Dirks, G. Eley, and S. Ortner, pp. 3–48. Princeton: Princeton University Press.

Douglas, Mary. 1966. *Purity and Danger.* New York: Routledge.

Douglas, Mary, and Baron Isherwood. 1979. *The World of Goods.* London: Allen and Lane.

Ebrey, Patricia. 1991. "Introduction." In *Marriage and Inequality in Chinese Society,* edited by R. Watson and P. Ebrey, pp. 1–24. Berkeley: University of California Press.

———. 1993. *The Inner Quarters: Marriage and the Lives of Chinese Women in the Sung Period.* Berkeley: University of California Press.

Eco, Umberto. 1982. "Critique of the Image." In *Thinking Photography,* edited by V. Burgin, pp. 32–38. London: Macmillan.

Edwards, Walter. 1989. *Modern Japan through Its Weddings.* Stanford: Stanford University Press.

Ehrenreich, Barbara, and Deirdre English. 1978. *For Her Own Good: 150 Years of Experts' Advice to Women.* Garden City, N.Y.: Anchor Press.

Elias, Norbert. 1978. *The History of Manners.* Translated by E. Jephcott. New York: Vrizen Books.

Engels, Friedrich. [1902] 1985. *Origin of the Family, Private Property, and the State.* London: Penguin Books.

Errington, Shelly. 1998. *The Death of Authentic Primitive Art.* Berkeley: University of California Press.

Escobar, Arturo. 1995. *Encountering Development.* Princeton: Princeton University Press.

Ewen, Stuart. 1988. *All Consuming Images.* New York: Basic Books.

Ewen, Stuart, and Elizabeth Ewen. 1982. *Channels of Desire: Mass Images and the Shaping of American Consciousness.* Minneapolis: University of Minnesota Press.

Fabian, Johannes. 1983. *Time and the Other.* New York: Columbia University Press.

Faludi, Susan. 1991. *Backlash: The Undeclared War Against American Women*. New York: Anchor Books.

Featherstone, Mike. 1991. "The Body in Consumer Society." In *The Body: Social Process and Cultural Theory,* edited by M. Featherstone, M. Hepworth, and B. Turner, pp. 170–96. London: Sage Publications.

Finkelstein, Joanne. 1991. *The Fashioned Self.* Cambridge: Polity Press.

Firestone, Shulamith. 1970. *The Dialectic of Sex: The Case for Feminist Revolution*. New York: Bantam.

Foucault, Michel. 1977. *Discipline and Punish: The Birth of the Prison*. Translated by A. Sheridan. New York: Vintage Books.

———. 1978. *The History of Sexuality.* Vol. 1. Translated by R. Hurley. New York: Random House.

Frank, Andre Gunder. 1998. *ReOrient*. Berkeley: University of California Press.

Freedman, Maurice. 1970. "Ritual Aspects of Chinese Kinship and Marriage." In *Family and Kinship in Chinese Society,* edited by M. Freedman, pp. 163–87. Stanford: Stanford University Press.

Freedman, Rita. 1986. *Beauty Bound.* Lexington, Mass.: Lexington Books.

Furman, Frida Kerner. 1997. *Facing the Mirror: Older Women and Beauty Shop Culture.* New York: Routledge.

Gallin, Rita. 1984. "The Entry of Chinese Women into the Rural Labor Force: A Case Study from Taiwan." *Signs* 9(3): 383–98.

———. 1986. "Mothers-in-Law and Daughters-in-Law: Intergenerational Relations within the Chinese Family in Taiwan." *Journal of Cross-Cultural Gerontology* 1(1): 31–49.

———. 1989. "Women and Work in Rural Taiwan." *Journal of Health and Social Behavior* 30(4): 374–86.

Gamson, Joshua. 1994. *Claims to Fame: Celebrity in Contemporary America.* Berkeley: University of California Press.

Garrett, Valery M. 1994. *Chinese Clothing: An Illustrated Guide.* New York: Oxford University Press.

Gates, Henry Louis Jr. 1985. "Writing 'Race' and the Difference It Makes." In *"Race," Writing, and Difference,* edited by H. L. Gates, Jr. Chicago: University of Chicago Press.

Gates, Hill. 1987. *Chinese Working-Class Lives: Getting By in Taiwan.* Ithaca: Cornell University Press.

———. 1992. "Small Fortunes: Class and Society in Taiwan." In *Taiwan: Beyond the Economic Miracle,* edited by D. F. Simon and M. Y. M. Kau, pp. 169–86. Armonk, N.Y.: M. E. Sharpe.

Gibson-Graham, J. K. 1996. *The End of Capitalism as We Knew It.* London: Blackwell.

Gillis, John R. 1988. "From Ritual to Romance." In *Emotion and Social Change,* edited by C. Stearns and P. Stearns, pp. 87–119. New York: Holmes and Meir.

Gilman, Sander L. 1998. *Creating Beauty to Cure the Soul: Race and Psychology in the Shaping of Aesthetic Surgery.* Durham, N.C.: Duke University Press.

Gilmartin, Christina. 1993. "Gender in the Formation of the Communist Body Politic." *Modern China* 19(3): 279–329.

Gilmartin, Christina, et al., eds. 1994. *Engendering China: Women, Culture, and the State*. Cambridge: Harvard University Press.

Goffman, Erving. 1973. *The Presentation of Self in Everyday Life*. Woodstock, N.Y.: Overlook Press.

———. 1979. *Gender Advertisements*. New York: Harper and Row.

Goldstein-Gidoni, Ofra. 1997. *Packaged Japaneseness: Weddings, Business, and Brides*. Honolulu: University of Hawaii Press.

Goody, Jack. 1996. *The East in the West*. Cambridge: Cambridge University Press.

Goody, Jack, and S. J. Tambiah. 1973. *Bridewealth and Dowry*. Cambridge: Cambridge University Press.

Government Information Office, Republic of China. 1999, 2001, 2002. http://www.gio.gov.tw.

Grosz, Elizabeth. 1994. *Volatile Bodies: Toward a Corporeal Feminism*. Bloomington: Indiana University Press.

Haiken, Elizabeth. 1997. *Venus Envy: A History of Cosmetic Surgery*. Baltimore: Johns Hopkins University Press.

Hall, Stuart. 1980. "Encoding/Decoding." In *Culture, Media, Language: Working Papers in Cultural Studies, 1972–79*, edited by S. Hall et al., pp. 128–38. London: Hutchinson.

Hansen, Joseph, and Evelyn Reed. 1986. *Cosmetics, Fashions, and the Exploitation of Women*. New York: Pathfinder.

Harrell, Stevan, and Chun-chieh Huang. 1994. "Introduction: Change and Contention in Taiwan's Cultural Scene." In *Cultural Change in Postwar Taiwan*, edited by S. Harrell and C. C. Huang, pp. 1–18. Taipei: SMC Publishing.

Harvey, David. 1989. *The Condition of Postmodernity*. Oxford: Basil Blackwell.

Hendry, Joy. 1981. *Marriage in Changing Japan*. New York: St. Martin's Press.

Hobsbawm, Eric, and Terrence Ranger, eds. 1992. *The Invention of Tradition*. Cambridge: Cambridge University Press.

Hochschild, Arlie Russell. 1983. *The Managed Heart: Commercialization of Human Feeling*. Berkeley: University of California Press.

———. 1989. *The Second Shift*. New York: Viking.

Holland, Dorothy, and Margaret Eisenhart. 1990. *Educated in Romance: Women, Achievement, and College Culture*. Chicago: University of Chicago Press.

Holland, Dorothy, et al. 1998. *Identity and Agency in Cultural Worlds*. Cambridge: Harvard University Press.

Hong, Zheng-shi. 1996. *Shiyong Hunsha Sheying & Yishuzhao Sheyingxue*. Gaoxiong: Huang Jia.

Honig, Emily, and Gail Hershatter. 1988. *Personal Voices: Chinese Women in the 1980's*. Stanford: Stanford University Press.

Hoodfar, Homa. 1997. *Between Marriage and the Market: Intimate Politics and Survival in Cairo*. Berkeley: University of California Press.

hooks, bell. 1992. *Black Looks: Race and Representation*. Boston: South End Press.

Hsiao, Hsin-huang Michael. 1993. "Discovering East Asian Middle Classes: Formation, Differentiation, Politics." In *Discovery of the Middle Classes in East*

Asia, edited by H. H. Hsiao, pp. 1–22. Nankang: Institute of Ethnology, Academia Sinica.

Hsieh, Shih-chung. 1994. "Tourism, Formulation of Cultural Tradition, and Ethnicity: A Study of the *Daiyan* Identity of the Wulai Atayal." In *Cultural Change in Postwar Taiwan,* edited by S. Harrell and C. C. Huang, pp. 184–202. Taipei: SMC Publishing.

Hsiung, Ping-chun. 1996. *Living Rooms as Factories: Class, Gender, and the Satellite Factory System in Taiwan.* Philadelphia: Temple University Press.

Hsu, Min-tao. 1998. " 'Fitting In' to the 'No Return Trip': Women's Perception of Marriage and Family in Taiwan." *Proceedings of the National Science Commission, ROC-C* 8(4): 527–38.

Hu, Tai-li. 1984. *My Mother-in-Law's Village: Rural Industrialization and Change in Taiwan.* Taipei: Institute of Ethnology, Academia Sinica.

Huang, Rui-chong. 1994. "Gaoxiongshimin Hunsha Sheying Shaofei Xingwei zhi Yanjiu." M.B.A. thesis, Zhongshan Daxue Qiye Guanli Yanjiusuo.

Illouz, Eva. 1997. *Consuming the Romantic Utopia: Love and the Cultural Contradictions of Capitalism.* Berkeley: University of California Press.

Ingraham, Chrys. 1999. *White Weddings: Romancing Heterosexuality in Popular Culture.* New York: Routledge.

Irigaray, Luce. 1985a. *Speculum of the Other Woman.* Translated by G. C. Gill. Ithaca: Cornell University Press.

———. 1985b. *This Sex Which Is Not One.* Translated by C. Porter. Ithaca: Cornell University Press.

Jameson, Fredric. 1991. *Postmodernism, or, The Cultural Logic of Late Capitalism.* Durham, N.C.: Duke University Press.

———. 2000. "Globalization and Political Strategy." *New Left Review* 4: 49–68.

Jankowiak, William. 1993. *Sex, Death, and Hierarchy in a Chinese City.* New York: Columbia University Press.

———. 1995a. "Introduction." In *Romantic Passion,* edited by W. Jankowiak, pp. 1–20. New York: Columbia University Press.

———. 1995b. "Romantic Passion in the People's Republic of China." In *Romantic Passion,* edited by W. Jankowiak, pp. 166–84. New York: Columbia University Press.

Jankowiak, W., and E. Fischer. 1992. "A Cross-Cultural Perspective on Romantic Love." *Ethnology* 31(2): 149–55.

John, Mary E. 1996. *Discrepant Dislocations: Feminism, Theory, and Postcolonial Histories.* Berkeley: University of California Press.

Johnson, Marshall. 1992. "Classification, Power, and Markets: Waning of the Ethnic Division of Labor." In *Taiwan: Beyond the Economic Miracle,* edited by D. F. Simon and Y. M. Kau, pp. 69–100. Armonk, N.Y.: M. E. Sharpe.

Kaw, Eugenia. 1994. " 'Opening' Faces: The Politics of Cosmetic Surgery and Asian American Women." In *Many Mirrors: Body Image and Social Relations,* edited by N. Sault, pp. 241–65. New Brunswick: Rutgers University Press.

Kendall, Laurel. 1996. *Getting Married in Korea.* Berkeley: University of California Press.

Kinsella, Sharon. 1995. "Cuties in Japan." In *Women, Media, and Consumption in Japan,* edited by L. Skov and B. Moeran. Honolulu: University of Hawaii Press.

Kuhn, Annette. 1991. "Remembrance." In *Family Snaps,* edited by J. Spence and P. Holland, pp. 17–25. London: Virago Press.

Kung, Lydia. 1983. *Factory Women in Taiwan.* Ann Arbor: UMI Research Press.

Lan, Pei-jia. 1995. "Xiaoshou de Zhengzhi: Xingbiehua de Laodong Shenti Guixun." M.A. thesis, Taiwan Daxue Shehuixue Yanjiusuo.

Lee, M. L., A. Thornton, and H. S. Lin. 1994. "Trends in Marital Dissolution." In *Social Change and the Family in Taiwan,* by A. Thornton and H. S. Lin, pp. 245–63. Chicago: University of Chicago Press.

Lee, Martyn J. 1993. *Consumer Culture Reborn: The Cultural Politics of Consumption.* London: Routledge.

Lee, Yean-Ju, William Parish, and Robert J. Willis. 1994. "Sons, Daughters, and Intergenerational Support in Taiwan." *American Journal of Sociology* 99(4): 1010–41.

Li, Xiu-lian. 1996. *Zhongguo Huazhuangshi Gaishuo.* Taibeishi: Yang-zhi Wenhua.

Liebes, Tamar, and Elihu Katz. 1990. *The Export of Meaning: Cross-Cultural Readings of Dallas.* New York: Oxford University Press.

Lin, Fang-mei. 1992. "Social Change and Romantic Ideology." Ph.D. dissertation, University of Pennsylvania.

Lin, H. S., M. L. Lee, and A. Thornton. 1994. "Trends in the Timing and Prevalence of Marriage." In *Social Change and the Family in Taiwan,* by A. Thornton and H. S. Lin, pp. 202–44. Chicago: University of Chicago Press.

Lin, Yu-ling. 1996. "The Ideal of Slenderness in Taiwan's Diet Ads from Foucault's Framework of Power/Knowledge." *Funü yu Liangxi Xuekan* 7: 1–26.

———. 1998. "The Concept of Slenderness Imposed upon Women in Taiwan from the 1940s to 1990s." Ph.D. dissertation, University of Wisconsin, Madison.

Liu, Hung-en. 2001. "Mother or Father: Who Received Custody? The Best Interests of the Child Standard and Judges' Custody Decisions in Taiwan." *International Journal of Law, Policy, and Family* 15: 185–225.

Lury, Celia. 1996. *Consumer Culture.* New Brunswick: Rutgers University Press.

Lutz, Catherine. 1988. *Unnatural Emotions: Everyday Sentiments on a Micronesian Atoll and Their Challenge to Western Theory.* Chicago: University of Chicago Press.

———. 1995. "The Gender of Theory." In *Women Writing Culture,* edited by R. Behar and D. Gordon, pp. 249–66. Berkeley: University of California Press.

Lutz, Catherine, and Jane Collins. 1993. *Reading National Geographic.* Chicago: University of Chicago Press.

Lutz, Catherine, and Geoffrey White. 1986. "The Anthropology of Emotions." *Annual Review of Anthropology* 15: 405–36.

Macfarlane, Alan. 1987. *Culture of Capitalism.* Oxford: Basil Blackwell.

Mann, Susan. 1991. "Grooming a Daughter for Marriage: Brides and Wives in the Mid-Ch'ing Period." In *Marriage and Inequality in Chinese Society,* edited by R. Watson and P. Ebrey, pp. 204–30. Berkeley: University of California Press.

Martin, Emily. 1987. *The Woman in the Body*. Boston: Beacon Press.

———. 1988. "Gender and Ideological Differences in Representations of Life and Death." In *Death Ritual in Late Imperial and Modern China*, edited by J. Watson and E. Rawski, pp. 164–79. Berkeley: University of California Press.

Marvullo, Joe. 1993. "Making Portraits." In *The Portrait: Professional Techniques and Practices in Portrait Photography*, edited by E. K. Company. Rochester: Silver Pixel Press.

McClintock, Anne. 1995. *Imperial Leather: Race, Gender, and Sexuality in the Colonial Contest*. New York: Routledge.

McVeigh, Brian. 1996. "Commodifying Affection, Authority, and Gender in the Everyday Objects of Japan." *Journal of Material Culture* 1(3): 291–312.

Meskill, Johanna Menzel. 1979. *A Chinese Pioneer Family: The Lins of Wufeng, Taiwan, 1729–1895*. Princeton: Princeton University Press.

Metz, Christian. 1985. "Photography and Fetish." *October* 34 (fall): 81–90.

Miller, Daniel. 1995a. "Introduction: Anthropology, Modernity, and Consumption." In *Worlds Apart: Modernity through the Prism of the Local*, edited by D. Miller, pp. 1–22. New York: Routledge.

———. 1995b. "Consumption and Commodities." *Annual Review of Anthropology* 24: 141–61.

———. 1995c. "Consumption as the Vanguard of History: A Polemic by Way of an Introduction." In *Acknowledging Consumption: A Review of New Studies*, edited by D. Miller, pp. 1–57. New York: Routledge.

———. 1997. *Capitalism: An Ethnographic Approach*. New York: Berg.

Miller, Laura. 1999. "Beauty Up: Aesthetic Salons in Japan." Paper presented at the Association for Asian Studies Annual Meeting, Boston.

Millett, Kate. 1970. *Sexual Politics*. Garden City, N.Y.: Doubleday.

Moeran, Brian. 1993. "A Tournament of Value: Strategies of Presentation in Japanese Advertising." *Ethnos* 58: 73–93.

Moore, Sally Falk. 1994. "The Ethnography of the Present and the Analysis of Process." In *Assessing Cultural Anthropology*, edited by R. Borofsky, pp. 362–74. New York: McGraw-Hill.

Mulvey, Laura. 1989. *Visual and Other Pleasures*. London: Macmillan.

Murray, Stephen O., and Keelung Hong. 1991. "American Anthropologists Looking through Taiwanese Culture." *Dialectical Anthropology* 16(3–4): 273–99.

"Nearly Half of Women in Taiwan Employed." 1998. *Central News Agency-Taiwan*, April 6. Accessed via Lexis-Nexis.

"New Law Mandates Premarital Counseling for Couples." 2003. *Taiwan News*. January 8. Accessed via Lexis-Nexis.

Newman, Katherine S. 1987. *Falling from Grace: The Experience of Downward Mobility in the American Middle Class*. New York: Free Press.

Newton, Julianne H. 1998. "Beyond Representation: Toward a Typology of Visual Behavior." *Visual Anthropology Review* 14(1): 58–72.

Ong, Aihwa. 1987. *Spirits of Resistance and Capitalist Discipline: Factory Women in Malaysia*. Albany: State University of New York Press.

————. 1997. "Chinese Modernities: Narratives of Nation and of Capitalism."
    In *Ungrounded Empires: The Cultural Politics of Modern Chinese Trans-
    nationalism*, edited by A. Ong and D. Nonini, pp. 171–202. New York:
    Routledge.

Parish, William, and Robert J. Willis. 1993. "Daughters, Education, and Family
    Budgets: Taiwan Experiences." *Journal of Human Resources* 28(4): 863–99.

Parrenas, Rhacel Salazar. 2001. *Servants of Globalization*. Stanford: Stanford
    University Press.

Peiss, Kathy. 1998. *Hope in a Jar: The Making of America's Beauty Culture*. New
    York: Metropolitan Books.

Perrin, John, and Trish Perrin. 1993. "Fashion Make-Overs." In *The Portrait:
    Professional Techniques and Practices in Portrait Photography*, edited by
    E. K. Company, pp. 92–111. Rochester, N.Y.: Silver Pixel Press.

Pinney, Christopher. 1997. *Camera Indica: The Social Life of Indian Pho-
    tographs*. London: University of Chicago.

Poole, Deborah. 1997. *Vision, Race, and Modernity: A Visual Economy of the
    Andean Image World*. Princeton: Princeton University Press.

Potter, Sulamith Heins. 1988. "The Cultural Construction of Emotion in Rural
    Chinese Social Life." *Ethos* 16(2): 181–208.

Radner, Hillary. 1995. *Shopping Around: Feminine Culture and the Pursuit of
    Pleasure*. New York: Routledge.

Radway, Janice. 1984. *Reading the Romance: Women, Patriarchy, and Popular
    Literature*. Chapel Hill: University of North Carolina Press.

Rebhun, L. A. 1993. "Nerves and Emotional Play in Northeast Brazil." *Medical
    Anthropology Quarterly* 7(2): 131–51.

————. 1995. "Language of Love in Northeast Brazil." In *Romantic Passion*,
    edited by W. Jankowiak, pp. 239–61. New York: Columbia University Press.

————. 1999. *The Heart Is Unknown Country: Love in the Changing Economy
    of Northeast Brazil*. Stanford: Stanford University Press.

Rofel, Lisa. 1994. "Yearnings: Televisual Love and Melodramatic Politics in
    Contemporary China." *American Ethnologist* 21(4): 700–722.

Rooks, Noliwe M. 1996. *Hair Raising: Beauty, Culture, and African American
    Women*. New Brunswick: Rutgers University Press.

Rosaldo, Renato. 1989. *Culture and Truth*. Boston: Beacon Press.

Rougemont, Denis de. 1956. *Love in the Western World*. Translated by M. Bel-
    gion. New York: Pantheon Books.

Said, Edward W. 1978. *Orientalism*. New York: Pantheon.

Sando, Ruth Ann. 1986. "Doing the Work of Two Generations: The Impact of
    Out-Migration on the Elderly in Rural Taiwan." *Journal of Cross-Cultural
    Gerontology* 1(2): 163–75.

Sassen, Saskia. 1991. *The Global City*. Princeton: Princeton University Press.

Schak, David. 1975. *Dating and Mate-Selection in Modern Taiwan*. Taipei: Ori-
    ent Cultural Service.

Schein, Louisa. 1994. "The Consumption of Color and the Politics of White Skin
    in Post-Mao China." *Social Text* 41 (Winter): 141–64.

Schor, Juliet. 1998. *The Overspent American*. New York: Basic Books.

Scott, James C. 1985. *Weapons of the Weak: Everyday Forms of Peasant Resistance*. New Haven: Yale University Press.

———. 1990. *Domination and the Arts of Resistance: Hidden Transcripts*. New Haven: Yale University Press.

Scott, Joan W. 1988. *Gender and the Politics of History*. New York: Columbia University Press.

Sekula, Allan. 1982. "On the Invention of Photographic Meaning." In *Thinking Photography*, edited by V. Burgin, pp. 84–109. London: Macmillan.

Shepherd, John. 1993. *Statecraft and Political Economy on the Taiwan Frontier, 1600–1800*. Stanford: Stanford University Press.

Sheu, Jia-You. 1993. "The Composition and Changes of Taiwan's Petty Bourgeoisie: 1976–1987." In *Discovery of the Middle Classes in East Asia*, edited by H. H. Hsiao, pp. 177–200. Nankang: Institute of Ethnology, Academia Sinica.

Simon, Scott. 2003. "From Hidden Kingdom to Rainbow Community: The Making of Gay and Lesbian Identity in Taiwan." In *Taiwan: The Minor Arts of Daily Life*, edited by M. Moskowitz and A. Morris. Honolulu: University of Hawaii Press.

Siu, Helen F. 1990. "Where Were the Women?" *Late Imperial China* 11(2): 32–62.

———. 1993. "Reconstituting Dowry and Brideprice in South China." In *Chinese Families in the Post-Mao Era*, edited by D. Davis and S. Harrell, pp. 165–88. Berkeley: University of California Press.

Snitow, Ann Barr. 1983. "Mass-Market Romance: Pornography for Women Is Different." In *Powers of Desire*, edited by A. Snitow, C. Stansell, and S. Thompson, pp. 245–63. New York: Monthly Review Press.

Sontag, Susan. 1977. *On Photography*. New York: Anchor Books, Doubleday.

Speare, Alden Jr., Paul K. C. Liu, and Ching-lung Tsay. 1988. *Urbanization and Development: The Rural-Urban Transition in Taiwan*. Boulder: Westview Press.

Stockard, Janice. 1989. *Daughters of the Canton Delta*. Stanford: Stanford University Press.

Stone, Lawrence. 1977. *The Family, Sex, and Marriage in England, 1500–1800*. New York: Harper and Row.

Strawn, Perri. 1999. *Teaching Nationalism in the Crucible: Changing Identities in Taiwan High Schools after Martial Law*. Ph.D. dissertation, Yale University.

Stuart, Jan, and Evelyn S. Rawski. 2001. *Worshiping the Ancestors: Chinese Commemorative Portraits*. Washington, D.C.: Smithsonian Institution.

Su, Kun-ming. 1988. "Taiwan Baisha Lifu zhi Meiguo Shichang Dingwei." M.B.A. thesis, Zhengzhi Daxue Qiye Guanli Yanjiusuo.

"'Tai Kong' Jiating Wenti Duo." 1984. *Funü Zazhi* (February): 87–91.

"Taiwan, Facts and Figures." 1999. Lexis-Nexis Country Profiles.

Taussig, Michael. 1993. *Mimesis and Alterity: A Particular History of the Senses*. New York: Routledge.

Thornton, A., and H. S. Lin. 1994. *Social Change and the Family in Taiwan*. Chicago: University of Chicago Press.

Thornton, A., J. S. Chang, and H. S. Lin. 1994. "From Arranged Marriage toward Love Match." In *Social Change and the Family in Taiwan*, by A. Thornton and H. S. Lin, pp. 148–77. Chicago: University of Chicago Press.

Tobin, J., ed. 1992. *Re-Made in Japan*. New Haven: Yale University Press.

Tomlinson, John. 1991. *Cultural Imperialism*. Baltimore: Johns Hopkins University Press.

Tsay, Rueyming. 1993. "Social Relations and Social Mobility in Taiwan." Ph.D. dissertation, Cornell University.

Tsui, Elaine Yi-lan. 1987. *Are Married Daughters "Spilled Water"?* Taipei: Women's Resource Program, Population Studies Center, National Taiwan University.

Turner, Victor. 1967. *The Forest of Symbols*. Ithaca: Cornell University Press.

Van Gennep, Arnold. [1909] 1960. *The Rites of Passage*. Translated by M. B. Vizedom. Chicago: University of Chicago Press.

Veblen, Thorstein. [1902] 1925. *The Theory of the Leisure Class*. London: Allen and Unwin.

Vergara, Benito M. Jr. 1995. *Displaying Filipinos: Photography and Colonialism in Early 20th Century Philippines*. Quezon City: University of the Philippines Press.

"Waiguoren de Zhongguo Taitai." 1974. *Funü Zazhi* (February): 52–54.

Wang, Flor. 1998. "Taiwan's Population Growth Said to Hit Zero in 40 Years." *Central News Agency-Taiwan*, October 1. Accessed via Lexis-Nexis.

———. 1999. "Premarital Sex Among Teens Seen Increasing." *Central News Agency-Taiwan*, January 9. Accessed via Lexis-Nexis.

Waters, Malcolm. 1995. *Globalization*. New York: Routledge.

Watson, James L. 1988. "The Structure of Chinese Funerary Rites: Elementary Forms, Ritual Sequence, and the Primacy of Performance." In *Death Ritual in Late Imperial and Modern China*, edited by J. Watson and E. Rawski, pp. 3–19. Berkeley: University of California Press.

———. 1997. "Introduction: Transnationalism, Localization, and Fast Foods in East Asia." In *Golden Arches East: McDonald's in East Asia*, edited by J. Watson. Stanford: Stanford University Press.

———. 1998. "Living Ghosts: Long-Haired Destitutes in Colonial Hong Kong." In *Hair: Its Power and Meaning in Asian Cultures*, edited by A. Hiltebeitel and B. Miller, pp. 177–94. Albany: State University of New York Press.

Watson, Rubie S. 1991. "Wives, Concubines, and Maids: Servitude and Kinship in the Hong Kong Region, 1900–1940." In *Marriage and Inequality in Chinese Society*, edited by R. Watson and P. Ebrey, pp. 231–55. Berkeley: University of California Press.

"Wedding Handbook." 1996. *Wei Wei Xinniang* (summer).

Whyte, Martin King. 1992. *From Arranged Marriages to Love Matches in Urban China*. Hong Kong: Chinese University of Hong Kong Press.

Wilk, Richard. 1995. "Learning to be Local in Belize: Global Systems of Common Difference." In *Worlds Apart: Modernity through the Prism of the Local*, edited by D. Miller, pp. 110–34. New York: Routledge.

Wilson, Rob, and Wimal Dissanayake. 1996. "Introduction." In *Global/Local: Cultural Production and the Transnational Imaginary*, edited by R. Wilson and W. Dissanayake. Durham, N.C.: Duke University Press.

Winship, Janice. 1987. *Inside Women's Magazines*. London: Pandora.

Wolf, Arthur. 1970. "Chinese Kinship and Mourning Dress." In *Family and Kinship in Chinese Society*, edited by M. Freedman. Stanford: Stanford University Press.

———. 1978. "Gods, Ghosts, and Ancestors." In *Studies in Chinese Society*, edited by A. Wolf, pp. 131–82. Stanford: Stanford University Press.

Wolf, Arthur, and Chieh-shan Huang. 1980. *Marriage and Adoption in China: 1845–1945*. Stanford: Stanford University Press.

Wolf, Eric. 1982. *Europe and the People without History*. Berkeley: University of California Press.

Wolf, Margery. 1968. *The House of Lim*. New York: Appleton Century Crofts.

———. 1972. *Women and the Family in Rural Taiwan*. Stanford: Stanford University Press.

———. 1975. "Women and Suicide in China." In *Women in Chinese Society*, edited by M. Wolf and R. Witke, pp. 111–42. Stanford: Stanford University Press.

———. 1984. "Marriage, Family, and the State in Contemporary China." *Pacific Affairs* 57(2): 213–36.

———. 1985. *Revolution Postponed: Women in Contemporary China*. Stanford: Stanford University Press.

Wolf, Naomi. 1991. *The Beauty Myth: How Images of Beauty Are Used against Women*. New York: W. Morrow.

Wollstonecraft, Mary. 1796. *Vindication of the Rights of Woman*. London: J. Johnson.

Wu, David Y. H. 1997. "McDonald's in Taipei: Hamburgers, Betel Nuts, and National Identity." In *Golden Arches East: McDonald's in East Asia*, edited by J. L. Watson, pp. 110–35. Stanford: Stanford University Press.

Wu, Feng-ji. 1996. "Mianxiang Kaiyun Huazhuang yu Zaoxingshu." Unpublished handbill at a fortune-telling exhibition at Taipei's Asia World Department Store.

Wu, Sofia. 1997. "More Taiwan Men Choose Mainland Brides." *Central News Agency-Taiwan*, November 7. Accessed via Lexis-Nexis.

———. 1998. "Poll Finds Many People Not Interested in Marriage." *Central News Agency-Taiwan*, December 26. Accessed via Lexis-Nexis.

———. 1999. "International Poll Finds Taiwan Women Least Romantic, Most Unhappy." *Central News Agency-Taiwan*, January 26. Accessed via Lexis-Nexis.

Yan, Yunxiang. 1996. *The Flow of Gifts: Reciprocity and Social Networks in a Chinese Village*. Stanford: Stanford University Press.

Yang, Mayfair Mei-hui. 1997. "Mass Media and Transnational Subjectivity in Shanghai: Notes on (Re)cosmopolitanism in a Chinese Metropolis." In *Ungrounded Empires: The Cultural Politics of Modern Chinese Transnationalism*, edited by A. Ong and D. Nonini, pp. 287–319. New York: Routledge.

———. 2000. "Putting Capitalism in Its Place." *Current Anthropology* 41(4): 477–509.

Ye, Lan-jing. 1996. *Nüxing Neiyi Chuanzhe Yishu*. Taibeishi: Guoji Cun.

Zhang, Wen-zhi. 1986. "Zhongguo Hunli Zhong Yanse de Xiangzheng yu Bian-
    qian." *Renlei yu Wenhua* 22: 15–19.
Zhang, Yuan-ling. 1997. "Taibei Hunsha Sheying de Shehuixue Yanjiu." M.A.
    thesis, National Taiwan University.
Zheng, Wei-wei. 1995. "Cong Hunsha Sheying Zhaopian Beijing Yunyong zhi
    Bianzheng Luoji Tan Taiwan Houxiandai Sheying Wenhua Biaozheng Yi Yu."
    In *Ziran yu Renwei de Duihua: Fengjing Sheying Xueshu Lunwen Ji,* edited
    by Z. Ling, pp. 65–72. Taipei: Zhonghua Sheying Jiaoyu Xuehui.
Zhuang, He-zhi. 1998. "Cong Shaonü Zazhi 'BEAUTY' Kan Nüxing Xingxiang."
    Funü yu Liangxing Yanjiu Tongxun 49(12): 17–20.
Zito, Angela, and Tani Barlow, eds. 1994. *Body, Subject, and Power in China.*
    Chicago: University of Chicago Press.
Zones, Jane Sprague. 1997. "Beauty Myths and Realities and Their Impact on
    Women's Health." In *Women's Health,* edited by S. Ruzek, V. Oleson, and A.
    Clarke, pp. 249–75. Columbus: Ohio State University Press.

Index

Page numbers in italics indicate illustrations.

Text: 10/13 Sabon
Display: Sabon
Compositor: Bookmatters, Berkeley
Printer and Binder: Sheridan Books, Inc.